Sensory Rhetorics

Sensory Rhetorics

Sensation, Persuasion, and the Politics of Feeling

Edited by Steph Ceraso and
Jonathan W. Stone

The Pennsylvania State University Press
University Park, Pennsylvania

Cataloging-in-Publication Data is on file with the Library of Congress.

Copyright © 2026 The Pennsylvania State University
All rights reserved
Printed in the United States of America
Published by The Pennsylvania State University Press,
University Park, PA 16802–1003

The Pennsylvania State University Press is a member of the Association of University Presses.

It is the policy of The Pennsylvania State University Press to use acid-free paper. Publications on uncoated stock satisfy the minimum requirements of American National Standard for Information Sciences—Permanence of Paper for Printed Library Material, ANSI Z39.48–1992.

Contents

List of Illustrations (vi)

Amuse-Bouche (vii)
CHRISTA J. OLSON

Acknowledgments (x)

Introduction: (Re)Mapping Rhetoric's Sensory Past, Present, and Future (1)
STEPH CERASO AND JONATHAN W. STONE

1 Red Tastes, Blue Tastes: Disgust and the Political Rhetoric of Moral Pollution (26)
MARGOT FINN AND BRYAN W. MOE

2 Rational Markets, Sensory Marketplaces: How Stock Imagery Shapes Digital Sense-Making (42)
KERRY BANAZEK AND KELLIE SHARP-HOSKINS

3 Reeking Revelations: How Olfaction Informs Rhetorical Processes in Environmental Injustice (61)
LISA L. PHILLIPS

4 The Sense of Soil: Antiracism and the Community Soil Collection Project (75)
NATALIE BENNIE AND KELLY WILLIAMS NAGEL

5 Feeling Through Numbness, Healing with Awe: Not-Knowing as a Methodology for Sensory Rhetorics (92)
AMES HAWKINS

6 Autokinesis and the Sense of Meaninglessness (112)
BENJAMIN FIRGENS

7 Unsettling Colonized Sensory Archives (128)
ROMEO GARCÍA AND KYLE S. BOND

8 In*form*ing Rhetoric: Pluriversal Lessons on *Différance* and Rhetorical Energy (146)
DAVID M. GRANT

After(WORD) (164)
JUSTIN ECKSTEIN

List of Contributors (171)

Index (173)

Illustrations

4.1 Benjamin Thomas's soil collection vessel (87)

4.2 Participants collecting soil (88)

5.1 Ames Hawkins, "Left Nipple, Week 1" (97)

5.2 Ames Hawkins, "Left Nipple, Week 3" (101)

5.3 Ames Hawkins, "Left Nipple, Week 6" (107)

Amuse-Bouche
CHRISTA J. OLSON

Soc.: Ask me now what art I take cookery to be.
Pol.: Then I ask you, what art is cookery?
Soc.: None at all, Polus.
Pol.: Well, what is it? Tell me.
Soc.: Then I reply, a certain habitude.
Pol.: Of what? Tell me?
Soc.: Then I reply, of production of gratification and pleasure, Polus.
Pol.: So cookery and rhetoric are the same thing?

—Plato, *Gorgias* 462 D–E

At the beginning of a multicourse restaurant dinner, a server will sometimes approach the table with a tiny treat from the chef, an amuse-bouche meant to engage the mouth before embarking on the larger meal. It seems wrong to begin a collection on sensory rhetorics with a fore*word*, so I am offering instead an amuse-bouche to help you prepare for the feast ahead.

And what would be a more classically appropriate amuse-bouche for a rhetoric book than a return to one of the earliest insults directed at rhetoric: that it is like cookery—a knack, a means of producing pleasure, and ultimately a practice of flattery. As a rhetorician who loves to cook and feed others, I adore the absurdity of the insult Plato has Socrates hurl. To denigrate rhetoric's value by aligning it with a fundamental human activity suggests Plato's own distance from the kitchen and from the complexities of everyday life. But I am not interested in taking Plato to task—others have done that so well, and, despite his lingering influence on Western cultures, the man has been dead a very long time. Instead, I ask us to revel in what rhetorical studies has become millennia later—a field immersed in the sensorium of life and equipped to help students and scholars understand the shaping force of sensory experience, a field that can bring into being a collection like *Sensory*

Rhetorics. I also invite us to ground ourselves in Ceraso and Stone's reminder that sensory rhetorics are crucial for "understanding and responding to the complexity of our current moment."

Cooking, eating, and hunger are full-sensory, rhetorical experiences. They are also, as Nathan Stormer (2015, 101) writes of hunger and rhetoric, "folded together in complex, dynamic layers, such that it is impossible to tell where one ends and the other begins." In this sense, hunger and eating are the first locus of rhetoric for all animals, including humans, in the form of cries for bottle or breast or teat. They are reminders that rhetoric is always sensory, whatever forms it takes. That point is foundational to the collection before you: "Sensory rhetorics" are not a particular class of a thing called "rhetoric" that can be contrasted with other, nonsensory, rhetorics; rhetoric is always, inevitably, fully sensorial; it is felt, heard, seen, smelled, and/or tasted in wonderful, impossible combination. I invite you to join me in sensing these pages and then carrying those sensations into the rest of your rhetorical wanderings.

For my part, reading the chapters of this collection led me to take sobering account of my own sensory engagement with the world around me. Sensory rhetorics, as presented in this collection, reminded me that cookery and rhetoric are kin in ways that Plato apparently could not grasp, not least in their profound consequence for everyday life. So, as I joined authors in considering political disgust, the stench of environmental racism, and the felt possibilities of not knowing, I also became increasingly aware of myself as what Stormer (2015, 102) once called a "rhetor whose belly is full."

Again and again, the chapters of *Sensory Rhetorics* remind us about the complex factors underlying each sensory experience—algorithms, markets, evolutionary selection—and so I cannot turn away from the irony that this amuse-bouche and the feast that follows it may well be read by rhetors whose bellies are empty, either for the moment or chronically. And the state of those bellies will shape the reading, the learning, and the uptake. Lest this point seem disconnected from likely readers of a scholarly connection, I point you toward the hunger crises simmering in our own places of work and learning. In a report on research into college student hunger between 2009 and 2022, Rebecca Hagedorn-Hatfield, Lanae Hood, and Adam Hege (2022, para. 3) write, "the reality is many college students are skipping meals or going hungry due to the inability to afford food in conjunction with all the other necessary college expenses (rent, textbooks, lab fees, tuition, etc.) and limited financial assistance." They continue, "Although the FI [food insecure] prevalence varies across campuses, consistently, rates are higher than the national US average. A recent review found an overall weighted average of 41% of students experience FI. No type of institution is immune from this issue, with evidence from every region of the US, at public and private universities, and both 2- and 4-year colleges" (para. 5). And, they report, "food-insecure college students have 42% lower odds of graduating" (para. 11).

Sensory rhetorics give us new ways to understand those hungry students and empty bellies as part of rhetorical cookery, not just text-based arguments about food policy. In concrete ways, then, the multicourse dinner of *Sensory Rhetorics* has led me to ponder a challenging, exciting next-step question: What can a full sensory rhetorical studies do for hungry students, hungry colleagues, hungry readers?

I hope that your own reading sparks equally generative, equally consequential questions for you.

References

Hagedorn-Hatfield, Rebecca L., Lanae B. Hood, and Adam Hege. 2022. "A Decade of College Student Hunger: What We Know and Where We Need to Go." *Frontiers in Public Health* 10 (February 24).

Plato. 1925. *Gorgias*. Loeb Classical Library. Cambridge, MA: Harvard University Press. https://www.doi.org/10.4159/DLCL.plato_philosopher-gorgias.1925.

Stormer, Nathan. 2015. "An Appetite for Rhetoric." *Philosophy and Rhetoric* 48 (1): 99–106.

Acknowledgments

Our shared interest in sensation blossomed from our shared obsession with sound. We begin, then, with a loud shout-out to the lively, generous community that has formed around sound, writing, and rhetoric. We have been lucky to be a part of this community since our graduate school years, and we have learned a ton about sensation from our colleagues/dear friends.

In many ways, this collection is an extension of the ideas we explored in Debra Hawhee and Vanessa Beasley's wonderful seminar on rhetoric and sensation at the 2015 RSA Summer Institute; we are forever grateful to them and to our fellow participants for fueling our interest in sensory rhetorics.

We owe a great debt of gratitude to Archna Patel for her editorial guidance, patience, and belief in this project. Simply put, this book would not exist without Archna. We are also very appreciative of editorial assistant Josie DiKerby and everyone at Penn State University Press for their support.

We want to thank David Howes and Jennifer LeMesurier for their enthusiasm and insightful feedback, which undoubtedly made this a better book.

Thanks as well to the University of Virginia and the University of Utah for providing funds that contributed to the production of this volume.

Last but certainly not least, a hearty thanks to our contributors, who stuck with us despite the long journey, and to the many brilliant scholars who pitched us chapters that did not make it into the final collection. Though it was impossible to include everything, glimpsing the range of vibrant in-progress scholarship on sensation in the field only reinforced that sensory rhetorics are alive and well and will be—we hope—for years to come.

Introduction

(Re)Mapping Rhetoric's Sensory
Past, Present, and Future

STEPH CERASO AND JONATHAN W. STONE

Jon: "Scratch and sniff!" the nurse said, and she handed me a small spiral notebook and a #2 pencil. A series of illnesses—beginning with a positive COVID diagnosis in January 2021, a hospital stint with a debilitating fever that March, and complete facial paralysis (Bell's palsy) in April—had landed me at an ear, nose, and throat clinic. I was seeking treatment for parosmia, a smell and taste disorder that had accompanied the various illnesses of early 2021 and had never gone away. By the summer of 2022, an alarming percentage of foods still smelled like burnt popcorn. More alarming, the sulfuric rotten-egg odor added to natural gas for safety didn't smell "bad" to me anymore. I was encouraged by my doctor to take the smell test contained in the notebook I was now holding. My task: scratch and sniff a little box and then try to guess the associated smell from a multiple-choice list. After the test, a doctor described my condition by comparing our olfactory nerves to a piano keyboard. "Different smells stimulate a series of different nerve endings, almost like a chord being played on a piano." I learned that parosmia knocks out a few of the "notes," and so the brain can't pinpoint and process odors as accurately as before the damage occurred. "There's no treatment," she said. "Your brain will eventually compensate for the loss." Perhaps seeing the concern on my face, she added that in the wake of COVID, tens of thousands are experiencing similar symptoms. She encouraged me to join an online support group and sent me on my way.

Steph: Breathing hurt. With each inhale, I felt like I was stoking embers in my chest cavity. No matter how I positioned my achy, burning body, I could not sleep. I had tested positive for COVID the day before. My excruciating sensory *experience was surprising to me, since at that point in the pandemic (November 2022) public discourse indicated most COVID cases were similar to a mild flu for those who were vaccinated with no underlying conditions or risk factors. Even close friends who had recently contracted COVID told me it was "no big deal," that they were actually relieved to have finally gotten it after years of worrying. Though I had taken COVID very seriously, still masking and avoiding crowds when the majority of people were not, I must have internalized this messaging because I was not particularly concerned when I got the positive test. I, too, felt a sense of relief knowing that I would have some immunity afterward. But by the second day, I started to feel scared. Despite the fiery sensation in my chest, though, I wondered if I was being overly sensitive. Maybe this was just how a "mild" case of COVID was supposed to feel. It wasn't until I saw the illuminated chest X-ray at Urgent Care, which displayed my lungs filled with a streaky, spectral concentration of COVID, that I fully trusted my bodily experience.*

As our personal stories illustrate, the pandemic forced us all to be more attentive to our own and others' bodily, sensory experiences. We wondered together if strangers' coughs were allergies or a potentially deadly virus; we questioned every sniffle or tickle in our throats—things we would have most likely ignored before March 2020. As COVID progressed, our scrutiny deepened. We felt for weakness in our limbs and heat on our faces. We monitored the quality of our taste and smell. Across the world, the sensory experiences of being human came into sharp relief.

For Jon, the experience of smelling was something he had taken for granted. The sudden missing olfactory "notes" challenged his perception of the world and necessitated (literally) new neural pathways for processing experience. Not being able to smell "right" was a reminder of just how reliant we are on our senses to construct our realities and, by extension, our sense of rationality. For Steph, the supposedly authoritative discourse from news outlets and friends' personal accounts made her question whether her own sensory experience was valid, illustrating how the rhetoric surrounding health crises (and other events) can affect how we actually perceive firsthand experiences of sensation. Additionally, it was not until she saw a visual representation—visual proof—of what was going on in her body that she trusted what she had been sensing. The entrenched cultural hierarchy of the senses, visual at the top, clearly influenced how she interpreted her bodily experience of illness.

We open with these stories to spotlight just a few ideas connected to what we call *sensory rhetorics*, or the ways that sensory engagements and experiences—including how sensation intersects with various discourses and logics—act as a suasive force that shapes and affects behaviors, environments, beliefs, feelings, and desires. "Sensory rhetoric(s)" is a phrase that has been circulating in the field for a number of years, emerging from the growing acknowledgment of sensation's relationship with rhetoric. We did not invent it, though in this introduction we are interested in pursuing a more concrete definition by considering what rhetoricians have already noticed about sensation. Sensory rhetoric is implied in terms such as "multimodal" and "multisensory," which have been linked to rhetoric and writing studies since the 1990s. "Sensory rhetoric" is rarer but crops up in scholarship inside and outside the field during that period, often associated with anthropology or religious studies. We use the pluralized "rhetorics" to capture the multiplicity and range of sensory experiences and their various capacities to influence.[1]

Beyond rhetorical studies, scholars across the disciplines are increasingly turning to sensation to understand the world, its occupants, and their relations in new ways. There is an ever-growing body of transdisciplinary scholarship on the senses and sensory studies is a well-established field of thought. Scholars such as David Howes, Constance Classen, Kathryn Geurts, and Ruth Finnegan started publishing extensively on the senses in the late 1990s and early 2000s. As Sarah Pink (2015, 3-4) observes in *Doing Sensory Ethnography*, this scholarly turn toward the senses includes a broad and disparate range of research, from "sensuous geography" to "a cultural history of the senses" to "sensory design and architecture." Sensory studies continues to be a thriving and capacious area of research. "It could be argued," Howes (2022, 10) writes in *The Sensory Studies Manifesto*, "that the sensory turn now rivals the . . . linguistic, pictorial, corporeal, and material turns in terms of its impact on scholarship in the humanities and social sciences. Rather than being just another turn, then, the uptake of the senses across the humanities and social sciences is revolutionary."

Where do scholars of rhetoric fit into this so-called sensory turn? This collection demonstrates that rhetorical scholarship is already contributing to such a turn in important ways and has been for a long time, though not always in the same terms as other fields. That said, like Howes, we find the concept of a scholarly "turn" to be limiting, particularly in relation to the senses (2022, 8). A turn toward something implies a turn away from something else. For instance, a sensory turn that emphasizes nonrational ways of being might imply that sensation is more relevant or significant than rationality, which we do not believe is the case—as we elaborate on below. A turn also refers to a specific time period when many scholars pay attention to something as opposed to acknowledging that certain ideas, practices, and epistemologies circulate in various ways throughout history, even if they are not deemed exciting or attention worthy. As Howes notes, "There is no Archimedean point, independent of any culture or period, from which to conceptualize the bounds of sense, or assess the different senses' contribution to the advancement of knowledge" (8). In the case of rhetoric, while there is a heightened interest in sensation at the moment, the senses have played an integral role throughout the rhetorical canon, as we outline in this introduction. Sensory rhetorical insights have, since ancient times, been at hand, under our noses, on the tip of our tongues, within earshot.

Rather than arguing that rhetoric should be included in the recent "sensory turn," our aim in this collection is to show why sensory rhetorics are vital for understanding and responding to the complexity of our current moment. We contend, that is, that this moment calls for a *resensing* of what the senses are and can do to help illuminate how rhetoric works or fails to work. By *resensing*, we are referring to both an attempt to reunderstand and retheorize sensation in relation to an ever-changing world and to reattune our bodyminds to sensory experience—to the ways everyday sensory encounters shape how we interpret rhetorical action (and vice versa).

Sensory Rhetorics offers readers in rhetorical studies and beyond nuanced approaches to recentering sensation as an important means for comprehending and intervening in thorny rhetorical situations. Echoing Candice Rai and Caroline Gottschalk Druschke's (2018, 2) sensuous conceptualization of fieldwork, we see sensory rhetorics as essential "for building interdisciplinary rhetorical theory and practice capable of responding to the contradictory, complex, shifting, and recalcitrant conditions of our world's salient exigencies." We are living during a time marked by unprecedented change that requires new kinds of bodily knowledge and sensory methods to help us make (literal and figurative) sense of constantly transforming rhetorics and ways of being in the world. For example, in "Sensing School Shootings," Justin Eckstein (2020) demonstrates how social media technologies have altered the way people experience tragedies like gun violence in schools and how such sensory shifts impact the political and rhetorical landscape of gun-control activism. In a similar manner, the chapters in this volume demonstrate how sensory rhetorical approaches open up new avenues for thinking about some of the most pressing issues in contemporary life: environmental and racial injustice, social and political divisions, digital consumption, and gender expression, among others. Indeed, more rhetorical approaches to sensation are especially needed given the repeated failure of rational deliberation to persuade people to rally around issues of climate threats, political demagoguery, and racist and gender-based violence. To put it simply, sensory rhetorics matter, and part of the work of this volume is to illustrate when, how, and why they matter.

This collection illuminates and interrogates how rhetoric "makes sense," focusing specifically on the ways sensory rhetorics act as a suasive force in everyday life. Encouraging rhetoric scholars to *resense* sensation, we argue, can offer ways of knowing, experiencing, and relating that are well suited to help us interpret and act in a world that is always changing. The work we present here offers an array of concepts and methods for sensory rhetorics that readers can take up and extend in their own work; the authors also challenge current conversations in sensory rhetorics and reimagine the future of this burgeoning subfield. One of the book's unique contributions is that it theorizes sensation not as separate from rationality but as an integral part of rationality. "Sensation" does related but different work than the term "rational" and its attendant antonyms, "irrational" and "nonrational." In *Rhetoric in Tooth and Claw*, for instance, Debra Hawhee (2019, 7) "seeks to alter persisting conceptions of rhetoric, or at least to emphasize the importance of the other than rational to rhetoric and rhetorical processes." "Sensation, feeling, and emotion," she continues, "have emerged as the positive counterparts to rationality and reason—positive, that is, in comparison with the term nonrational" (7). Many of the chapters in *Sensory Rhetorics* complicate the relationship between sensation and rationality, breaking down the false and unproductive barriers between these concepts.

We also make a point to treat the senses holistically. We are attentive to another observation of Hawhee's (2015, 5), namely, that the study of sensory rhetorics invites an expansion "from the individual to the collective." As Hawhee notes, "the idea of the sensorium refuses to separate the senses [or] to cordon them off into a 'subfield' (e.g., visual studies or sound studies)" (5). Further, this collectivity "may help us move past commonplace conditional observations," including a productive extension from embodiment (the most obvious realm of the senses) to the "connective, participatory dimensions of sensing" (5). Thus, if the sensorium names an integrated system of parts that work together to aid the interpretation of meaning and experience, sensory rhetorics might be understood as the study of how this system works, including the ways it is made to work, or composed by sensing individuals and collectives that produce rhetoric. In short, the authors in this volume crystallize the significance of sensation in rhetorical studies and demonstrate how a deeper understanding of sensing might produce novel answers to vexing rhetorical problems.

Before getting to the specifics of this collection, however, we offer a more detailed account of how the senses have figured into rhetoric to show that the work featured in *Sensory Rhetorics* stems from a long and rich disciplinary history. With the notion of *resensing* in mind, below we provide a chronological, though not comprehensive, overview of the long-standing relationship between rhetoric and the senses. After establishing the importance of sensation in the ancient Western rhetorical tradition, we touch on key moments in rhetorical history when a renewed attention to the senses coincided with major changes in the world. In each era we focus on, rhetoricians' theories of sensation seem to be in response to or in conversation with significant technological, social, and/or political upheaval. Rhetoricians turn to sensation during these considerable shifts in part because they must seek new ways of understanding how rhetoric works in relation to these changes. Like the historical precedents we note, *Sensory Rhetorics* is responding to another significant moment in our cultural and planetary history that requires us to rethink rhetoric in relation to a world in flux—a moment when strictly rational ways of doing rhetoric often fail.

Rhetoric and the Senses

While rhetorical scholarship is not often included under the umbrella of sensory studies, rhetoric has an enduring connection to sensation, intermittently expressed in related concepts such as emotion, feeling, and affect. We recognize the importance of distinguishing these terms, as each carries significant implications for various academic theories and disciplines.[2] However, we also want to ensure that conceptual or disciplinary politics do not overshadow efforts at a better understanding of rhetoric's relationship with the senses. Without the space to offer a full accounting of these differences and their intellectual histories, we do hope to put "sensory rhetorics" within a legible, if not comprehensive, scholarly context and trajectory.

We begin, predictably, with the Greeks. This is for the obvious reason of Western rhetorical genesis but also because when examining sensation in early Greek rhetoric, translations yield concepts that are similar but not identical to the modern distinctions (and possible complications) mentioned above. This provides us with the semblance of a fresh start and the opportunity to assert, straightforwardly, that rhetoric and sensation have always been intrinsically intertwined. In the West, the art of rhetoric evolved as orators skillfully combined the strategic arrangement of their arguments with the eloquent style of their delivery, all performed through voice and gesture. Therefore, it is no surprise that the early rhetorical texts are saturated with sensory language. This is most evident, perhaps, in Aristotle's rhetorical appeals, which acknowledged the power and potential of *pathos*, or the rhetorician's consideration of an audience's emotions, including how to change them. "Rhetoric is concerned with making a judgment," Aristotle posits, and "emotions [*pathē*] are those things through which, by undergoing change, people come to differ in their judgements" (1991, 1378a7, 1378a20–21). These two elements, judgment and change, describe well the purview of rhetoric, and as Aristotle states, emotion is key to both.³

Further, the sophist Gorgias's insights on rhetoric in his *Encomium of Helen* demonstrate the mutability of judgment by way of emotion, or embodied multisensory experience. Rhetoric can "stop fear and banish grief and create joy and nurture pity" (2001, 45). Its effects are not unlike drugs in their influence, affecting both body and mind with power enough to alter Helen's (and, by extension, our) ability to judge (46). For Plato, rhetoric is suspect because of its ability to change or confuse the senses through visual (cosmetics/self-adornment), gustatory/olfactory (cookery), or sonic (poetic rhythm/meter) means (1961, 464b–66a, 502c). Indeed, whether or not to trust our nonrational senses and feelings over the trained logic of the rational mind is at the heart of the debate between the ancient sophists and the philosophers.

Later in Rome, Cicero draws on the senses to elucidate the strength and scope of rhetoric. In relation to the canon of memory, he writes in *De oratore* that the most successful rhetors were those with a speech before the "mental eye . . . most strongly fixed in [their] minds, which are communicated to them, and imprinted upon them, by the senses" (1860, 2.357). When composing a speech, the senses should guide everything from audience appeal (3.96–100) to the selection of rhetorical devices. For example, Cicero writes that "every metaphor that is adopted with judgment is directed immediately to our senses, and principally to the sense of sight, which is the keenest of them all. For such expressions as the odour of urbanity, the softness of humanity, the murmur of the sea, and sweetness of language, are derived from the other senses" (3.160–61). Present in this consideration are each of the five senses, and rhetoric has power to evoke each in the mind and heart of an audience.

This "mental eye" is akin to what Aristotle called *phantasia* and comes up often across Greek and Roman literature on rhetoric. As Hawhee (2019,

43) notes, Quintilian drew "a direct line from *phantasia* to the emotions," one resounded by a later Roman rhetorician, Longinus, in his sensory-laden descriptions of the sublime. *Phantasia* tracks from the "enthusiastic, frenzied emotion (of the speaker or writer) through words and to the ears, minds, and bodies of listeners or readers" (43). *Phantasia* is the ability to capture vivid emotion in the mind so as to motivate enthralled action/change, or *enargeia*, in an audience. This is related to the observation Thomas Rickert (2013, 43) makes in advancing his theory of ambient rhetoric, that "minds are at once *embodied*, and hence grounded in emotion and sensation, and dispersed into the environment itself, and hence no longer autonomous actants but composites of intellect, body, information, and scaffolding of material artifacts."

As these examples show, within the ancient Western rhetorical tradition, rhetoric is bound to sensation—constitutive of it in ways evident whenever rhetoric is described or critiqued. Emerging from this constitutive relationship are at least two ways of employing sensory rhetorics, one with practical applications and others with more theoretical possibilities. Practical use draws on what might be called "sensory modality," or the recognition of five major human senses and their individual and combined rhetorical characteristics and powers. The exploration of these sensory modes has been a consistent thread through centuries of scholarship on the topic. Plato's classifications noted above provide a starting point, and Cicero's offhand comment about the sense of sight being the "keenest of them all" preambles one of the key debates in the history and politics of sensory modality studies. Close and prolonged scholarly attention to individual modalities has inspired manifold theories, so the distinction we are making here is a porous one.

(Neo-)Sophistic and Feminist Rhetorical Connections
Hailing from an overlapping ancient rhetorical context, the Sophists offer a more nuanced, sensorial understanding of rhetoric. Indeed, Sophism is a convenient, if incomplete, way of recognizing the long presence of sensory rhetorical theory. As John Poulakos (1983, 36) writes, "the Sophists were the first to infuse rhetoric with life. Indebted only to the poetry of their past, not to any formal rhetorical theory, they found themselves free to experiment playfully with form and style and to fashion their words in the Greek spirit of excellence." Coalescing with deconstruction and the work of Jacques Derrida, a renewed interest in the Sophists in the second half of the twentieth century reified curiosity in rhetoric's contingent, contextual, and cultural embeddedness. Unlike the persisting narrow and prescriptive Aristotelian

approach to rhetoric, neo-Sophists sought to expand the scope and range of rhetorical processes (Leff 1999, 53). Echoing Sharon Crowley's (1989) verbiage, various pleas for the revival of the Sophists were very impactful, breaking rhetorical studies out of long-standing traditional ruts and broadening the way for diverse and frequently sensual rhetorical perspectives, including those outside the Western tradition itself.

For example, in *Rereading the Sophists: Classical Rhetoric Refigured*, Susan Jarratt (1991, xix) argued that the Sophists recognized "human perceptions as the only source of knowledge in all fields" and, given this radical contingency, advocated for the "possibilities for nonrational and emotional responses to the whole range of discourse types." Beyond these sense-conscious Sophistic affirmations, Jarratt's distinctly feminist approach shows the intentional exclusion of Sophists and women from the history of rhetoric by the ancient gatekeepers of Western philosophy. Both "are trivialized by identification with sensuality, costume, and color—all of which are supposed to be manipulated in attempts to persuade through deception" (65). It is impossible to conceive of a sensory rhetorical tradition without such feminist incursions of the oh-so-masculine, rational, and "objective" inheritances of the philosophic rhetorical tradition. Almost twenty years earlier, in Karolyn Kohrs Campbell's (1973, 84) classic essay, "The Rhetoric of Women's Liberation: An Oxymoron," she argued that "traditional or familiar definitions of persuasion [i.e., those inherited from the Aristotelian and neo-Aristotelian traditions] do not satisfactorily account for the rhetoric of women's liberation." Such an argument recognizes in a neo-Sophistic way the limitations of rhetoric without nonrational affordances, including sensation. It also hints at the importance of creating *new* rhetorical traditions and suggests how sensory rhetorical incursions have catalyzed the growth and maintenance of transformative political movements such as feminism, which, in turn, have propelled rhetorical theory well beyond the parameters set by the Greeks.

The *resensing* of sophistic rhetoric championed by Poulakos, Crowley, and Jarratt (among others) paved the disciplinary roads of the late twentieth century, leading to the bright and still-burgeoning proliferation of diverse rhetorical theories, histories, and traditions that have emerged during the first decades of the twenty-first century. Taking up the feminist ethic of Jarratt and Campbell, disability, queer, and critical race histories and theories of rhetoric have become central to the study and practices of the field, as has work that considers environmental, nonhuman, and material rhetorics. So much of this scholarship, as we show in the next section, intersects with sensation, and much of it is non-Western. Sorry (not sorry!) Quintilian, but the art of rhetoric can no longer be summed up quaintly as "a good man speaking well" (2006, 12.1.1).

New (Media) Sensations

Of course, as mentioned at the beginning of this introduction, sensation and its attendant theories are not the purview of a single discipline. They can be found both at the heart of a singular field like rhetoric (as is our argument here) and also undergirding transdisciplinary fields like media studies and digital humanities. The work of Marshall McLuhan (1964) and Walter J. Ong (1982), which bridges both media and rhetorical studies, provides instructive examples of this interplay.[4] Both were interested in the impact of media and technology on communication and particularly technology's ability to transform human experience. Responding to the sudden ubiquity of television in the 1960s, they also examined the role of visuality in shaping the everyday lives of people participating in industrialized societies. And while McLuhan tended to focus on the human sensory "extensions" of the technological moment (he wrote that "new electric media are direct extensions of sight and sound and touch and kinesthesia" [1961, 51]), Ong's interest was most often on the historical sensorium. In *The Presence of the Word* (1967), such work led him to the prescient claim that the senses are not just biological but cultural: "given sufficient knowledge of the sensorium exploited within a specific culture, one could probably define the culture as a whole in all its aspects" (28). Ong was interested in what he termed the "great divide," or the differences between oral/aural and visual cultures and the emergence and implications of ocularcentrism. He attempted to demonstrate how the visuality of literacy (i.e., alphabetic text and writing) changes human cognition, culture, and experience, including what was lost when aurality ceased being the primary sensory means of communication.[5]

The intellectual heritage of McLuhan and Ong's sensorium, interwoven with other scholarly influences, has inspired a number of advancements in rhetoric. Some of that work has originated in classrooms, where evolving technology is always prompting new methods for teaching. In communication, this can be seen in the extension of speech pedagogies into the teaching of media production (radio, television, advertising, etc.). In rhetoric and composition, a pedagogical exploration of writing's multimodalities (Kress and Van Leeuwen 2001; Yancey 2004) has included a careful accounting of the affordances of various sensory modalities in the classroom (Shipka 2011), including the ways digital rhetorics change what it means to write (Hawisher and Selfe 1991; Eyman 2015). Scholars working at the intersection of multimodality and disability have also made crucial contributions to the field's understanding of sensation. Their work has amplified "the need to incorporate redundancy across multiple channels" to enable an audience with various sensory capacities to engage with multimodal and digital work (Kerschbaum 2013, para. 7); it has also highlighted how an uncritical celebration of the senses in multimodal pedagogy (e.g., assuming that everyone has/wants access to all senses at all times) privileges able-bodiedness (Yergeau 2014).

Outside the classroom, research on the rhetorics of sensory modalities has also followed pathways at least partially blazed by McLuhan and Ong. Visual rhetoric (C. Finnegan 2003, 2021; Olson 2013; Gries 2015) has long held a prominent position in the field and was instrumental in pushing rhetorical studies beyond speech and text as its primary domains. Visual rhetoric also helped to propel the work of sonic rhetoricians, who have developed novel theories and methods to reexamine (or resound) rhetorical histories, cultural practices, and public discourses (Selfe 2007; Gunn 2008; Comstock and Hocks 2016; Hawk 2018; Ahern 2018). In turn, work on the visual and sonic in rhetoric has enabled rhetoricians to think more broadly and inclusively about sense and sensation—spurring work on touch, olfaction, taste, and more (Conley and Eckstein 2020; S. Barnett 2022; DiCaglio 2022). And, echoing a broader movement in sensory studies writ large, in addition to studying particular sensory modes, there has been an increased interest in relational approaches to the senses in rhetorical studies. For instance, sound studies work on listening, affect, embodiment, and materiality (Henriques 2011; Dyson 2009; Daughtry 2015; Sun Eidsheim 2015) has led to a more nuanced treatment of sound and listening as full-bodied, multisensory experiences in rhetoric scholarship (Ceraso 2018; Hawk 2018; Stone 2021). Indeed, as this volume demonstrates, relational, multisensory approaches have become a salient feature of contemporary sensory rhetorical work.

Sensory Rhetorical Emergence and Intersections in the Twenty-First Century

Over the past two and a half decades, it is accurate to say that rhetorical studies has again come to its senses. This emphasis on the senses is a continuation of the long and robust engagement with sensation in the history of rhetoric just rehearsed but also mirrors evolving approaches in the humanities and social sciences, where tools for making sense of complex sociocultural, environmental, and political changes are urgently needed. In this section, we trace a number of recent sensational through lines in an effort to show both the diversity and the strength of these conversations as they thread in and out of rhetoric's disciplinary and subdisciplinary scholarship. We again acknowledge the limits of such an exploration but invite readers to join us in further embroidering and expanding the tapestry of sensory rhetoric we are weaving here.

One legible scholarly thread focuses on the body (Selzer and Crowley 1999; Bennett and Dickerson 2000; Hawhee 2005). Springing from a rich genealogy of feminist theory and method, work on rhetorical embodiment encourages scholars of speech and writing to reexamine rhetorics of perception and representation, particularly (though not limited to) the visual and sonic. This focus on embodiment has also expanded efforts for greater diversity and inclusion. Rhetorical scholars counter myths and retheorize notions of normalized bodies, converging with work in disability (Dolmage 2014; Yergeau 2018; Cedillo 2018), gender and sexuality (Carey 2016; Jensen 2016; VanHaitsma 2019), and cultural rhetoric, decolonial, and critical race studies (Powell 2020; Hidalgo 2016; García and Cortez 2020; Martinez 2020; Ore 2019). This scholarship collectively reconceives rhetorical subjectivity—moving away from paradigms privileging white, ableist, cis-, heterosexual perspectives and toward the bodies, sensations, and voices of historically marginalized populations.

Much of the work cited in the previous paragraph draws on or contributes to a growing body of global rhetorical scholarship, including important non-Western rhetorical contributions. Such work acknowledges the presence of rhetorics "elsewhere and otherwise" (García and Baca 2019) and utilizes decolonial and other theories not originating from the ancient Greeks to amplify the epistemologies and ontologies of non-Western and Indigenous rhetors. This work is critical to a sensory rhetorical perspective because it is not encumbered by the baggage of Western rational thought. Indeed, in light of such work, the term "nonrationality" can seem outright absurd, so steeped is it in the orthodoxies of Western modernity's ideological inheritances.

Materialist, digital, and environmental scholars in the field also offer perspectives that stretch the tradition—this time beyond human bodies. A growing area of scholarship examines how nonhuman machines, animals, environments, and ecosystems contribute to sense-making via complex rhetorical ontologies (Pezzullo 2009; Rice 2012; Rickert 2013; Brown 2015; Boyle 2018; Hawhee 2019; J. Barnett 2025). Additionally, field methods like oral history, case study, interview, and participant observation play a major role in rhetorical research; these methods also heighten researchers' attention to sensory experiences and ecologies. As Candice Rai and Caroline Gottschalk Druschke (2018, 3) write,

Fieldwork allows researchers to study both rhetoric's emplacement and fieldwork's complexity by offering access to and insight into a wider range of texts, perspectives, and experiences than we might otherwise discover. This might include the narratives and arguments offered through interviews and observations; the extra-textual aspects of persuasion and rhetorical performance that require our sensory facilities to perceive, like the sour stench of an alleyway, the sweat on a clam digger's brow, and the bodily warmth of a quick embrace; or the situated rhetorical forces that can be observed only through inhabitation, such as how place, power, materiality, embodiments, texts, and rhetoric intermesh and matter in particular situations.

The kinds of methods amplified in Rai and Gottshalk Druschke's text have deep roots in anthropology, a field that helped to galvanize the multidisciplinary interest in sensation. Though the goals of rhetorical and anthropological research are clearly different, we see strong resonances among these fields' sensory-rich methods. For instance, the description of rhetorical fieldwork above shares elements with Sarah Pink's (2015, 7) notion of "sensory ethnography," which "involves the researcher self-consciously and reflexively attending to the senses throughout the research process." As we discuss below, several chapters in this collection offer sensory methods and methodologies that can be taken up in diverse contexts.

We are inspired by recent scholarship within rhetorical studies that merges the various threads discussed in this section to create vibrant, intersectional, and transdisciplinary work—scholarship that uses sensation in its methodological and analytical frameworks to elevate social and political awareness (Muller 2020; Cram 2022; Brooks 2024). Such work is essential for addressing complex contemporary issues. In an illustrative example that demonstrates this intersectionality, Jennifer Lin LeMesurier describes the racialized epideictic rhetorics of taste in a chapter from her book *Inscrutable Eating* (2023). LeMesurier recounts a scene from David Chang's television show *Ugly Delicious* in which Chang and the historian Ian Mosby conduct a study with participants who claimed a sensitivity to MSG in Chinese food. Participants were unaffected by the MSG in provided snacks like Doritos—foods with similar amounts of the ingredient. "Even with this direct experience," LeMesurier writes, "several of them attempted to argue that their lack of symptoms meant that the dosage in Doritos was much lower than that in Chinese food. More than mere rationalizations, these contradictions demonstrate that the power of the sensory can be framed according to ideological assumptions that bypass whatever neutrality of sensation exists" (97). Sensations, she continues, "are made legible through patterned, socially normative understandings of the relationship between feeling and bodily states as either praiseworthy or blameworthy." In the book's preface, LeMesurier outlines her commitments to scholarship in Asian American studies, cultural studies, history, and rhetoric (9). This is just one example of many that bring together these interdisciplinary fields in the service of sensory rhetorical analysis.

While we see a reliance on and theorizing with sensation in all the scholarship cited above, that term does not always show up explicitly like it does in Rai and Gottschalk Druschke's or LeMesurier's texts. Part of the work we are interested in doing here, then, is curational. We want to show how and why terms and theories circulating in the field might be understood as and incorporated within a more formalized "sensory rhetorics" subdiscipline.

Clearly, the senses are implicated across rhetorical studies and baked into its earliest Western theorizations. They are also found within non-Western traditions and in the borderlands intersecting them all. Indeed, sensation always seems to crop up as a method for coping with and attempting to understand rapid cultural change. As we have discussed, sensation is also central to the technological innovations at the heart of multimodal studies and pedagogy; it is vital to rhetorical innovations like "ambience" and "attunement" (Rickert 2013); it is central to "field rhetoric," or the field methods that rely on researchers "being there," immersed "in the dynamic, living, breathing ecologies that give rise to rhetoric and its work" (Rai and Gottschalk Druschke 2018, 1); and it is integral to understandings of cultural rhetorics as dependent on situated embodied practices and traditions (Bratta and Powell 2016). Additionally, sensation is about thinking-feeling and collective experience—two ideas that have been significant in our conception of *Sensory Rhetorics*—which we turn to now.

Making Sense Together with Sensory Rhetorics

In Debra Hawhee's book *A Sense of Urgency* (2023), she sums up the province of sensory rhetorics with the colloquial expression "to make sense." Making sense is a process of recognizing and harnessing the rhetorical power of feeling. As she writes, "To make sense cuts in two different directions. The first is to understand and clarify. But even those actions can cut away from representational meaning, which adheres too closely to logical certainty.

To 'make sense,' here, is also to engage with, activate, and in some cases speak the senses. To make sense is a matter of deep and sometimes visceral feeling. Rather than viewing these related categories—feeling, emotion, affect—as factors that 'short-circuit' rational deliberation, I approach them as indispensable constituents of rhetoric. Feeling and its bodily, sensuous manifestations matter for rhetoric—always have, always will" (16). This indelible affective-cognitive pairing is part of her larger point: Thinking is inseparable from feeling, not distinct from it.[6] Echoing Hawhee's approach, then, our intention in this book is not to create a hierarchy between rationality (thinking) and nonrationality (feeling) but instead to blur the distinction between them. Along with the neo-Sophists, we suggest that, like truth, rationality is contingent, contextual, and constitutive of nonrational sensory experience. So-called rational discourse—even discourse used to explain scientific processes or material reality—is based on sensory input, embodied interpretation, social identification (in the Burkean sense), and rhetorical output.

This brings us to another key insight from Hawhee, specifically from her article "Rhetoric's Sensorium," where she describes *sensorium* as a concept rooted in multiplicity, collectivity, and participation rather than individuation. She writes, "The idea of a sensing package, a bundle of constitutive, participatory tendrils, may help us press past commonplace conditional observations . . . and could offer a way to think about connective, participatory dimensions of sensing" (5). Christa Olson (2021, 23) expands on this idea in her book *American Magnitude*, framing sensation as a participatory "public feeling." Olson explains, "Publics are always about feeling. They are made of sensation, shared risk, affiliation, and affection. Thinking of publics through the visceral and as spaces of individual and collective feeling enables us to notice how sensations that churn, ripple, tear, and flash as well as those that whisper, brush, flicker, and seep work to form public affiliation, give it staying power, and lend it consequence" (23). Such public feeling, Olson concludes, "is the base material of *common sense*. . . . How and what we feel leaves marks on us, and those marks, in turn, mark our public and private orientations. Over time, those sensations become habitual" (23–24; emphasis added).

Brian McNely furthers this line of thinking in his book *Engaging Ambience*, where he examines the impact of photography and describes the "participatory tendrils" of habitual, public sensation in Heideggerian terms as a "worlding." Echoing Steph's work on multimodal listening (Ceraso 2014, 2018), McNely (2024, 13) conceptualizes seeing as an embodied, multisensory experience: "We *see*, which is to say that we feel and hear and touch and take in the world with our eyes and with our bodies." "Seeing photographs," he continues, "is an affective exchange, touching, worlding unbracketed. Worlding may be *felt*: in our skin, in our throats, with our hands and bellies and eyes" (14). Drawing on Gilles Deleuze, McNely acknowledges the "haptic sense of sight" and reminds us that such multisensory touching—or Hawhee's "sensing package" (2015, 5)—situates us within the world and thus in relationship with the humans, objects, and nonhuman animals around us. To be in relationship, McNely suggests, is to participate in a sensory exchange wherein new sensations are created and shared.

Building on the work of Hawhee, Olson, and McNely, *Sensory Rhetorics* illustrates that sensory exchanges are always rhetorical, and thus, we *make sense* together. We see this collection as an invitation for readers to make sense together—to reify a commitment to sensory education, to "consider more deeply the constitutive roles of sensation in participatory, rhetorical acts" (Hawhee 2015, 13) so that we might work collectively toward novel and creative ways of addressing salient social, political, and environmental issues. To that end, the following chapters provide readers with a range of approaches and possibilities for how rhetoric can be brought to bear on sensation, as well as how a focus on sensation can provide new pathways for understanding how and why rhetoric works. Additionally, making sense together requires rhetoricians to mesh knowledge with other disciplines; a sustained relationship with the senses requires widening the lens of rhetorical work to seek more opportunities for transdisciplinary rhetorical research. Indeed, our authors draw on scholarship from across the humanities and social sciences to theorize sensation in various contexts. As the following pages make clear, rhetoric's—and this volume's—distinct contribution within this transdisciplinary conversation is that it treats sensation as a form of suasion. Ultimately, *Sensory Rhetorics* offers methods and orientations for understanding the role the senses play in shaping beliefs, environments, feelings, behaviors, and desires.

Plan of the Book

This book brings together seasoned and emerging scholars in rhetoric and communication studies to examine the concept of sensory rhetorics through a range of (multi)sensory modes and experiences. In choosing chapters for this project, we were mindful of the experiential inability to isolate the senses. Thus, while some chapters have a specific sensory focus—olfaction, for instance—all chapters highlight the interconnectivity of the senses. That said, it is important to acknowledge that interconnectivity does not necessarily mean harmony. As Howes (2022, 12) puts it, "The senses overlap and collaborate, but they may also conflict. The unity of the senses should not be presupposed." In Lisa L. Phillips's chapter on environmental injustice, for instance, she points out that complaints regarding smell often get ignored or overshadowed because visual and sonic threats are taken more seriously. She writes, "olfactible violence garners such rhetorical neglect because it reflects an archaic sensory hierarchy that privileges sight and hearing" (see chapter 3). We invite readers, then, to notice when and how different senses mix and mingle, as well as how they clash and compete—both within individual chapters and across the collection as a whole—and how these interactions affect the efficacy of different kinds of sensory rhetorics.

Sensory Rhetorics also features scholarship that explicitly addresses sensation in situated, embodied ways. As Hawhee (2015, 12) acknowledges, it is incredibly challenging to write about the senses without "thinking in terms of communal sensation, without presuming sameness." Many of our chapters center on highly specific and contextual bodily experiences—from white researchers grappling with their own complicity as they participate in a soil collection ceremony for two Black men who were lynched in the nineteenth century to the awe-inspiring sensations and physical transformations related to one of our author's experience with gender-affirming top surgery. Indeed, part of what makes the concept of sensory rhetorics so powerful is that it calls attention to the fact that sensation is *not* identical or neutral—that the ways people experience and interpret sensation is dependent on a range of factors, such as culture, race, ethnicity, gender, sexuality, physical and mental capacities, and ideological beliefs, to name just some. As the following chapters demonstrate, sensory rhetorical work enables us to tease out the complexity and specificity of sensation, including how our nonrational, embodied responses intersect with and shape how we make (figurative) sense of our experiences.

To honor sensation's complexity and specificity, we made a deliberate choice to showcase an array of writing styles and approaches to research in this collection. Some chapters resemble more traditional academic scholarship, and others take risks when it comes to style and form. For example, several of our authors foreground personal sensory experiences, while others write about the senses from a more objective stance. Some chapters focus on case studies, some focus on methods, and others are theoretically inclined. One author—Ames Hawkins—also pushes the boundaries of academic writing with a creative-critical approach to their subject. This eclectic mix is intended to present readers with a variety of models for engaging with and writing about the senses. There are many ways to examine sensory rhetorics, and we hope this book provides different possibilities for or "ways into" sensory rhetorical work for future scholars.

While the chapters may not look uniform from a writing standpoint, as an ensemble they offer a unified argument: that sensory rhetorical work is central to understanding and intervening in some of the most perplexing, urgent issues of our time, from political polarization to environmental disasters. The order of the chapters is intended to move readers through the volume in a way that allows them to gradually gain exposure to critical concepts and methods for sensory rhetorics before being introduced to approaches that challenge and reimagine the future work of sensory rhetorics. Chapters 1 and 2 offer readers a clear sense of why sensory rhetorical approaches are needed to comprehend the complexity (and absurdity) of contemporary life—including the politicization of taste and digital consumption practices. In "Red Tastes, Blue Tastes: Disgust and the Political Rhetoric of Moral Pollution," Margot Finn and Bryan W. Moe focus on the Cracker Barrel culture war, Alex Jones's claims about who smells of sulfur, and the liberal response to Trump's tastes to explore how disgust shapes political rhetoric across the left-right divide. Drawing largely from contemporary journalism, their accessible, public-facing chapter illustrates how disgust is a primal response to offensive tastes and smells *and* a moral and social sentiment—and in both cases is a response to perceived pollution. As both an embodied sensory experience and form of social boundary drawing, Finn and Moe argue, disgust accentuates the interplay between the senses and the rhetoric of political division and helps illuminate how and why bad smells and tastes are so useful for identifying and distancing oneself from threats.

In "Rational Markets, Sensory Marketplaces: How Stock Imagery Shapes Digital Sense-Making," Kerry Banazek and Kellie Sharp-Hoskins examine how consumption, commercialization, and the logics of capital exert pressure on sensory rhetorics through a case study of the stock image industry. They consider how sense is made not only by sensuous objects (including commercial images) that circulate through digital spaces but also by speed as a logical function that structures digital circulation. Banazek and Sharp-Hoskins propose "acceleration" as a key term for sensory rhetoric that allows us to understand multisensory digital marketing in its complexity, arguing that understanding acceleration in this context requires attention to how patrons in digital marketplaces are hailed via repetition and abundance—rhetorical features that contribute to the creation of immersive experiences with their own forms of rationality. The stock photo industry, they contend, participates in a style of sensory world-making where aesthetics, embodied sensations, and consumption are distributed asymmetrically in service of market rationality. This case study exposes how even seemingly singular moments of digital consumption draw on sensory multiplicity, and it serves as a model for future explorations of how digital industries participate in the rhetorical construction of sensory experiences and norms—and their cultural influence.

Chapters 3, 4, and 5 model for scholars a range of innovative research methods for engaging in and with sensory rhetorical work in relation to environmental injustice, antiracism, and gender-affirming surgery. Lisa L. Phillips's "Reeking Revelations: How Olfaction Informs Rhetorical Processes in Environmental Injustice" reveals how reeking smellscapes shape lived experiences, catalyze environmental justice activism and advocacy, and inform sensory rhetorical tactics used to address environmental risks. Phillips lays out a theoretical approach to assess the impact of olfaction and olfactory rhetoric on environmental injustice mitigation and outlines a procedural method to evaluate how people sense and perceive environmental injustices and their subsequent engagement through sensory-rhetorical activism and advocacy efforts. Ultimately, this chapter offers keen insights about sensation to demonstrate how we can bridge academic and activist work in service of environmental justice.

In "The Sense of Soil: Antiracism and the Community Soil Collection Project," Natalie Bennie and Kelly Williams Nagel write about their experience attending a soil collection ceremony in memory of Joseph McCoy and Benjamin Thomas, two Black men lynched in Alexandria, Virginia, in the late nineteenth century. This ceremony culminated in a communal act of soil collection in which over one hundred attendees physically moved soil taken from the historical lynching sites into urns for McCoy and Thomas. Methodologically, the authors focus on the sensory input of rhetorical fieldwork, moving beyond the speeches and text of the ceremony toward the soil itself as a sensory agent of public memory. Bennie and Williams Nagel argue that rhetorical fieldwork methodologies ought to grapple with the senses of researchers to better understand how meaning making in antiracist activism becomes salient. This chapter will be of particular importance to white scholars engaged in antiracist scholarship, public intellectuals engaged in unsettling legacies of racial violence, and scholars from a diverse range of disciplines that utilize sensory fieldwork methodologies.

In a creative-critical autoethnographic essay, "Feeling Through Numbness, Healing with Awe: Not-Knowing as a Methodology for Sensory Rhetorics," Ames Hawkins writes about their personal experience of gender-affirming top surgery to explore the potential of "not-knowing" as a critical concept for sensory rhetorics. This chapter seeks to illustrate the relevance of "not-knowing" to sensory rhetorics in both content and form. Hawkins combines evocative personal narrative, images, and scholarly reflection to model an embodied research method for sensory rhetorical work. In short, Hawkins reimagines what sensory rhetorics scholarship might look like, offering writing that mixes rigorous intellectual inquiry with exciting creative possibilities. Ultimately, Hawkins advocates for a sensory rhetoric that values ambiguity, embodied experience, and the refusal of definitive conclusions. By embracing not-knowing as a methodology, scholars are invited to reconsider how we craft, convey, and engage with knowledge in ways that honor the complexity of human experience.

Finally, chapters 6, 7, and 8 leave readers with provocative questions and ideas—regarding received notions of sense and meaning in rhetorical theory and decolonial approaches to sensation—that have the potential to transform the field's understanding of sensory rhetorics going forward. Benjamin Firgens's "Autokinesis and the Sense of Meaninglessness" argues that "autokinesis," an optical illusion of seeing movement where none exists, exemplifies how sight plays a more complicated role in the sensorium than previously acknowledged and that illusions in general require rhetoricians to reckon with the social norms that define certain responses to meaninglessness as sensible and others illusory. Normative habits that delimit the neurodivergent from the neurotypical persist not only in our ablest societies and publics but also in received traditions of rhetorical theory, specifically the pretense that consensus—literally, "shared sense"—is possible as an end goal for rhetorical practice. Firgens demonstrates that meaninglessness is not a failure or loss but the fundamental condition of sense prior to the normative imposition of meaning.

In "Unsettling Colonized Sensory Archives," Romeo García and Kyle S. Bond explore the relationships among colonization, sensory archives, and sonic rhetoric. Using early Latter-day Saint hymnody as a case study, this chapter examines how sensory experiences are archived and mobilized to sustain dominant religious orthodoxies and control. This exploration not only illustrates the ways these sensory archives are constructed to perpetuate power but also advocates for a critical disconnection—or delinking—of the senses from entrenched colonial aesthetics. This interrogation challenges the foundational sensory models and processes that uphold epistemic authority and compliance, urging a reevaluation of our inherited sensory frameworks.

In "In*form*ing Rhetoric: Pluriversal Lessons on *Différance* and Rhetorical Energy," David M. Grant argues that both decolonial and Continental philosophies point toward a more complex theorization of sensation and sense-making. Following a central metaphor in sensory rhetorics scholarship—energy—this chapter argues that relative rhetorical energies are inherent in all things, including rocks. Grant's chapter demonstrates how common approaches to sensation as biological energy may reinscribe a colonial vision of reality. Through an examination of rocks as energy-transducing rhetorical agents, he makes a case for extending notions of sensory rhetoric beyond the living. Grant's bold argument has the potential to reshape the future of sensory rhetorical work.

Collectively, the chapters in *Sensory Rhetorics* make an overarching argument about the need for a sustained attention to the senses in rhetorical studies, which will enable us to make (fuller) sense of the constantly changing, often precarious rhetorical situations and ecologies we encounter in everyday life. As with any edited volume, *Sensory Rhetorics* is not intended to be representative of sensory rhetorical work as a whole. Rather, our hope is that this collection will help to establish sensory rhetorics as a thriving and diverse area of research and provide readers with theories, concepts, and methods that carve out new pathways for scholarship on rhetoric and the senses. To that end, we encourage readers to build on, complicate, and transform the ideas presented in this volume.

Notes

1. In 2015, the phrase "sensory rhetoric" began to gain momentum with the completion of Justine B. Wells's dissertation "A Taste for Things: Sensory Rhetoric Beyond the Human" and an RSA summer institute at the University of Wisconsin–Madison led by Debra Hawhee and Vanessa Beasley on the topic (Steph and Jon were both participants). Since then, sensory rhetorical work has proliferated in the scholarship, with nearly one hundred publications in the past ten years (according to Google Scholar), the majority of which are works by rhetoricians.

2. For example, the distinction between affect and emotion is commonly understood as one of cognitive awareness, where "knowable concepts of emotion organize otherwise inchoate though no less visceral affective intensities" (Hawhee 2019, 6). This particular distinction is useful on its own but has also wrought, in affect theory, the development of a significant multidisciplinary field, which—due to its popularity and impact—might overwhelm the aims of a project on sensation. It is therefore important that we both acknowledge the conceptual overlap of the above terms while also working to distinguish them from each other when such distinctions are meaningful and/or useful.

3. Aristotle's epideictic mode is another example of sensory-based judgment. Epideictic, in its most basic form, is a judgment of what is or is not "honorable," intuited at a cultural, sensory level that registers as praise or blame (1991, 2.20.26). See also Jeffery Walker, *Rhetoric and Poetics in Antiquity* (2000), where epideictic's sensory history is mapped. Walker shows rhetoric's

emergence alongside (and wrapped up within) the rhythmic sound of poetry and song. These sensorial productions undergirded early Greek ideology as "the basic codes of value and belief by which a society or culture lives" (9), or what Aristotle would later call epideictic.

4. McLuhan is also notably one of David Howes's primary intellectual influences, and Howes builds on McLuhan's sensorium in each of his major works. In reviewing the literature for this introduction, we thought it was interesting that the cultural/anthropological sensory work of Howes has not been of more interest to rhetoricians. But that may be at least partly because of McLuhan's position as a lodestar in the field. The work of Howes may have been less conspicuous when McLuhan himself is so embedded in the overlapping histories of communication and rhetoric, including his place in a lineage of sensory-minded scholars (including Harold Inis, Eric Havelock, and Walter Ong), not to mention his influence on the creation of subdisciplines like computers and writing and digital rhetoric.

5. As Jon has explored elsewhere (Stone 2018, 2021), Ong's work was not without its problematic conclusions, not the least of which was ascribing to oral cultures a certain mystical authority even while categorizing them as technically inferior (see Ong 1982, 170).

6. In Hawhee's 2015 article "Rhetoric's Sensorium," she draws out this (in)distinction, pointing to the rise of "epistemic rhetoric" in the 1960s that elevated rhetoric above sensation as "a—if not the—way of knowing" (10). In the article, she briefly summarizes the history of postmodern rhetoric influenced by Nietzsche that emphasized the limitations of the senses for accessing knowledge. She traces the development of a false dichotomy between aesthetic and epistemic rhetoric, with authors John Poulakos and Steve Whitson (1995, 382) eventually stating, "An aesthetic rhetoric counts on, attends to, and takes into account the body and its senses; an epistemic rhetoric tries to bypass them but cannot." This debate is reminiscent of a much earlier observation from the moral philosopher David Hume ([1739] 1987, 462) that "reason is, and ought only to be the slave of the passions."

References

Ahern, Kati Fargo. 2018. "Understanding Learning Spaces Sonically, Soundscaping Evaluations of Place." *Computers and Composition* 48 (June): 22–33.

Aristotle. 1991. *On Rhetoric: A Theory of Civic Discourse.* Translated by George Kennedy. New York: Oxford University Press.

Barnett, Joshua Trey. 2025. *Ecological Feelings: A Rhetorical Compendium.* East Lansing: Michigan State University Press.

Barnett, Scott. 2022. "Violence and Beneficence in the Rhetorics of Touch." In *Bodies of Knowledge: Embodied Rhetorics in Theory and Practice*, edited by A. Abby Knoblauch and Marie E. Moeller, 23–42. Logan: Utah State University Press.

Bennet, Michael, and Vanessa D. Dickerson. 2000. *Recovering the Black Female Body: Self-Representations by African American Women.* New Brunswick: Rutgers University Press.

Boyle, Casey. 2018. *Rhetoric as a Posthuman Practice.* Columbus: The Ohio State University Press.

Bratta, Phil, and Malea Powell. 2016. "Introduction to the Special Issue: Entering the Cultural Rhetorics Conversations." *Enculturation*, April 20. https://www.enculturation.net/entering-the-cultural-rhetorics-conversations.

Brooks, Earl H. 2024. *On Rhetoric and Black Music.* Detroit: Wayne State University Press.

Brown, James. 2015. *Ethical Programs: Hospitality and the Rhetorics of Software.* Ann Arbor: University of Michigan Press.

Campbell, Karolyn Kohrs. 1973. "The Rhetoric of Women's Liberation: An Oxymoron." *Quarterly Journal of Speech* 59 (1): 74–86.

Carey, Tamika. 2016. *Rhetorical Healing: The Reeducation of Contemporary Black Womanhood.* Albany: SUNY Press.

Cedillo, Christina V. 2018. "What Does It Mean to Move? Race, Disability, and Critical Embodiment Pedagogy." *Composition Forum* 39 (Summer). https://compositionforum.com/issue/39/to-move.php.

Ceraso, Steph. 2014. "(Re)Educating the Senses: Multimodal Listening, Bodily Learning, and the Composition of Sonic Experiences." *College English* 77 (2): 102–23.

———. 2018. *Sounding Composition: Multimodal Pedagogies for Embodied Listening*. Pittsburgh: University of Pittsburgh Press.

Cicero, Marcus Tullius. 1860. *De oratore*. Translated by J. S. Watson. https://www.attalus.org/info/deoratore.html.

Classen, Constance. 1998. *The Colour of Angels: Cosmology, Gender and the Aesthetic Imagination*. New York: Routledge.

Comstock, Michelle, and Mary E. Hocks. 2016. "The Sounds of Climate Change: Sonic Rhetoric in the Anthropocene, the Age of Human Impact." *Rhetoric Review* 35 (2): 165–75.

Conley, Donovan, and Justin Eckstein. 2020. *Cookery: Food Rhetorics and Social Production*. Tuscaloosa: University of Alabama Press.

Cram, E. 2022. *Violent Inheritance: Sexuality, Land, and Energy in Making the North American West*. Berkeley: University of California Press.

Crowley, Sharon. 1989. "A Plea for the Revival of Sophistry." *Rhetoric Review* 7 (2): 318–34.

Daughtry, J. Martin. 2015. *Listening to War: Sound, Music, Trauma, and Survival in Wartime Iraq*. Oxford: Oxford University Press.

DiCaglio, Sara. 2022 "Towards an Olfactory Rhetoric." In *Bodies of Knowledge: Embodied Rhetorics in Theory and Practice*, edited by A. Abby Knoblauch and Marie E. Moeller, 57–73. Logan: Utah State University Press.

Dolmage, Jay Timothy. 2014. *Disability Rhetoric*. Syracuse: Syracuse University Press.

Dyson, Frances. 2009. *Sounding New Media: Immersion and Embodiment in the Arts and Culture*. Berkeley: University of California Press.

Eckstein, Justin. 2020. "Sensing School Shootings." *Critical Studies in Media Communication* 37 (2): 161–73.

Eyman, Douglas. 2015. *Digital Rhetoric: Theory, Method, Practice*. Ann Arbor: University of Michigan Press.

Finnegan, Cara A. 2003. *Picturing Poverty: Print Culture and FSA Photographs*. Washington, DC: Smithsonian Institution Scholarly Press.

———. 2021. *Photographic Presidents: Making History from Daguerreotype to Digital*. Urbana: University of Illinois Press.

Finnegan, Ruth. 2022. *Communicating: The Multiple Modes of Human Connectedness*. New York: Routledge.

García, Romeo, and Damián Baca, eds. 2019. *Rhetorics Elsewhere and Otherwise: Contested Modernities, Decolonial Visions*. Urbana: National Council of Teachers of English.

García, Romeo, and José M. Cortez. 2020. "The Trace of a Mark that Scatters: The Anthropoi and the Rhetoric of Decoloniality." *Rhetoric Society Quarterly* 50 (2): 93–108.

Geurts, Kathryn Linn. 2003. *Culture and the Senses: Bodily Ways of Knowing in an African Community*. Berkeley: University of California Press.

Gorgias. 2001. "Encomium of Helen." In *The Rhetorical Tradition: Readings from Classical Times to the Present*, 2nd ed., edited by Patricia Bizzell and Bruce Herzberg, 42–46. New York: Bedford / St. Martin's.

Gries, Laurie. 2015. *Still Life with Rhetoric: A New Materialist Approach for Visual Rhetorics*. Logan: Utah State University Press.

Gunn, Joshua. 2008. "Speech Is Dead; Long Live Speech." *Quarterly Journal of Speech* 94 (3): 343–64.

Hawhee, Debra. 2005. *Bodily Arts: Rhetoric and Athletics in Ancient Greece*. Austin: University of Texas Press.

———. 2015. "Rhetoric's Sensorium." *Quarterly Journal of Speech* 101 (1): 2–17.

———. 2019. *Rhetoric in Tooth and Claw: Animals, Language, Sensation*. Chicago: University of Chicago Press.

———. 2023. *A Sense of Urgency: How the Climate Crisis Is Changing Rhetoric*. Chicago: University of Chicago Press.

Hawisher, Gail E., and Cynthia L. Selfe. 1991. *Evolving Perspectives on Computers and Composition Studies: Questions for the 1990s*. Urbana: National Council of Teachers of English.

Hawk, Byron. 2018. *Resounding the Rhetorical: Composition as a Quasi-Object*.

Pittsburgh: University of Pittsburgh Press.

Henriques, Julian. 2011. *Sonic Bodies: Reggae Sound Systems, Performance Techniques, and Ways of Knowing*. New York: Bloomsbury Academic.

Hidalgo, Alexandra. 2016 "Family Archives and the Rhetoric of Loss." In *Provocations: Reconstructing the Archive*, edited by Patrick W. Berry, Gail E. Hawisher, and Cynthia L. Selfe. Logan: Computers and Composition Digital Press / Utah State University Press. https://ccdigitalpress.org/book/reconstructingthearchive/hidalgo.html.

Howes, David. 2003. *Sensual Relations: Engaging the Senses in Culture and Social Theory*. Ann Arbor: University of Michigan Press.

———. 2022. *The Sensory Studies Manifesto: Tracking the Sensorial Revolution in the Arts and Humanities*. Toronto: University of Toronto Press.

Hume, David. (1739) 1987. *A Treatise of Human Nature*. Edited by Ernest Campbell Mossner. London: Penguin.

Jarratt, Susan. 1991. *Rereading the Sophists: Classical Rhetoric Refigured*. Carbondale: Southern Illinois University Press.

Jensen, Robin. 2016. *Infertility: Tracing the History of a Transformative Term*. University Park: Pennsylvania State University Press.

Kerschbaum, Stephanie. 2013. "Modality." In "Multimodality in Motion: Disability in Kairotic Spaces," edited by M. Remi Yergeau, Elizabeth Brewer, Stephanie Kerschbaum, Sushil Oswal, Margaret Price, Michael J. Salvo, Cynthia L. Selfe, and Franny Howes. Special issue, *Kairos: A Journal of Rhetoric, Technology, and Pedagogy* 18 (1). https://kairos.technorhetoric.net/18.1/coverweb/yergeau-et-al/pages/ableism/tech.html.

Kress, Gunther, and Theo Van Leeuwen. 2001. *Multimodal Discourse: The Modes and Media of Contemporary Communication*. London: Hodder Arnold.

Leff, Michael. 1999. "The Habitation of Rhetoric." In *Contemporary Rhetorical Theory, A Reader*, edited by John Louis Lucaites, Celeste Michelle Condit, and Sally Caudill, 52–64. New York: Guilford.

LeMesurier, Jennifer Lin. 2023. *Inscrutable Eating: Asian Appetites and the Rhetorics of Racial Consumption*. Columbus: The Ohio State University Press.

Martinez, Aja Y. 2020. *Counterstory: The Rhetoric and Writing of Critical Race Theory*. Urbana: National Council of Teachers of English.

McLuhan, Marshall. 1961. "Inside the Five Sense Sensorium." *Canadian Architect* (6): 49–54.

———. 1964. *Understanding Media: The Extensions of Man*. New York: McGraw-Hill.

McNely, Brian. 2024. *Engaging Ambience: Visual and Multisensory Methodologies and Rhetorical Theory*. Denver: University Press of Colorado.

Muller, S. Marek. 2020. *Impersonating Animals: Rhetoric, Ecofeminism, and Animal Rights Law*. East Lansing: Michigan State University Press.

Olson, Christa J. 2013. *Constitutive Visions: Indigeneity and Commonplaces of National Identity in Republican Ecuador*. University Park: Pennsylvania State University Press.

———. 2021. *American Magnitude: Hemispheric Vision and Public Feeling in the United States*. Columbus: The Ohio State University Press.

Ong, Walter J. 1967. *The Presence of the Word: Some Prolegomena for Cultural and Religious History*. New Haven: Yale University Press.

———. 1982. *Orality and Literacy: The Technologizing of the Word*. London: Methuen.

Ore, Ersula J. 2019. *Lynching: Violence, Rhetoric, and American Identity*. Jackson: University Press of Mississippi.

Pezzullo, Phaedra C. 2009. *Toxic Tourism: Rhetorics of Pollution, Travel, and Environmental Justice*. Tuscaloosa: University of Alabama Press.

Pink, Sarah. 2015. *Doing Sensory Ethnography*. 2nd ed. Los Angeles: Sage.

Plato. 1961. *The Gorgias*. Translated by W. D. Woodhead. In *Plato: The Collected Dialogues*, edited by Edith Hamilton and Huntington Cairns, 229–307. Princeton: Princeton University Press.

Poulakos, John. 1983. "Toward a Sophistic Definition of Rhetoric." *Philosophy and Rhetoric* 16 (1): 35–48.

Poulakos, John, and Steve Whitson. 1995. "Rhetoric Denuded and Redressed: Figs and Figures." *Quarterly Journal of Speech* 81 (3): 378–85.

Powell, Malea. 2020. "Rhetoric on Native Land." *Journal for the History of Rhetoric* 23 (1): 115–16.

Quintilian. 2006. *Institutes of Oratory*. Edited by Lee Honeycutt. Translated by John Selby Watson. https://kairos.technorhetoric.net/stasis/2017/honeycutt/quintilian/.

Rai, Candice, and Caroline Gottschalk Druschke. 2018. *Field Rhetoric: Ethnography, Ecology, and Engagement in the Places of Persuasion*. Tuscaloosa: University of Alabama Press.

Rice, Jenny. 2012. *Distant Publics: Development Rhetoric and the Subject of Crisis*. Pittsburgh: University of Pittsburgh Press.

Rickert, Thomas. 2013. *Ambient Rhetoric: The Attunements of Rhetorical Being*. Pittsburgh: University of Pittsburgh Press.

Selfe, Cynthia. 2007. *Multimodal Composition: Resources for Teachers*. New York: Hampton.

Selzer, Jack, and Sharon Crowley, eds. 1999. *Rhetorical Bodies*. Madison: University of Wisconsin Press.

Shipka, Jody. 2011. *Toward a Composition Made Whole*. Pittsburgh: University of Pittsburgh Press.

Stone, Jonathan W. 2018. "Rhetorical Folkness: Reanimating Walter J. Ong in the Pursuit of Digital Humanity." In *Digital Sound Studies*, edited by Mary Caton Lingold, Darren Mueller, and Whitney Trettien, 65–80. Durham: Duke University Press.

———. 2021. *Listening to the Lomax Archive: The Sonic Rhetorics of African American Folksong in the 1930s*. Ann Arbor: University of Michigan Press.

Sun Eidsheim, Nina. 2015. *Sensing Sound: Singing and Listening as Vibrational Practice*. Durham: Duke University Press.

VanHaitsma, Pamela. 2019. *Queering Romantic Engagement in the Postal Age: A Rhetorical Education*. Columbia: University of South Carolina Press.

Walker, Jeffrey. 2000. *Rhetoric and Poetics in Antiquity*. Oxford: Oxford University Press.

Wells, Justine Beatrice. 2015. "A Taste for Things: Sensory Rhetoric Beyond the Human." Ph.D. diss., University of South Carolina.

Yancey, Kathleen Blake. 2004. "Made Not Only in Words: Composition in a New Key." *College Composition and Communication* 56 (2): 297–328.

Yergeau, M. Remi. 2014. "Shiny Rhetorics." Keynote address at the 21st Century Englishes Graduate Student Conference, Bowling Green State University. Bowling Green, OH, October 4.

———. 2018. *Authoring Autism: On Rhetoric and Neurological Queerness*. Durham: Duke University Press.

1

Red Tastes, Blue Tastes
Disgust and the Political
Rhetoric of Moral Pollution

MARGOT FINN AND BRYAN W. MOE

Iconic Southern restaurant and gift shop Cracker Barrel probably did not expect to ignite controversy with its August 1, 2022, Facebook post announcing a new menu offering: Impossible brand vegan sausage. Cracker Barrel uses Facebook to communicate with roughly three million followers about seasonal specials and holiday offerings. For example, a September 2022 post advertised, "As a small token of our appreciation, on #VeteransDay tomorrow, we're giving away a free slice of Double Chocolate Fudge Coca-Cola® Cake* to veterans and active duty military" (Cracker Barrel 2022). The new menu offering was introduced in the same cheerful, placeless marketing voice scrubbed of all personality: "Discover new frontiers. Experience the out of this world flavor of Impossible Sausage Made From Plants time you Build Your Own Breakfast [sic]." The post was anchored by a picture of scrambled eggs and hash browns with two sausage patties.

Although the Impossible brand of meat substitutes is only about a decade old, it has established a nationwide presence in grocery stores and chain restaurants without causing any noteworthy outcry. White Castle started serving an Impossible version of its iconic slider in 2018, and the Impossible brand worked with Little Ceasars to develop its first version of Impossible sausage to serve on its pizzas in 2019. Burger King has been serving Impossible burgers and sausage patties nationwide since 2019, and by 2020, Carl's Jr. / Hardys, Dunkin Donuts, and Subway all had meat alternatives on their menus (Chayes 2020). However, for some people, hearing that the plant-based meat alternative would be served at a chain more firmly associated with the conservative American heartland was a bridge too far.

Within three days, the Facebook post received six thousand comments when it is rare for Cracker Barrel's posts to get more than five hundred, and it had been retweeted 115,000 times (Lamour 2022). Much of the outraged response used the word "woke" pejoratively to describe the sausage and suggested the move was out of touch with the company's customer base. For example, Catherine Blanke Witt replied to the original post, "Keep your Bill Gates sausage! Are you all really prepared to go woke and go broke? Your customer base is the South!! We don't eat plant based meat in the South! I hope this crap falls flat!! (Cracker Barrel 2022). Others welcomed the company's decision. Brandon Hilton wrote, "It truly gives me hope for our future, when even Cracker Barrel starts offering vegan options! It is so disgusting to see these comments and how ignorant people can be when they're losing NOTHING . . . and for the 100 ignorant people you may lose, you'll gain 1,000's more!!"

Many flabbergasted vegetarians pointed out that, like Hilton the chain was not proposing to get rid of pork sausage or force anyone to try the new menu option. But its mere presence on the menu was enough to make some people swear off the restaurant forever. "We don't eat in an old country store for woke burgers," read one reply to the company's Facebook announcement quoted in *Salon*'s coverage, and another added, "I just lost respect for a once great Tennessee company" (Stevens 2022).

The consumer response to Cracker Barrel's introduction of Impossible sausage is just one recent example of how the United States' bitter political and social divisions affect our sensory experiences and, in particular, the multisensory experience of disgust. "Disgust," a word built on Latin roots meaning "bad taste," evokes both a sensorial response to perceived pollution or contamination and also social or moral judgment. Repulsion can be elicited by the physical or the conceptual, and the two are often mingled in experience and rhetoric. In the Cracker Barrel example, we see both conservatives and liberals expressing disgust.

In what follows, we elaborate further on the Cracker Barrel controversy, focusing specifically on the role of context in perceptions of disgust. Then we consider a more quintessentially conservative example and a more quintessentially liberal example, offering some preliminary speculations on the partisan tendencies one might find in a more robust survey of political disgust. What the three examples together make clear is that the revulsion associated with bad tastes and smells is used across the partisan divide to distance and demean others seen as dangerous or polluting. Better understanding the use of disgust in political rhetoric may have implications for people wishing to communicate effectively with audiences on the right or left. Ultimately, though, we hope this exploration of disgust accentuates how sensory rhetorics figure into the increasingly contentious arena of US politics.

Moral Pollution and Woke Sausage

In *The Expression of the Emotions in Man and Animals*, Charles Darwin (1899) argues that disgust is essentially rooted in the rejection of bad, contaminated food that would make us sick to eat. However, his discussion reveals how easily an offensive taste can be induced by things besides food: "In Tierra del Fuego, a native touched with his finger some cold preserved meat which I was eating at our bivouac, and plainly showed utter disgust at its softness; whilst I felt utter disgust at my food being touched by a native savage, though his hands did not appear dirty. A smear of soup in a man's beard looks disgusting, though there is of course nothing disgusting in the soup itself" (qtd. in Miller 2020, 1). The passage explores multiple potential sources of disgust: the texture of the meat that offends the native, the nakedness of the man touching Darwin's potted meat, and in the case of soup in a beard, food that is not offensive to anyone but is in the wrong place. Sufferers of an anxiety disorder named "trypophobia" are disgusted by patterns with repetitive holes, like the ones found in sponges and some cheeses. Even people without a diagnosable disorder sometimes find patterns like lotus seed pods disgusting, especially when projected onto human skin (Martinez-Aguayo et al. 2018). Disgust is possible wherever we are offended by a perceived category error. Rather than being merely the experience of tasting something bad, disgust might be better described as an experiential sense of *wrongness*.

Darwin's passage about soup in a beard recalls the anthropologist Mary Douglas's (1966, 44) definition of dirt as "matter out of place." According to Douglas, "there is no such thing as absolute dirt," and "no single item is dirty apart from (i.e., outside of) a particular system of classification in which it does not fit." She offers examples like shoes, which might not be dirty in themselves, "but it is dirty to place them on the dining table" (44). Soup itself is not polluted, but soup in a beard is doubly polluted: The hair contaminates the soup, and the soup contaminates the man. When the concern is contamination, context is crucial. For example, the smell of butyric acid can be delicious, as it is for many people when it wafts from a plate of pasta covered in parmesan cheese, or disgusting, as when its origin is known to be underarms or vomit. The chemical does not change, but depending on the context, it can make us either salivate or gag.

The importance of context to the experience of disgust helps make sense of the outraged reaction to Impossible sausage being served at Cracker Barrel. Cracker Barrel has a deeply rooted ethos as a representative food establishment for the US South. Dan Evins, a Shell Oil salesman, started the restaurant in 1969 in Lebanon, Tennessee, as a way to encourage the sales of gasoline and recreational travel by car (Broome and Boone 2022). This is why many Cracker Barrel establishments are connected to gas stations and located off highways. The South is still far more dependent on the interstate system than are regions with more major airline hubs or that are better connected by passenger rail. Between the prominence of highway travel in southern experience and the ubiquity of Cracker Barrel restaurants along the routes connecting major southern cities, the chain has become a highly visible part of the southern landscape and foodscape.

The décor of the restaurant also deliberately evokes general stores in a sort of regionally nonspecific pastiche. As described in *The Atlantic*, "The elements don't really obey any kind of historical order, or any geographical one. The stores' peaked facade, reaching above the roof of the building, is a classic design element of Northern country stores. The front porch, with its rocking chairs, would more likely have been found in the South. Taken together, all these elements signal 'general store' to the average American" (Chertoff 2013). Despite the regional incoherence of the architecture, general stores and rural agricultural communities are themselves associated with the South. The menu's emphasis on comfort foods associated with the South, like chicken and dumplings, grits, greens cooked with bacon, and biscuits and cornbread, along with flourishes like folksy wooden games on every table and the cast-iron dishes it serves its baked beans in all work to solidify the chain's regional identity.

Cracker Barrel also earned a reputation for being a hostile workplace for queer people after an overtly homophobic purge of sixteen employees in the early 1990s. According to *Mashed*, "There was a company-wide directive to fire any Cracker Barrel workers 'whose sexual preferences fail to demonstrate normal heterosexual values.' . . . Stockholders (the company had gone public in 1981) of Cracker Barrel organized resistance. Cracker Barrel founder Danny Evins eventually apologized and retracted the policy" (Broome and Boone 2022). The company made public efforts to portray itself as a reformed and more tolerant employer, but the incident encouraged many people to see the company as a promoter and protector of the kind of bigotry associated with southern, white, Christian Republicans.

All of this helps to explain why Cracker Barrel's introduction of Impossible meat was more controversial than its appearance was in less regionally and culturally marked chains like Little Caesars or Burger King. Plant-based meat is only a contaminant in this supposed refuge from the demonic spirits of progressive wokeness. Probably satirizing the conservative response, one woman quoted in *Salon*'s coverage replied to the initial Facebook post, "This is the future us leftists want. For the domain of all right winged red necks to turn on them and force veganism upon them. Next they'll be donating proceeds to BLM and trans youth. After that we're coming for Waffle House and Walmart. You've been warned. The revolution is nigh" (Stevens 2022). Many of the people opposed to the menu change attribute the decision to outsiders and assume that its target must also be people who would not have previously eaten at the chain. Plant-based meat and the people who eat it are seen as so antithetical to the brand that many could confidently assert that Cracker Barrel's existing customers could not possibly want it.

Relatively few of the people opposed to the menu change complained about the taste of plant-based meats, perhaps because few had tried them. In one of many responses on the Cracker Barrel Facebook page that conflated the sausage more typically made of pork with burgers more typically made of beef, Brian Peplinski wrote, "All natural humanely raised beef, 1 ingredient. Impossible burger 50. Go ahead and tell yourself it's healthier. I don't care what people eat really. I'll stick to normal food and eat less of the bad rather than put manufactured things into my body" (Cracker Barrel 2022). His concern for how "humanely raised" the beef is seems especially noteworthy, indicating that what is distasteful about the new plant-based sausage is not anyone's attempt to reduce the ecological, ethical, or nutritional harms associated with their diets but instead a rejection of the notion that products like the Impossible sausage are better in those ways than "normal food."

Alison Perelman (2013, 17) argues, in her work on the rhetoric of food in US politics, "Taste, in the most comprehensive sense of the term, is at the root of how identity is made visible." Variations on this theme are the stuff of cross-cultural cliché, from Jean Anthelme Brilliat-Savarin's most-cited bon mot, "Dis-moi ce que tu manges, je te dirai ce que tu es" (tell me what you eat, and I will tell you what you are), to the koan typically attributed to the twentieth-century Chinese poet and philosopher Lin Yutan: "What is patriotism but the love of the food one ate as a child?" Attempting to account for differences in *taste* conceived broadly and identity is the project of Pierre Bourdieu's landmark text *Distinction*, which documented how preferences in everything from food to music to clothing to interior decorating reflected people's class position and upbringing in 1970s France. Bourdieu (1984, 11) argued that exhibiting the right tastes serves as a form of currency, or "cultural capital." However, what tastes confer cultural capital depend crucially on context, as the controversy over plant-based sausage at a conservative southern chain highlights.

The widespread assumption that people who eat and like plant-based meat could not possibly be the kinds of people who eat and like the food at Cracker Barrel helps illustrate how contemporary partisan politics in the United States influence taste preferences that inevitably communicate information about who we are. The conservative heartland generally commands less cultural respect and status than do the cities and coasts associated with the liberal elite, but the divide here is less one of class than of political valence. The problem is not that the sausage is too fancy or gourmet to be accepted in fast food chains. Rather, it contaminates Cracker Barrel because it carries connotations of liberal "bleeding heart" responses to concerns about animal welfare and the environment like eating vegetarian food.

Disgust is one of the ways our senses are involved in creating and reinforcing social boundaries to separate us from who and what we do not like. In an analysis of gay rights activism in the 1990s, Shana Kushner Gadarian and Eric van der Vort (2018, 521) note that disgust is a "powerful rhetorical tool" in shaping public opinion. Cindy Kam and Beth Estes (2016, 493) also argue that one's sensitivity to disgust is "strongest on policies that most overtly lend themselves to concerns about bodily and societal contamination." Building on these ideas, our analysis finds that smells related to bodily contamination may sometimes be used rhetorically regardless of whether the policies they are actively espousing have any connection to literal contamination. As we discuss in the next section, especially on the political right, rhetorically linking those who are disliked for other reasons to physically disgusting stimuli may defy reason but draw some efficacy from the power of bad smells—real or imagined—to evoke physical revulsion.

Literal Demons That Smell Like Sulfur

The rhetorical use of disgust in US politics today illustrates how taste and smell make identity not only visible but visceral. As the example of butyric acid suggests, even our involuntary physiological responses like salivating or gagging depend crucially on the context where we perceive tastes and smells. However, there are a handful of aromas that have taken on particular cultural significance due to both the most typical sources of the odor and perhaps the modal physiological response they inspire. The warm, sweet smells of cinnamon, vanilla, and saffron and their widespread use in cooking make them generally associated with home, desserts, and holidays. Conversely, although many people who love to eat durian also come to like the smell, the fruit has been infamously banned from public transit in Singapore because to the uninitiated, it is typically described as a mixture of raw sewage and rotting flesh.

Associations with putrefaction are probably part of the reason the smell of sulfur is so consistently associated both physiologically and culturally with badness. The stench of rotting eggs in particular is dominated by sulfuric compounds formed by the decomposition of the proteins globulin and keratin. Anyone who has gotten hit with a whiff upon cracking one open will not soon forget it, but modern egg production and refrigerated commodity chains have made the experience uncommon. The sense memory lingers in idioms like "he's a bad egg" or "the last one is a rotten egg," where children who may never in their lives smell an egg going bad still connect the shame of being the slowest one in a playground game with what is for them a wholly imaginary stink.

Sulfur is also to blame for the historical association between the smell of cabbage and poor, low-status immigrant groups in the United States in the nineteenth and twentieth centuries. The sulfuric compounds in cabbage become especially redolent the more they are chopped and the longer they are cooked, when they form the hydrogen sulfide we associate with rotting eggs and trisulfides present in large amounts in human feces. The relative cheapness of cabbage, the reliance of the poor on soups and stews that stretch ingredients, and the prevalence of cabbage in the diets of Irish and central European immigrants to the United States at the turn of the twentieth century all combined to promulgate associations between cabbage in general and the smell of boiled cabbage in particular with destitution and despair.[1]

According to the geologist Salomon Kroonenberg's *Why Hell Stinks of Sulfur* (2013), the association between sulfur and evil may be due to volcanic vents and springs. Many underground caves, springs, and human quarries—especially in regions where humans live above limestone—emit both odorless carbon dioxide, sometimes lethal to birds and other passing animals, and highly odiferous sulfur, wrongly blamed for the caves' lethal effects.[2]

This network of cultural associations was available for Alex Jones to draw on when he started claiming that both sitting president Barack Obama and Democratic nominee Hillary Clinton smelled like sulfur during the lead-up to the 2016 US presidential election. Jones has never been affiliated with any major news organization, but the website and company he founded in 1999, called InfoWars, built a substantial audience and distinctive rhetorical style outside the traditional means (Akmut 2022). By 2017, his site was getting approximately ten million monthly visitors, more than *Newsweek* or *The Economist* at the time. The lawsuit brought against him in 2022 by the families of children killed in the Sandy Hook elementary school shooting further solidified his reputation for being one of the political far right's most shameless hucksters and peddlers of malicious fake news.

In October 2016, with mere weeks to go before Americans would first elect Donald Trump president, Jones first brought up the way Obama and Clinton smell on his radio show: "Imagine how bad she smells, man? I'm told her and Obama, just stink, stink, stink, stink. You can't wash that evil off, man. Told there's a rotten smell around Hillary. I'm not kidding, people say, they say—folks, I've been told this by high up folks. They say listen, Obama and Hillary both smell like sulfur. . . . I've talked to people that are in protective details, they're scared of her. And they say listen, she's a frickin' demon and she stinks and so does Obama. I go, like what? Sulfur. They smell like hell" (Kline 2016). The claims became an internet sensation and meme, to the point that CNN at least once reported ironically that Obama had "passed the smell test" (Wright 2016). As outlandish as Jones's claims about Clinton and Obama smelling like sulfur may be, they are emblematic of the strategy of using stimuli generally regarded as disgusting regardless of context to taint an ideological opponent.

The connection between unpleasant smells and avoidant behaviors in the sensory-emotional experience of disgust is probably due to the role of the senses, and specifically smell, in alarm systems that may predate the development of language and reasoning. According to brain-imaging research completed in the early 2000s, sharply unpleasant smells trigger disproportionately strong responses in the amygdala and ventral insula.[3] Steven Johnson explains, "the human brain appears to have evolved an alert system whereby a certain class of extreme smells triggers an involuntary disgust response that effectively short-circuits one's ability to think clearly—and produces a powerful desire to avoid objects associated with the smell" (2006, 128–29). This nose-gut-brain alarm system requires no neocortical involvement and may even possess the capacity to override language-based reasoning. Jones's claims that Clinton and Obama smell "like hell" were never connected in any way to anything they said or did that he might disagree with. While we can conceptually distinguish between the material/physical, spiritual/moral, and ideological/intellectual registers of disgust, they are not experienced as separate phenomena but instead amplify and bleed into each other.

Our sensitivity to disgust is also linked to our moral judgments. In a series of experiments by the psychology professor Jonathan Haidt and his colleagues, undergraduate students exposed to disgusting stimuli including fart spray, a disgusting room, recalling a physically disgusting experience, or watching a disgusting video scene increased the severity of the moral judgments they made about behaviors like eating a pet dog or lying on a résumé in order to get a job. They also found that the higher students scored on a measure of sensitivity to their own bodily sensations, the stronger the connection between their experience of disgust and the strength of their moral judgments (Schnall et al. 2008). The strength of the connection between bodily disgust and moral judgment may help explain the rhetorical efficacy of political discourse that draws on smells that evoke fears of contamination.

This rhetorical invocation of the smells of biological threat may be particularly effective with conservative-leaning audiences. Experimental data have so consistently found that conservatives display a higher disgust response than liberals that a 2021 *New York Times Magazine* article on disgust, largely based on Haidt and his mentor Paul Rozin's work, described the two groups as inhabiting entirely different moral universes: "These two types of human—which broadly map onto 'liberal' and 'conservative,' or 'relatively disgust-insensitive' and 'relatively disgust-sensitive'—live in separate moral matrices. If it seems bizarre that disgust sensitivity and politics should be so closely correlated, it's important to remember that disgust sensitivity is really measuring our feelings about purity and pollution. And these, in turn, contribute to our construction of moral systems, and it is our moral systems that guide our political orientations" (Young 2021). According to this research, then, it would make sense that more disgust-sensitive conservatives might be more apt to invoke and be moved by rhetorical gestures to physically repellent smells and the experience of bodily disgust. As our last example demonstrates, liberals also use disgust rhetorically to express political distaste and distance, but they seem to do so in a strikingly different way than conservatives.

With Ketchup, Like a Damn Child

President Donald J. Trump's tastes were the subject of liberal scorn long before he embarked on a political career. As a real estate mogul, he was portrayed as a living caricature of recently amassed wealth starting in the 1980s, when he began making cameos in television shows like *The Jeffersons* and later in *Sex in the City*, *The Simpsons*, *Home Alone II*, and *Zoolander*. But despite achieving the celebrity he aspired to, he never managed to win the respect of the cultural and intellectual elites who ran institutions like Le Club, where he repeatedly and unsuccessfully sought membership, or the very hip satirical *Spy* magazine, which described him as a "short-fingered vulgarian" in 1988 (Coppins 2016, para. 17). One of the editors of *Spy*, explaining his antipathy for Trump after he had been elected, told *Buzzfeed* that the problem with Trump was that he did not "behave according to the old protocols of wealth. . . . [Trump] was this kind of bridge-and-tunnel guy who the Manhattan establishment rejected. They saw him as a guy trying to punch too far above his weight; who was rude and classless and desperate for attention" (para. 18). Nearly three decades later, he was still getting the cold shoulder from the Manhattan aristocracy. In October 2016, after Trump was booed at the Al Smith Dinner, a charity event for elite Manhattan Catholics, the *Washington Monthly* correspondent Martin Longman (2016, para. 5) wrote, "Trump has never been able to mix at these white tie events in Manhattan, which I suspect is a source of both his ostentatious striving and his bottomless resentment."

One of the more obvious gaps between Trump and the Manhattan establishment, despite them both occupying the financial super-elite, were his tastes, which received the sneering treatment always directed at the nouveau riche. Shortly before his election, the *Vanity Fair* contributing editor Fran Lebowitz (Fox 2016, para. 3) described Trump as "a poor person's idea of a rich person." She continued, "They see him. They think, 'If I were rich, I'd have a fabulous tie like that. Why are my ties not made of 400 acres of polyester.' All that stuff he shows you in his house—the gold faucets—if you won the lottery, that's what you'd buy" (para. 3). Like many people historically labeled as having "new money," Trump has faced criticism and exclusion from certain elite circles he appears to seek acceptance in, largely due to perceptions of his coarse manners and overtly conspicuous displays of wealth.

Judgments about good and bad taste are where the social work of distinction and the aesthetic and sensory experiences of foods, smells, décor, and behaviors we admire or despise collide (Bourdieu 1984). The scorn heaped on Trump by liberals for his literal tastes reached its apogee in a play-by-play account of the president's dinner at the BLT Steakhouse in the DC Trump Hotel published in February 2017 on the site *Independent Journal Review* (*IJR*). The article was written by *IJR*'s content director, Benny Johnson, who had gotten a reservation at the next table over based on a tip about where Trump would be dining that evening. The post was over twenty-two hundred words long, featuring detailed descriptions of Trump stopping to take a picture with a woman who said it was her birthday and discreetly tipping one of the busboys $100 on the way out. But the detail that the twitterati seized on was how he had ordered his steak (B. Johnson 2017).

When Colin Campbell, *Yahoo! News* politics editor, shared Johnson's post on X (formerly Twitter), he led with, "last night, President Trump reportedly ate a well-done steak with ketchup" (Rousselle 2017). The *Gawker* offshoot *Jezebel* based a post on Campbell's tweet with the title, "Donald Trump Eats His Steak Well Done with Ketchup, Like a Damn Child" (Cote 2017). In addition to infantilizing the president's choice, the article also declared his order "completely unappetizing." The problems with his condiment choice are so obvious that the author does not even need to insult it, only repeat it: "he ate it with ketchup. Ketchup," assuming that her audience will find the application of this condiment to steak as intrinsically offensive as she does. Julia Thomson (2017, para. 2), writing for *The Huffington Post*, explains for anyone who might not know that to order a steak *well done*, "according to experts in the food world is simply the wrong way to order meat." She continues, "But eating it with ketchup just adds insult to injury. Ketchup, a beloved condiment among children, has a powerfully sweet flavor. So strong that it overpowers other foods, such as the subtle umami flavors that can only be found in a $54 28-day dry-aged steak."

Making the opposite argument about ketchup, Helen Rosner (2017, para. 15) of *The New Yorker* and *Eater* noted that the condiment "adds back much of the moisture, sweetness, and flavor that the overcooking removed in the first place." But rather than praising his condiment choice as an appropriate remedy for the effects of how fully cooked he likes his meat, she declares his steak order evidence of "risk aversion, timidity, defensiveness, and insecurity." What is remarkable is that she attempts to reason about her judgment at all. Rosner seemingly cannot cast aspersions on Trump's tastes unless they can be taken as evidence of ethical, personal, or professional failings.[4]

Unlike the smell of hydrogen sulfide, seemingly a close-to-universal stimulus for disgust that preempts cognition, the idea that eating well-done steak with ketchup is disgusting depends on highly contextual moral, aesthetic, and political assumptions. The disgust about Trump's tastes is not the sort that overrides neocortical systems; it is instead generated by language-based reasoning and the storytelling mind. The reasoning does not have to be particularly sound or consistent, as seen in the competing theories about why ketchup is disgusting on steak; the presence of any reasoning at all offers a striking contrast to Alex Jones's visceral use of disgust. In these examples, the kind of disgust invoked by liberals seems to look down the nose from above instead of being governed from below by a gut sensation triggered by a noxious smell.

Sensual Relations Are Social Relations

The rhetorical use of disgust shows how inextricable the judgments we associate with our higher minds and cognitive faculties are from the body, senses, and instinctual reactions. A feeling of revulsion can be elicited by an idea, and that alone may be enough to trigger a violent physical reaction like vomiting. Conversely, the smells we associate with putrefaction and underground evils can metaphorically evoke everything from disease to shame to distrust—associations that may have helped our species survive. Whether disgust is being used to identify a contaminant we want removed or to inspire dislike for something in others by associating the target with bad tastes and smells, it calls our attention to how we recognize that which we do not want—from foods to people to political agendas. It is one of our most vivid reminders of David Howes's (2003) claim that sensual relations are social relations.

For the same reasons disgust is so deeply tied to division, the deeply rooted nature of taste might also make sharing mutually agreeable foods a particularly powerful way to build trust and affinity between unfamiliar or even divided groups. *The Economist* coined the term "gastrodiplomacy" to describe efforts like the Global Thai Initiative, launched in 2002 by the Thai government in part to counter the country's reputation as a destination for sex tourism by increasing the number of Thai restaurants around the world. The Thai government signed agreements to make it easier for Thai chefs to get work visas and created a "Thai Select" certification system for restaurants that employed Thai cooks and staff, included particular dishes like pad thai on their menus, and used ingredients and tableware imported from Thailand. These efforts are widely credited with increasing interest in and tourism to Thailand in countries like the United States and Germany (Parasecoli 2022). The restaurant Conflict Kitchen in Pittsburgh and other mostly pop-up "Conflict Cafés" use a similar principle to introduce diners to the foods of Syria, Nepal, Columbia, Turkey, and Armenia, while also teaching them something about the migrant crises, earthquakes, civil wars, and genocidal conflicts that have driven refugees to adopted lands that are not always entirely welcoming.

From state departments to pop-up restaurants, these efforts point to the ways even unfamiliar foods can sometimes invite and entice connection. However, the Impossible sausage controversy should remind us that not everyone finds novel foods equally appealing. Culinary cosmopolitanism tends to be celebrated by people with the resources to acquire and learn about novel foods and to easily replace anything that turns out to be inedible (Finn 2017). One reason we might see a greater prevalence of disgust in US political rhetoric today is the historically unusual level of partisan division and the trend of negative partisanship documented by the political scientists Alan Abramowitz and Steven Webster. For decades and with increasing speed since around 2000, Americans have been forming political loyalties based more on their loathing for the opposition than inherited preferences, for example, that daddy was a Democrat (Chait 2015). Partisan loyalties have also gotten stronger, with swing voters all but disappearing since the 1970s and Americans reporting increasingly negative sentiments about the possibility of their children marrying someone affiliated with the opposite party and seeing the other party as a threat to the nation's well-being (Azari 2019).

While we only had space to touch on a limited number of examples in this chapter, we encourage further research on the effects of disgust in political rhetoric in the media—especially for audiences with different partisan leanings. On the basis of our preliminary exploration of these three test cases, we would expect to find more references to sources of bodily disgust on right-wing radio and in books by conservative pundits and politicians and more attempts to justify taste judgments with moral and policy justifications on shows like *Last Week Tonight* and *The Rachel Maddow Show*. Related connections to characteristics like authoritarian leanings and religiosity would also be worth exploring.

We have also touched on the connection between sensory rhetoric and biological science. Rhetoric's influence extends beyond the rational mind and into the biological processes that shape sensory responses. Steven Johnson (2006, 129) describes disgust as "a form of evolutionary pattern recognition," explaining that "the brain evolved a system for setting off an alarm whenever [hydrogen sulfide and cadaverine] molecules were detected. Nausea itself [is] a survival mechanism." The fact that certain political rhetoric can elicit a visceral reaction akin to a microbial threat vividly underscores how deeply rhetoric is interwoven with biological embodiment. Further study might explore rhetoric that resonates at similar instinctual levels.

Much like Cracker Barrel, contemporary political communication—though likely to be met with resistance—is in need of its own kind of Impossible Burger. We need healthier ways of understanding political difference and new strategies for illuminating and challenging deeply ingrained sensibilities.

Notes

1. In George Orwell's novel *1984*, the smell of cabbage in the hall of Victory Mansions is part of what reveals the irony of the name, and in *A Clergyman's Daughter*, he describes the "melancholy smell of boiled cabbage and dishwater" seeping under a parishioner's front door (Sutherland 2016).

2. A cave excavated in Turkey in 2013 with inscriptions to the god Pluto, ruler of the underworld, is believed to be the same one described by the Greek geographer Strabo two thousand years ago: "[It is] full of a vapor so misty and dense that one can scarcely see the ground. Any animal that passes inside meets instant death. I threw in sparrows and they immediately breathed their last and died" (Dickey 2013). A similar phenomenon is likely behind the name of the "foul-smelling gorge of Avernus," which Virgil identified as the entrance to Hades in the *Aeneid* and whose name derives from the Greek *aornos* or "birdless" (Kroonenberg 2013). From the Greek Hades to Christian Hell, dying birds and the smell of sulfur have heralded doorways and descents into spiritual evil and punishment, the obvious antithesis to rising toward celestial paradise and divine goodness.

3. As Steven Johnson (2006, 128–29) notes, "The amygdala is an evolutionarily ancient part of the brain, much older than the mammalian higher functions of the neo-cortex; raw instinctual responses to threats and emotionally charged stimuli emanate from the amygdala. The ventral insula appears to play an important role in biological urges like hunger, thirst, and nausea, as well as in certain phobias. Both regions can be thought of as alarm centers of the brain; in humans, they possess the capacity to override the neocortical systems where language-based reasoning occurs."

4. It is noteworthy that the conservative response to Trump's use of ketchup was quite different, as exemplified by an article in *The National Review* titled "Freedom Is Eating Steak Well Done with Ketchup" (Continetti 2017).

References

Akmut, Camille. 2022. "Documentary: Infowars Beginnings." *Computer Science and Technology: Historiography* 8 (7): 1–7.

Azari, Julia. 2019. "The Puzzle of Weak Parties and Strong Partisanship." *Library of Congress Blog: Insights*, March 15. https://blogs.loc.gov/kluge/2019/03/the-puzzle-of-weak-parties-and-strong-partisanship/.

Bourdieu, Pierre. 1984. *Distinction: A Social Critique of the Judgement of Taste*. Translated by Richard Nice. Cambridge, MA: Harvard University Press.

Broome, Mary Patterson, and Brian Boone. 2022. "The Untold Truth of Cracker Barrel." *Mashed*, September 26. https://www.mashed.com/158983/the-untold-truth-of-cracker-barrel/.

Chait, Jonathan. 2015. "How 'Negative Partisanship' Has Transformed American Politics." *New York Magazine*, April 17. https://nymag.com/intelligencer/2015/04/negative-partisanship-has-transformed-politics.html.

Chayes Wida, E. 2020. "These Popular Fast-Food Chains Are All Serving Plant-Based Meats." *Today*, March 5. https://www.today.com/food/all-popular-fast-food-chains-offering-plant-based-meats-t171328.

Chertoff, Emily. 2013. "Cracker Barrel's Oddly Authentic Version of American History." *The Atlantic*, March 2. https://www.theatlantic.com/national/archive/2013

/03/cracker-barrels-oddly-authentic-version-of-american-history/272826/.

Continetti, Matthew. 2017. "Freedom Is Eating Steak Well Done with Ketchup." *National Review*, March 17. https://www.nationalreview.com/2017/03/donald-trump-steak-liberals-show-their-elitism-while-mocking-trump/.

Coppins, McKay. 2016. "Inside the Fraternity of Haters and Losers Who Drove Donald Trump to the GOP Nomination." *Buzzfeed*, October 25. https://www.buzzfeednews.com/article/mckaycoppins/how-the-haters-made-trump.

Cote, Rachel Verona. 2017. "Donald Trump Eats His Steak Well Done with Ketchup, Like a Damn Child." *Jezebel*, February 26. https://jezebel.com/donald-trump-eats-his-steak-well-done-with-ketchup-lik-1792770173.

Cracker Barrel. 2022. "As a small token of our appreciation . . ." Facebook, August 1. https://www.facebook.com/crackerbarrel/.

Darwin, Charles. 1899. *The Expression of the Emotions in Man and Animals*. New York: D. Appleton.

Dickey, Colin. 2013. "Subterranean Homesick Blues: Salomon Kroonenberg's 'Why Hell Stinks of Sulfur.'" *Los Angeles Review of Books*, July 14. https://lareviewofbooks.org/article/subterranean-homesick-blues-salomon-kroonenbergs-why-hell-stinks-of-sulfur/.

Douglas, Mary. 1966. *Purity and Danger*. New York: Routledge.

Finn, Margot. 2017. *Discriminating Taste: How Class Anxiety Created the American Food Revolution*. New Brunswick: Rutgers University Press.

Fox, Emily Jane. 2016. "Let Fran Lebowitz Soothe All Your Election-Related Worries." *Vanity Fair*, October 20. https://www.vanityfair.com/news/2016/10/fran-lebowitz-trump-clinton-election.

Gadarian, Shana Kushner, and Eric van der Vort. 2018. "The Gag Reflex: Disgusting Rhetoric and Gay Rights in American Politics." *Political Behavior* 40:521–43.

Howes, David. 2003. *Sensual Relations: Engaging the Senses in Culture and Social Theory*. Ann Arbor: University of Michigan Press.

Johnson, Benny. 2017. "Inside Trump's Secret Dinner: A Side of the President You Don't Ever See." *Independent Journal Review*, February 26. https://web.archive.org/web/20180224162843/https://ijr.com/2017/02/810965-trump-ditched-the-press-to-have-dinner-heres-how-the-president-acts-when-no-one-is-watching/.

Johnson, Steven. 2006. *The Ghost Map*. New York: Riverhead Books.

Kam, Cindy D., and Beth A. Estes. 2016. "Disgust Sensitivity and Public Demand for Protection." *Journal of Politics* 78 (2): 481–96. https://www.jstor.org/stable/10.2307/26550726.

Kline, Ezra. 2016. "Trump Ally Alex Jones Thinks Barack Obama and Hillary Clinton Are Literally Demons from Hell." *Vox*, October 10. https://www.vox.com/policy-and-politics/2016/10/10/13233338/alex-jones-trump-clinton-demon.

Kroonenberg, Salomon. 2013. *Why Hell Stinks of Sulfur: Mythology and Geology of the Underworld*. Chicago: University of Chicago Press.

Lamour, Joseph. 2022. "Cracker Barrel Posted About Its New Meatless Sausage, Causing Major Beef with Its 'Customer Base.'" *NBCBoston*, August 4. https://www.nbcboston.com/news/national-international/cracker-barrel-posted-about-its-new-meatless-sausage-causing-major-beef-with-its-customer-base/2799492/.

Longman, Martin. 2016. "Donald Trump Again Fails to Mix in High Society." *Washington Monthly*, October 21. https://washingtonmonthly.com/2016/10/21/donald-trump-again-fails-to-mix-in-high-society/.

Martinez-Aguayo, Juan Carlos, Renzo C. Lanfranco, Marcelo Arancibia, Elisa Sepúlveda, and Eva Madrid. 2018. "Trypophobia: What Do We Know So Far? A Case Report and Comprehensive Review of the Literature." *Front Psychiatry* 9:9–15.

Miller, William Ian. 2020. "Darwin's Disgust." In *Empire of the Senses: The Sensual Culture Reader*, edited by David Howes, 335–56. Oxford, UK: Berg.

Parasecoli, Fabio. 2022. "How Countries Use Food to Win Friends and

Influence People." *Foreign Policy*, August 20. https://foreignpolicy.com/2022/08/20/food-diplomacy-countries-identity-culture-marketing-gastrodiplomacy-gastronativism/.

Perelman, Alison. 2013. "Political Appetites: Food as Rhetoric in American Politics." PhD diss., University of Pennsylvania.

Rosner, Helen. 2017. "Actually, How Donald Trump Eats His Steak Matters." *Eater*, February 28. https://www.eater.com/2017/2/28/14753248/trump-steak-well-done-ketchup-personality.

Rousselle, Christine. 2017. "For Some Reason the Internet Is Very Concerned with How President Trump Eats Steak." *Townhall*, February 27. https://townhall.com/tipsheet/christinerousselle/2017/02/27/for-some-reason-the-internet-is-very-concerned-with-how-president-trump-eats-steak-n2291277.

Schnall, Simone., Jonathan Haidt, Gerald. L Clore, and Alexander. H. Jordan. 2008. "Disgust as Embodied Moral Judgment." *Personality and Social Psychology Bulletin* 34 (8): 1096–109.

Stevens, Ashlie D. 2022. "After Cracker Barrel Adds Vegan Sausage to Its Menu, Some Customers Say the Chain Is Too 'Woke.'" *Salon*, August 5. https://www.salon.com/2022/08/05/after-cracker-barrel-adds-vegan-sausage-to-its-menu-some-customers-say-the-chain-is-too-woke/.

Sutherland, John. 2016. *Orwell's Nose: A Pathological Biography*. Chicago: University of Chicago Press.

Thomson, Julie, R. 2017. "Donald Trump Eats His Steak with Ketchup, and Twitter Isn't Happy." *Huffington Post*, February 27. https://www.huffpost.com/entry/donald-trump-steak-ketchup_n_58b43bf2e4b0a8a9b7845b25.

Wright, David. 2016. "Obama Smells Himself." *CNN*, October 12. https://www.cnn.com/2016/10/12/politics/obama-sulfur-smell-alex-jones/index.html.

Young, Molly. 2021. "How Disgust Explains Everything." *New York Times Magazine*, December 27, https://www.nytimes.com/2021/12/27/magazine/disgust-science.html.

2

Rational Markets, Sensory Marketplaces
How Stock Imagery Shapes
Digital Sense-Making

KERRY BANAZEK AND KELLIE SHARP-HOSKINS

The sugar and cinnamon scent of Auntie Anne's Pretzels beckons with familiarity. The taste of samples lingers as we stroll through Costco. At the farmers' market, we make small talk with vendors, kettle corn popping in the background. Physical marketplaces engage us as potential customers through a range of appeals that not only direct sensory attention but invite sensation into evaluation. Our senses corroborate and are corroborated by what makes sense. *Is the pretzel worth the price? Who doesn't need one hundred bagel bites? Will that handmade satchel hold up to use, or does it just look cool styled for Instagram on the shoulder of a mannequin?*

Western paradigms that disarticulate bodies from knowledge, pathos from logos, the senses from good sense allow for these kinds of market experiences by suggesting an inevitable two-part audit: Bodies collect information through sensory inputs, and minds organize and assess that information. At the mall, at the superstore, at the local market, this "fact" is understood and exploited: We gather information through sights and sounds, smells and feel, compare relative qualities and pleasures, and select the best option based on our values and resources. In a marketplace defined by abundance, placing products side by side facilitates the deliberation necessary for rational choices to become obvious.

This idealization of (normative) comparative evaluation is consistent with work that grounds contemporary capitalism and thus legislates market rationality writ large. John Stuart Mill ([1859] 1978) compared rational deliberation with marketplace logics, imagining a marketplace of ideas, where each is tested and comparatively judged, a process that ultimately leads to truth. Markets, as real and theoretical spaces, are the proving ground of rationality. This framing is neither limited to economic thought nor relegated to history; rather, the connection between markets and rationality is persistent in its cultural influence, deeply embedded in the American imagination as both inevitable and morally good, and wholly dependent on ableist conceptualizations of mind and body. So even as economic and marketing literature invokes experiential models—and their attendant focus on sensation and feeling—to explain consumer behavior, it causally links such experiences to reasoned interpretation and evaluation. Consumers have experiences and then make choices: They are rational economic actors. As evidenced by this collection, however, bodies and minds, causes and effects, cannot be so easily disarticulated.

In short, an input-output model of sensory information and reasoning has never been adequate to account for how sensation or reasoning materialize and matter—not in the marketplace and not more generally. Understanding the sensuous stakes of markets thus requires other ways of accounting for their rhetorical work. In this chapter, we argue that digital marketplaces call this rhetoric's failure to match material conditions into relief in unique ways and thus provide a useful starting place for reconfiguring related methods and theories.

Below, we show how attention to digital marketplace logics, rhetorics, and practices affords the field of rhetoric a better understanding of relationships between sensation and consumption by theorizing how patrons in digital marketplaces are hailed via repetition and abundance. Input-output models, we argue, fail in part because they do not fully account for how sensation shapes the conditions of possibility that enable sense-making. Sense is made not only as sensuous objects circulate but also via the combined *styles* and *speeds* that characterize different forms of circulation. Even seemingly singular moments of digital consumption, we argue, draw on sensory multiplicity, a fact digital marketers exploit to create immersive sensory experiences with their own forms of rationality. We pursue these arguments by centering "acceleration" as a key term for sensory rhetoric that allows us to understand "multisensory" digital marketing in its complexity. We then apply it—and the related terms "accumulation" and "proliferation"—to a case study of the stock image industry and its marketplaces.

We foreground this industry's infrastructural role in shaping visual culture and rhetoric in order to argue that identifying how—and to what ends—digital platforms invite consumer sense-making requires attention not only to studies attuned to highly visible market shapers like Amazon or Netflix but also to everyday ambient media and the less visible industries and marketplaces that support their production, circulation, and influence. Respecting the history of the stock image industry allows us to bring specificity to this argument, implicitly affirming that "there is no turn to the digital that does not already rely on previous technological arrangements" (Boyle et al. 2018, 252). It also aids us in showing more broadly how cultural objects that seem to facilitate their own sensory appeal, accumulating rhetorical force as they gather rhetorical speed, are always functioning in relation to industry infrastructures designed with this exact function—and related economic benefits—in mind.

Because rhetorical tactics that emerge in digital marketplaces—including stock image marketplaces—are filtered through the demands of global capitalism but also moderated by digital interfaces and infrastructures, we argue that understanding the impact that logics of acceleration, accumulation, and proliferation have on cultural forms requires bringing together economic rhetorics, digital rhetorics, and sensory rhetorics in novel ways, a bringing together our analysis models. Ultimately, we argue that challenges associated with accounting for sensuous, bodily experiences under regimes of global capitalism require analyses that proceed along similar lines and that such analyses are, conversely, essential to understanding how sensation operates in the digitally inflected rhetorical situations that characterize not only explicit acts of buying and selling online but much contemporary life.

"Acceleration": A Key Term for Understanding Rhetorics of the Digital Marketplace

Speed has long been cited as a goal and feature of technology development. Companies like IBM and Intel thrive on reputations for engineering fast experiences. A 1941 IBM advertisement extolls benefits—speed, accuracy, and control—of Punched Card Accounting for managing "progressive municipalities." In the 1960s, IBM sold Selectric Typewriter performance via virtues of the typeball, an "element that dances across the paper at incredible speed, faster even than the eye can see" (Dul 2022). We call attention to these technologies (and marketing logics that propelled their sales) to signal our attunement to a perhaps obvious but still crucial point: Fast is a moving target, especially in the computing world. This is an issue of engineering but also embodied, sense- and experience-informed perceptions. What felt fast twenty-five years ago is different from what feels fast now. What feels fast to individual users varies widely.

Importantly, this feeling is not simply registered through the ocular nerve: Speed strikes not just the eye but the ear and the skin, assessed as bodies aggregate multisensory experiences via cultural (including market) narratives and forms. The sensuous story of the typewriter's speed is always told in relation to its technological kin: It seems slower than handwriting before we learn touch typing; it feels faster once we habituate. And just because we can measure some aspects of speed—1998's Pentium desktop processors offered speeds up to 300 MHz, while 2023's Intel processor family promises more than 5 GHz—does not mean we understand its significance. Rather, contextual and cultural dimensions of how humans and objects operate together make evaluation of sensory meanings possible. Accordingly, evaluating the sensory work of speed in electronic marketplaces requires attention to their cultural forms (Bradshaw 2018): The speed at which we encounter products, and the effects of that speed on our sense of their value, is always relational.

The rhetorical effects of speed are well articulated by Jim Ridolfo and Dànielle DeVoss (2009) as "rhetorical velocity," defined as "a conscious rhetorical concern for distance, travel, speed, and time, pertaining specifically to theorizing instances of strategic appropriation by a third party." Whereas Ridolfo and DeVoss center uptake and consequent circulation of rhetorics, Charles Lowe (2010) highlights the importance of attending to acceleration to consider how—and at what speeds—rhetorics travel. Likewise, in this chapter, we emphasize theoretical and practical roles that acceleration plays in understanding how technologies build on one another. For example, a 2023 visit to the Intel website assured us, "The Future of Acceleration Has Arrived." This campaign builds on the premise that growth in areas like AI, market analytics, and social networking means major corporations and entrepreneurs alike are troubled by the same set of "fastest growing workloads," which are changing how all business happens. Moving *fast*, we can infer, is not adequate to the needs of producers, sellers, marketers, or consumers under late capitalism. We must keep moving faster. To stay at constant speed in the contemporary marketplace is to fall behind—the sensory equivalent of waiting for dial-up in a 5G world. Indeed, in this fixation with acceleration, we identify a culturally saturated interest in specific kinds of speed and associated sensory experiences.

Building on Lowe's argument about the need to attend to acceleration in rhetorical accounting work, we go one step further. In digital marketplaces, we argue, acceleration not only makes sense to the market but does so via sense-making—by provoking multisensory experiences that accord with cultural logics of market accumulation and proliferation. Before delving into more specific examples below, we further argue that understanding sensory implications of rhetorical acceleration (as a feature of electronic marketplaces) is linked in complex, meaningful ways to understanding processes of accumulation and proliferation. Exposing the rhetorical work of accumulation and proliferation necessary to the sense-making function of acceleration is critical to identifying how digital markets participate in global capitalist arguments, the asymmetrical effects of which mediate not only access to or representation within such markets but the livability of all bound to their inexhaustible appetites.

We center "accumulation" as a key term for understanding digital acceleration because it immediately invokes a capitalist logic of growth by any means available—the dogged pursuit of more as its own rationale; it also, as Jonathan L. Bradshaw (2020, 4) reminds, can refer "to the buildup of rhetorical elements in parts of discourse in order to heighten the effect." Bradshaw juxtaposes accumulation with virality and speed in his account of digital amplification and affective experience. For him, accumulation—not speed—"affords [a] heightened emotional connection" and, ultimately, generates exhaustion, which is "weaponize[d]" as a "digital communication strateg[y], . . . a way of immobilizing audiences" (6).

By contrast, we see a relationship between acceleration—shifting genres of speed—and accumulation whereby what accumulates and how is directly correlated with the ease with which speeding up and slowing down can be accomplished. While we, like Bradshaw, see rhetorical exhaustion as a potential effect of rhetorical accumulations, we also see how accumulationist logic and rhetorics contribute to a capitalist agenda, surging through consumers as they attempt to make choices that make sense in a digital milieu of overabundance. For example, we might make an impulsive, "unreasoned" digital purchase because we are too tired to evaluate more options; we might buy three similar things with intent (never fulfilled, statistically) to return two after testing side by side; or we might simply buy three things we "don't need" because their slick visual appeal caused a surge of pleasure when perfectly (personally) calibrated ads showed up in succession on our social media feed. Following these examples, we note a connection to scholarship on media effects, which articulates how "numerous (often, but not necessarily, small) effects accumulate over time as individuals use a certain medium or specific media contents repeatedly" (Koch and Arendt 2017).

This connection is particularly useful as we consider electronic marketplaces because the sensory appeal happens over time.

In short, cultural objects that seem to facilitate their own sensory appeal, accumulating rhetorical force as they gather rhetorical speed, are always functioning in relation to industry infrastructures designed with this exact function—and related economic benefits—in mind. Accordingly, we cannot account for the speed of digital marketplaces without a concomitant account of digital accumulation.

But accumulation is also critical in revealing politics of acceleration, a critical component of sense-making. To rhetorically equate speeding up with keeping up means not only matching global markets and their insatiable appetite for production and consumption but also identifying normative expectations associated with this participation. Keeping up requires bodies attuned to markets, bodies that move at the speed of global capitalism, bodies physically able to go without rest, unimpaired by cultural baggage or geographic distance. This is largely true because processes of accumulation rely fundamentally, as David Harvey (2004) argues, on practices of dispossession. He explains "accumulation by dispossession" in terms of a "given territorial system," whereby "surpluses of labor" and "surpluses of capital" are "absorbed by (a) temporal displacement, ... (b) spatial displacement, ... or (c) some combination" (63). It could be tempting to restrict this theory to material accumulation, holding that category separate from both digital and cultural accumulations like media effects.

To be sure, digital accumulation of images, for example, feels somewhat different than the accumulation of land, water, or wealth. Whereas it is clear who is dispossessed in these instances—Indigenous peoples, minoritized peoples, peoples of the global majority—the effects of digital accumulation are not as immediately evident. But this relationship is no less persistent or pernicious in digital contexts, which not only rely on material infrastructures that take up space, take over land, pollute waterways, and restrict lifeways but also dispossess people of self-representation and rhetorical sovereignty (Lyons 2000) and disarticulate cultural products from the cultures and bodies by which they were produced (allowing, for example, downloads of Black musicians to accumulate significant profits for Spotify without offering a living wage to the artists). Accumulation, following the logic of capital, then, is a cultural, material, and *rhetorical* phenomenon that speaks explicitly to what happens for persistent consumers of commodities—including ideas and media—as well as to those not conceptualized as ideal consumers (i.e., those whose economic circumstances are inadequate to keep up with market trends or those whose sensory processing makes commodities challenging, maddening, or unusable).

We argue that a strong, rhetorical understanding of accumulation requires the companion term "proliferation." A name for rapid reproduction and distribution, proliferation helps account for both the production that drives consumption and also how mis- and redirection of production processes complicate our understanding of consumption and accumulation. It signals attention to market logics where "more" signals differences not just in quantity but in kind—that is, differences in *consequences* and *sensibilities*. Because extractions that permit accumulation in certain geographic and cultural places operate in relation to production and distribution—not just consumption and storage—attending to interplays between proliferation and accumulation connects cases where material discards pile up to cases where speed, consumption, and intellectual production seem merely to permit social or cultural "keeping pace." In these cases, traditions of materialist and environmental rhetoric help us understand how sense and sensation operate in complex relation to digital markets and their wares.

Commodities, we know, directly generate storage issues for consumers, fueling markets for custom closet organizers and file-management services alike. Upgrade tactics that participate in "planned obsolescence" and corporate measures that make personal maintenance of tools and devices difficult cause waste-management problems—physical pileups—that are geographically hidden from the consumers. For example, copper and cadmium poison soils near a "typical" e-waste area in Southeast China (Chen et al. 2022). Scholarship on human impacts of sorting jobs at the e-waste market in Seelampur and the Agbogbloshie scrap yard in Accra, Ghana, call attention to the specific problem of heavy-metal poisoning in workers as well as the "broader postcolonial terrain of plural injustices and violence producing the[se] toxic urban landscape[s]" (Akese and Little 2018, 53). Heavy-metal poisoning, it is worth noting in a collection on sensation, is a well-known cause of peripheral neuropathy—which, among other serious effects, transforms the sense of touch by damaging the nerves of the hands and feet.

Such effects are not peripheral to but proliferated by accumulation and acceleration of sensory appeals made in the digital marketplace. They are also well hidden from our (sensory) view. The physical pileups and associated health issues are not present for their one-time users but shipped away from centers of market activity. An upgrade to the latest iPhone, for example, with its hyperfast processing and seemingly limitless capacity for storage, provides its consumer with the pleasurable sensory experiences of unboxing a carefully packaged product and marveling over its camera's ability to capture light and movement. We feel like we need its speed and capacity, and we relish its other sensory perks (sleek design, sensitive—but not too sensitive—touch screen, no waiting for image loading, etc.). This experience does not require said consumer to pick apart the old phone, sorting it into reusable and unusable parts, or to smell its deterioration over time. But one sensory experience is predicated on the other. Accordingly, we see a need to rhetorically recast conceptualizations of market sense-making to account for how sensory accelerations accumulate and proliferate benefit and harm under the guise of good economic sense.

In foregrounding digital markets in our accounts of sense-making, we also foreground the necessity of addressing global capitalism's influence on rhetorical bodies; this builds on existing digital rhetoric scholarship that asserts, "We cannot assume distance from the digital since even the most innocuous of activities, such as grocery shopping, now rely on computational procedures that connect local purchases to global supply chains" (Boyle et al. 2018, 251). Seemingly innocuous commercial activity, as rhetoric scholars interested in embodiment and environment further show, haunts not only our digital interfaces but the field itself; such activity "haunts because it surfaces what we attempt to repress: that the technologies of the digital age do not stand outside processes destroying the earth (and thus enable us to comment from that position) but participate in those very processes" (Sharp-Hoskins and Stagliano 2022, 243–44).

Electronic Marketplaces in the Experience Economy

Identifying sensory engagement as a feature of marketplaces—physical or electronic—is not a uniquely rhetorical contribution to their study. In this section, we pick up David Howes's (2021, 288) argument that convergence of design for multisensory engagement with marketing is a critical function of late capitalism, which has "made it its business to engage as many senses as possible in its drive for product differentiation and the distraction/seduction of the consumer." This is because, as Regina Lee Blaszczyk and David Suisman (2023, 2) explain, "seeing, hearing, tasting, smelling, and touching have shaped, and been shaped by, business enterprise from the turn of the twentieth century to our own time." For these scholars and for us, the stakes of such sensory appeals are not only economic but worldly, (re)creating what we might otherwise imagine to be "unchanging, hard-wired, and outside history" (Blaszczyk and Suisman 2023, 3). Such sensory work does not merely enlist our senses—as if they were static or stable—but participates in the sociocultural production of sensory experiences and sense-making itself. This phenomenon is conceptualized in business scholarship by Joseph Pine II and James Gilmore as "the experience economy," a concept they elaborate synecdochally via appeals designed into a once-popular restaurant: "The mist at the Rainforest Cafe appeals serially to all five senses. It is first apparent as a sound: Sss-sss-zzz. Then you see the mist arising from the rocks and feel it soft and cool against your skin. Finally, you smell its tropical essence, and you taste (or imagine that you do) its freshness. What you can't be is unaffected by the mist" (Pine and Gilmore 1998, 104). Howes identifies related tactics with the "hyperesthesia" of physical marketplaces in the late twentieth century, a term with unique implications for electronic marketplaces that we address in more detail below. Importantly, "hyperesthesia" is not a synonym for "hyperrealism": The multisensory appeal of the café is seductive, in part, because forest sounds are not accompanied by actual animals or insects, the mist cool, never cold. The "experience economy" requires imperfect imitations—immersive but not uncomfortable.

Articulated through the Rainforest Cafe and related enterprises, like Disney resorts or adventure glamping venues (see, for example, Mack 2014), the experience economy can seem to rhetorically operate through opposition to a digital culture premised on speed and abstraction—thriving on attention from consumers bored of spending workdays looking at screens. As Richard Lanham (2006) has persuasively argued, attention is not infinite; it can be rhetorically manipulated toward particular ends. However, popularity of electronic marketplaces and popularity of physical experiences packaged in hypersensual, hypercommodified ways (saturated in the details of the real but without exposure to real dangers or too much novelty) are motivated structurally by the same cultures of attention; both are driven by capitalist, accumulation- and proliferation-based logics and rhetorics, persuading consumers through appeals to embodied cues, comforts, and cravings. Both immerse consumers in a world of sensation. Electronic marketplaces, however, rely more acutely on sense images—complex, residual impressions that follow from seemingly singular (often image-centric) sensory stimulation and integrate input from multiple sense organs with nuances drawn from embodied memory. Sense images act affectively (not consciously) to anchor the virtual to material referents and conspire with fantasy, which invokes sensations that presage or promise future experiences (often by offering to amplify or reduce sensory stimulation in service of pleasure, comfort, or luxury).

Accumulated rhetorical exposure to targeted sense images, in other words, immerses consumers in worlds where sensory possibilities also proliferate.

Implicitly helping articulate how immersion conspires to create hyperesthetic appeals, Brian L. Ott and Greg Dickson (2019, 58–59) explain how sensation is activated by something's "unique aesthetic qualities," our experience of which "depends to a large extent upon which of our senses the thing most actively engages." In other words, the multisensory appeals of immersive technologies and electronic marketplaces are just as "present" as those we more easily recognize in physical markets. A consumer wearing a virtual reality headset experiences "unique aesthetic qualities" produced in an electronic marketplace as different but not less sensuous than the qualities of a shopping mall, for example. This is because, as Ott and Dickinson go on to explain, "Strictly speaking, the aesthetic qualities of things do not signify.... Aesthetic qualities like rhythm, temperature, scale, pungency, and intensity do not operate referentially; they do not directly signify or 'stand in' for something else" (60). One might even argue that the indirect signification of aesthetics acts as its own form of personalized advertising: Here is a signal, strong but abstract—attach your own referent, please. Private, embodied logics of connection are allowed influence without having to be understood, let alone explained.

It is worth noting here that as a category, "hyperesthesia" also includes more mundane examples like the artificial scents added to crayons, the Muzak of department stores, and the algorithmically driven repetition of online advertisements. The everydayness of these examples helps us understand that this is not simply a feature of objects; rather, it shapes, through repeat exposure (a kind of accumulation), our cultural ways of making sense. In other words, we expect products to carry with them hyperintense, multisensory appeals; and in preparing to make purchases, we look for evidence that this expectation will be met—even online.

Multisensory marketing has, consequently, emerged as a critical (rhetorical) strategy for developers of electronic marketplaces that aim to complement and/or replace physical markets and malls. Indeed, rapid development of immersive technologies designed to target the whole sensorium serves as one testament to marketing professionals' investment in capitalizing on how sense images shape digital markets and interactions, promising full participation in the "hypersensuality of the contemporary marketplace" and thus "the likelihood of the[ir] message being registered and acted upon by the customer" (Howes 2021, 288).

Augmented and virtual reality "solutions" in particular play established roles in electronic marketplaces. Three-hundred-and-sixty-degree views let us "pick up" a product and turn it around before we click "buy now." Three-dimensional tours mean homes for sale are always "open." Simulations let us "see" a new couch positioned amid our things or "try on" a pair of glasses (courtesy of AI-supported computer vision models that separate foregrounds from backgrounds). As Shen Bingqing et al. (2021, 3) elucidate, these experiences are designed to "create the perception of being there, i.e., the sense of presence," made possible by combinations of "computer software and hardware that stimulate the five senses of humans . . . in a simulated environment." Here our rhetorical conceptualization of presence must expand to account for its sensuous work. Presence is established not only through repetition but through sensory confirmation: It is when we feel the fit of the glasses on our face or sense the rightness of the couch in our room and click "buy it now."

Polysemy as an Agent of Acceleration: Lessons from the Stock Image Market

In order to understand how our key terms facilitate a shift away from conceptualizing sensation as a precursor to rational economic audit and toward a more complex accounting of its constitutive economic work, we turn to a short case study of the stock image industry, which reveals cultural stakes and logics of acceleration that co-implicate velocity and sensation in the rhetorical work of electronic marketplaces. This industry and its marketplaces offer a particularly useful example because it is an infrastructural culture industry—one rarely thought of unless a sloppy design or technical failure allows its seams to show. Notably, this industry's history exposes how business-to-business marketplaces mediate business-to-consumer possibilities, and its specific structures highlight complex relationships between sensation and acceleration that enable its rhetorical work.

Put simply, the business of stock photography is the business of selling ready-made images for commercial and editorial use. Most buyers in stock image marketplaces are culture-industry intermediaries—often but not exclusively designers and advertising professionals—who work under tight deadlines and have regular reason to deploy images. Because speed and frequency define their professional "need" to visit image marketplaces (instead of permitting them, for example, to hire photographers each time they want images), stock companies that capitalize on technologies that allow faster access to more images are positioned to gain market share. As above, "fast" is an insufficient descriptor for what motivates this model. Access must always seem to be speeding up, keeping pace with the cultural demands of a marketplace of ideas and media driven by oversaturation—a world in which we are surrounded by images.

To understand the impact and effects of acceleration on (and in) this industry, some articulation of its history is useful. This history extends to photography's very early days. Given constraints of space, below we attend to two moments when cultural and technical shifts enabled new kinds of rhetorical acceleration and thus sponsored new industry forms and infrastructures, circumscribing visual cultures and their associated regimes of sensation.

Stock imagery's "modern era" began in the 1970s and evolved through the 1980s. Notably, while photographers and illustrators populate "modern" stock marketplaces with images, the industry thrives because their role as sellers stays indirect. Abundant images from many sources are conglomerated and made available for purchase via infrastructure provided by companies that specialize in organizing catalogues and promoting sales, resale, and reuse. In short, the primary commodity that cultural intermediaries are purchasing is the logic that allows fast access to organized images. This industry form was not inevitable. Whereas earlier "picture agencies" drew primary revenue from editorial images—selling to magazines like *Life*—modern agencies thrived on ties to advertising. Abbott Miller (1994) historicizes cultural and material shifts in this era, documenting how magazine staff photographers were supplanted by freelance photographers (who "owned" and could thus sell images merely used by others, supported by 1987 copyright law changes) and how Kodak duping film (debuted in 1985 and permitting "limitless" prints) changed industry possibilities by replacing transparencies—often good for just five print runs.

In the late 1990s, another major industry shift began: Improved sensors allowed digital cameras to capture higher-quality images; agency catalogues migrated to CDs, then online databases—both able to hold more images than classic look books. As differently curated, higher-volume image stocks became possible, they drove logics of accumulation and archival overabundance.

This second shift presages industry changes that, we argue, have salience for understanding many kinds of electronic marketplaces. While stock companies have been explicitly selling themselves as purveyors of fast, affordable access to many versatile images for a long time, this is now even truer—structurally circumscribed by digital infrastructure and industry profit modeling—than ever. Competing stock image companies and other copyright-free digital image sources seem to offer limitless options. Consequently, while electronic stock image marketplaces as a whole rely on the potential velocity of images, in this saturated market, both individual sellers and companies must "argue" sensuously for attention. Such arguments reveal the rhetorical stakes of sensation in the industry: Attention must be carefully courted in the context of market saturation.

"Microstock" companies like Shutterstock that take the logic of their predecessors to an extreme now shape market expectations. Rather than selling themselves based on photographer reputation—common in earlier versions of the industry—these companies invite anyone to submit catalogue photos. As long as a reviewer approves a photo, it can be sold again and again, ad infinitum (or so contributor recruitment intimates), making both photographer and distributor money across time. Image success is measured even more emphatically via accumulation and proliferation, since individual sales generate far less revenue than they did in the "classic age." Indeed, it is only by selling a huge number of photos that a photographer finds economic reward.

The "best" stock—and especially microstock—images are not the most "original" or "artistic" images in a portfolio; they are images that can be sold many times to different buyers, who need those images to perform different functions and provoke differential affects. The smiling face of a teenager with braces, for example, might appear on orthodontia brochures in several countries while simultaneously advertising a Christian summer camp and a community program for queer teens. Economically successful images in this kind of marketplace thus share a perplexing rhetorical feature: the ability to seem simultaneously general (easy to imagine deploying in a variety of ways) and specific (easy to deploy in service of particular rhetorical appeals); Paul Frosh (2003, 73) encompasses this industry quality via the phrase "parsimoniously polysemic." We suggest that for an image to be "parsimoniously polysemic," it cannot rely on a neat appeal to one sense, a visuality mediated by the eye, but rather must encompass a full body of sensory connotations. This suggestion follows the media ecology tradition and W. J. T. Mitchell's (2005, 343) assertion that "there are no visual media. All media are mixed media, with varying ratios of senses and sign types," a reality that has only been amplified by digital culture's influence.

Notably, the sensuous rhetorical work of digital stock images also cannot be explained as a simple, temporal precursor to some kind of rational audit like those described in the introduction to this chapter. Decisions made at various points by image purveyors, cultural intermediaries acting as image buyers, and consumers of the multimedia end products necessarily contaminate one another. Visual cultural studies have long grappled with how individual reactions, desires, and interpretations are influenced heavily by things like memory, experience, culturally trained concepts of taste, and elements of exposure dictated by media industries; in this industry, such complexity is further compounded by the ways both sensation and evaluation are distributed across the industry. Cultural stakes emerge at this nexus because the speed associated with availability and desirability of images contributes to the sense experiences of businesses buying and then using those images in support of other (economic and cultural) activities. Consumer sensation (and evaluation) is always already mediated by the speed at which a business recognizes and procures marketing material, even as such processes are hidden from consumers.

This is consequential for digital rhetoric, and rhetoric more generally, because it suggests how approaches to rhetorical analysis like the one we model can account practically and simultaneously for individual communicators making trained, expert choices that follow discernible logics and the principle that messages influence in a great many ways that are not—and cannot be—well described by rational or ahistorical logics. Notably, the rhetorical analysis modeled here is not one where the body decides before the mind catches up (as described in early digital rhetorics that followed affect theory fully). Neither is it a model where decisions are always (or even often) based on rational comparisons. It is a messy rhetoric, embedded in cultural and material systems, one that takes its lead from calls attuned to complexity and infrastructure.

Making Sense in a Stock Sensorium

"Acceleration," "accumulation," and "proliferation" as rhetorical key terms describe a deeply influential cultural logic driven simultaneously by aspects of economic, digital, and sensuous rhetorics. Taken together, these terms help us grapple with the fact that "the digital is not only irreducible to what we see, it also exceeds that which we feel—in any traditional sense—and extends far out to what helps organize our collective bodies" (Boyle et al. 2018, 252). They also help us account for how sensuous bodies participate in digital, commercial, and cultural infrastructures—a move that responds to Jonathan Adams's theory of infrastructural rhetoric, which asks communication studies to hold more space for persuasive influence infrastructures, as "relational networks of social interaction around objects" have in a variety of communication settings (2022, 46).

We began our study of this logic by asking the (deceptively straightforward) questions, What happens when consumer experiences are moderated by screens and digital infrastructures? and How, in particular, does paying close, rhetorical attention to these experiences put pressure on existing theories of sensation, consumption, and digital culture? We conclude by, again, calling special attention to the infrastructural work done by digital marketers and other rhetorical agents active in shaping the markets where dramas associated with these questions unfold. In short, we believe it important to end by observing that infrastructural communication industries, like the stock image industry, exacerbate cultural risks associated with how individual digital images and popular categories of imagery produce differential effects.

In the previous section, we focused on describing the stock image market, showing some ways images sold there are entangled with the infrastructures of digital culture. When this particular class of images participates in collective and individual sense-making, including consumer decision-making, there are a variety of human stakes worth additional emphasis—not all of them strictly financial. We think here about the differentially distributed climate impact of internet infrastructures, including energy costs associated with high-volume file storage, without which this image market would collapse. We thus hope readers will connect our work to rhetorical studies like Dustin Edwards's (2021, 1) investigation of big data, which "positions the infrastructural dynamics of big data storage and circulation as a concern for social and environmental justice," or Karrieann Soto Vega's (2020, para. 1) crucial call for rhetorical work that foregrounds ethical engagement and "emphasize[s] the importance of attending to colonial causes and consequences in studying climate change," given the degree to which digital life is entangled with the same colonial projects driving climate change more broadly.

We also think about differential impacts that take place at the level of representation, a rhetorical implication too often elided when the senses are foregrounded in analysis. When sensory and digital rhetorics emerged as subfields, being taken seriously required resisting "traditional" forms of analysis that overvalued visual and semiotic content. Yet the important work of making space for our fields to study affects, unruly bodies, temperamental infrastructures, ambient media, nonhuman coconspirators, and multisensory experiences requires us to continue holding space for how these things interact with the representational aspects of visual media; this is easy to acknowledge, and many have, but space often makes it hard to enact—presenting the need for continued interdisciplinary rhetorical work, like ours, that engages image-making industries in their complexity.

A useful example of how the infrastructural role of stock industries (elaborated above) can promote differential impacts at the level of representation comes from the proto-stock-image industry of the 1930s and 1940s, when it was already understood that freelancers benefited from producing "generic pictures [that] could be sold to either liberal or conservative publications" (Miller 1994). In short, the emergent logic of the "picture agency" discouraged production of political imagery, with concrete consequences for what stories were being told, who appeared in them, and how appearances were skewed. This, of course, remains true. Similarly, we might critique the role stock images play in promoting rhetorical "bothsidesism," where the amount of evidence on each side of an argument is not weighted and journalists' attempts to balance perspectives introduce new biases rather than accounting for existing ones (see Boudana 2016).

Additionally, when end users interface with an image, the speed at which it can be interpreted (or ignored, in the case of background imagery) heightens its sensory appeal. When photographers are spurred to upload ever more images in faster succession for an industry that rewards visual shorthand and gimmicks, there is increased risk of stereotyping. If you need an image of a family at a picnic, how fast a particular image shows up and what style of filtering you do before finding it can shape your sense of its desirability. When the first page of picnic images that a search engine spits out features only happy white or light-skinned biracial families, cultural ideas about who picnics are for—which is to say, who is permitted to enjoy a leisure activity in a public place—are reinforced; localized representation is quietly usurped by "efficient" imagery.

In today's stock image marketplaces, these dynamics are driven by industry logics that have persisted over a century but also by development of specialty search engines, AI-driven lightboxes, and other tools that extend and distort that logic even further. The time and money that companies put into developing these tools suggests their importance; the speed at which searches unfold—how fast a marketing team can find good-enough images to meet its needs—confirms images' appeal in relation to the projects marketers are working on. In short, digital tools that dictate how and when individual images become visible and thus available to potential buyers act as important agents in the marshaling of representation and sensation alike. Consequently, we suggest the need for more sustained attention to how algorithmic logics that enable speed and access in this industry perpetuate algorithmic bias (Noble 2018). We also assert that this industry's long history of engineering image search experiences holds lessons deeply relevant to a world in which digital search functions are being invited into an ever-increasing array of daily activities.

Resensing the Digital Marketplace

Algorithmic rendering cannot be accounted for when sensation is disarticulated from making (economic) sense. Algorithmic bias persists, in part, because the speed at which accumulated images are curated and presented sensorily confirms their appeal: This must be the right way to represent a picnic—there are so many variations on the theme, and they showed up so fast. This is not simple (visual) input that precedes (rational) output but an embodied resonance between culturally situated expectations and speed. To account for our sense of (and senses in) the electronic marketplace, then, we should imagine how it not only parallels more traditional markets but recombines aesthetic appeals for sensory impacts irreducible to five discrete senses.

Returning to Ott and Dickinson (2009, 60, 58) we see how although "the aesthetic qualities of things do not signify," they nevertheless "activate and engage our senses." We find this both exciting for reimagining the roles sensation can and does play in seemingly boring or esoteric industries and a necessary invitation to look closer at how not just judgment but also responsibility, agency, and image desirability grow entangled in complex ways that are not ideologically or culturally neutral.

By considering the rhetorical commingling of acceleration, accumulation, and proliferation, we have shown how senses are conscripted into the differential work of capital markets. Digital tools, infrastructures, demands, and artifacts shape contemporary communal and sensory life through layered and complex appeals to sense-memory and imagery, making rhetorically present and appealing images that move fast and ever faster and, in so doing, infiltrate and organize our sense of rationality and desirability. These terms can thus be enlisted across economic, digital, and sensory rhetorics to identify and intervene in the curious appeal of the mundane and sensational alike. We hope, however, that they will be used to call attention to the necessary overlap of these often-discrete subfields, such that the senses are understood as embodied and economic, that economics are understood as argumentative and sensory, and that the digital is no longer disarticulated from its complicity in economic or sensory audits of rationality.

References

Adams, Jonathan. 2022. "A Theory of Infrastructural Rhetoric." *Communication Design Quarterly Review* 10 (3): 46–55.

Akese, Grace A., and Peter C. Little. 2018. "Electronic Waste and the Environmental Justice Challenge in Agbogbloshie." *Environmental Justice* 11 (2): 53–94.

Blaszczyk, Regina Lee, and David Suisman. 2023. *Capitalism and the Senses*. Philadelphia: University of Pennsylvania Press.

Boudana, Sandrine. 2016. "Impartiality Is Not Fair: Toward an Alternative Approach to the Evaluation of Content Bias in News Stories." *Journalism* 17 (5): 600–618.

Boyle, Casey, James J. Brown Jr., and Steph Ceraso. 2018. "The Digital: Rhetoric Behind and Beyond the Screen," *Rhetoric Society Quarterly* 48 (3): 251–59.

Bradshaw, Jonathan L. 2018. "Slow Circulation: The Ethics of Speed and Rhetorical Persistence." *Rhetoric Society Quarterly* 48 (5): 479–98.

———. 2020. "Rhetorical Exhaustion and the Ethics of Amplification." *Computers and Composition* 56:1–14.

Chen, Hanrui, Lu Wang, Bifeng Hu, Jianming Xu, and Xingmei Liu. 2022. "Potential Driving Forces and Probabilistic Health Risks of Heavy Metal Accumulation in the Soils from an e-Waste Area, Southeast China." *Chemosphere* 289:133–82.

Dul, Lucas. 2022. "The IBM Selectric: The Typewriter That Defined an Era." *ETCetera* 137:14.

Edwards, Dustin. 2021. "Critical Infrastructure Literacies and/as Ways of Relating in Big Data Ecologies." *Computers and Composition* 61 (September): 1–13.

Frosh, Paul. 2003. *The Image Factory: Consumer Culture, Photography and the Visual Content Industry*. London: Bloomsbury.

Harvey, David. 2004. "The 'New' Imperialism: Accumulation by Dispossession." *Socialist Register* 40:63–87.

Howes, David. 2021. "Hypesthesia, or, The Sensual Logic of Late Capitalism." In *Empire of the Senses: The Sensual Cultural Reader*, edited by David Howes, 281–303. New York: Routledge.

IBM (International Business Machines Corporation). 1941. "Get All the Accounting Facts of All Departments Through Punched Cards." Advertisement in *The American City* 56:78.

Koch, Thomas, and Florian Arendt. 2017. "Media Effects: Cumulation and Duration." In *The International Encyclopedia of Media Effects*, edited by Patrick Rössler, Cynthia A. Hoffner, and Liesbet van Zoonen. Chichester, UK: Wiley. https:// doi.org/10.1002 /9781118783764.wbieme0217.

Lanham, Richard A. 2006. *The Economics of Attention: Style and Substance in the Age of Information*. Chicago: University of Chicago Press.

Lowe, Charles. 2010. "Considerations for Creative Commons Licensing of Open Educational Resources: The Value of Copyleft." *Computers and Composition Online*, September. http://www.cconline journal.org/open/index.html.

Lyons, Scott Richard. 2000. "Rhetorical Sovereignty: What Do American Indians Want from Writing?" *College Composition and Communication* 51 (3): 447–68.

Mack, Adam. 2014. "The Senses in the Marketplace: Commercial Aesthetics for a Suburban Age." In *A Cultural History of Senses in the Modern Age*, edited by David Howes, 77–100. New York: Bloomsbury.

Mill, John Stuart. (1859) 1978. *On Liberty*. Edited by Elizabeth Rapaport. 8th ed. Cambridge: Hackett.

Miller, Abbott. 1994. "Pictures for Rent." *Eye* 14 (4). https://www.eyemagazine.com /feature/article/pictures-for-rent.

Mitchell, W. J. T. 2005. *What Do Pictures Want? The Lives and Loves of Images*. Chicago: University of Chicago Press.

Noble, Safiya Umoja. 2018. *Algorithms of Oppression: How Search Engines Reinforce Racism*. New York: New York University Press.

Ott, Brian L., and Greg Dickinson. 2019. "Redefining Rhetoric: Why Matter Matters." *Berlin Journal of Critical Theory* 3 (1): 45–81.

Pine, B. Joseph, II, and James H. Gilmore. 1998. "Welcome to the Experience Economy." *Harvard Business Review* 76 (4): 97–105.

Ridolfo, Jim, and Dànielle Nicole DeVoss. 2009. "Composing for Recomposition: Rhetorical Velocity and Delivery." *Kairos* 13 (2). https://kairos.technorhetoric.net/13.2/topoi/ridolfo_devoss/velocity.html.

Sharp-Hoskins, Kellie, and Anthony Stagliano. 2022. "Matters That (Em)Body." In *Bodies of Knowledge: Embodied Rhetorics in Theory and Practice*, edited by A. Abby Knoblauch and Marie E. Moeller, 236–52. Logan: Utah State University Press.

Shen Bingqing, Weiming Tan, Jigzhi Guo, Linshuang Zhao, and Pen Qin. 2021. "How to Promote User Purchase in a Metaverse? A Systemic Literature Review on Consumer Behavior Research and Virtual Application Design." *Applied Sciences* 11:1–23.

Soto Vega, Karrieann. 2020. "Colonial Causes and Consequences: Climate Change and Climate Chaos in Puerto Rico." *Enculturation: A Journal of Rhetoric, Writing, and Culture* 32. https://www.enculturation.net/colonial_causes_consequences.

3

Reeking Revelations
How Olfaction Informs Rhetorical Processes in Environmental Injustice

LISA L. PHILLIPS

If it is difficult to imagine . . . olfactory persuasiveness, that is only because we are unused to analyzing [the affiliated] behaviors as argument.
—Alex Parrish, *Adaptive Rhetoric*

Reek in the planetary lungscape damages bodies in its wake. In my neighborhood, on a bad day, southeast winds deliver visceral stink bombs. Imagine sulfurous ammonia-laced air that bombards, burns, and chokes. Nausea and retching distort and jerk me if I am caught outdoors. Rage ensues. Adrenaline floods. Blood pressure and cortisol levels elevate. The immune system pauses. Digestion halts. Mood depresses. Motivation implodes. Fear activates (Mayo Clinic 2023). Memory and olfaction share and accent both nerves—axon and anxiety. My neighbor who grew up in a funeral home says it smells like ammonia mixed with rotting flesh and embalming fluid. Trauma triggers. Another neighbor, a US Army veteran, says a medium day smells like Agent Orange and a bad day smells like the "Hanoi Hilton," his hellish prison during the Vietnam War. Our noses, minds, bodies, hair, and clothing remain affected hours after exposure, making everything taste and smell foul. Hot, humid weather adds frequency, length, and intensity to the visceral effects. Fumes and stench rendered the Vietnam veteran unconscious on a hot hazy summer evening when a temperature inversion concentrated poor air quality issues. A massive seventeen-thousand-plus hog-breeding facility built less than a mile from my rural Illinois home spawns these stench events.

The Illinois Environmental Protection Agency delivers no alleviating nosegay because olfaction appears unimportant to human health—patent nonsense—and a few folks' suffering matters little when political and environmental fires stir air elsewhere (see Roberts et al. 2020). The "law of the senses" is also subjective (Valverde 2019). Yet forced exposure to graphic pornography, ear-piercing noise, and physical assault equal illegal violences, and perpetrators of such sensory injuries face fines, jail, and accountability. Why are noisome attacks disregarded rhetorically when the stress response does such visceral violence and leaves lasting embodied effects? My distinct thesis is that olfactible violence garners such rhetorical neglect because it reflects an archaic sensory hierarchy that privileges sight and hearing in much the same way that white men enjoy unearned privileges that allow them to remain at the apex of power. One hierarchy reflects the other within western culture's Great Chain of Being.[1]

Sniffing Out Environmental Injustice Through Intersectional Ecofeminism

I argue that we must rethink and redress this faulted sensory hierarchy and its masculinized counterpoints to address a range of environmental injustices. To do so, I blend intersectional and ecofeminist frameworks and attend specifically to olfactory rhetoric designed to rectify environmental injustices. The intersectional ecofeminist framing of the chapter emphasizes inequitable environmental risk distribution and interrogates overlapping and mutually reinforcing forms of oppression that inform environmental injustice and how it is sensed and subsequently embodied (Singer 2020). The Black legal scholar Kimberlé Crenshaw (2020) first coined the term "intersectionality" in 1989, noting that intersectionality is "a lens, a prism, for seeing [how] various forms of inequality often operate together and exacerbate each other." Hence, intersectional approaches interrogate how layered discrimination works and disclose sites of multiple marginalization. For example, queer Black women face discrimination in cisgender-heteronormative (cis-het) Black-majority contexts that differ markedly from discrimination faced in cis-het white environments. Ecofeminism merges ecological care with gender-inequity concerns, confronting patriarchal approaches to environmentalism. The environmental communication scholar N. Ross Singer (2020, 269) situates intersectional ecofeminism as "an anti-essentialist heuristic [that] overtly rejects any singular, universal categorization of identity as a covering explanation of agency and experience, . . . [which] helps to account for variables of experience and power" that extend to both "human [and] more-than-human" entities in a given environment. An intersectional ecofeminist approach evaluates how various forms of oppression restrict and divert attention directed to environmental concerns raised by Black, Indigenous, and other people of color (BIPOC), women, and additional historically marginalized groups. The approach aims to address and amend these injustices. It also recognizes that proximal senses like olfaction, touch, and taste are granted less credibility in western contexts than are their distal counterparts of vision and hearing, which impacts what people pay attention to and why. The hierarchy of the senses informs and is informed by similar intersecting axes of oppression that circulate in rhetorical ecologies. History and universal design combined with disability studies principles also tell us that improving living conditions for the most vulnerable results in better living conditions across the board (see, e.g., Kerr et al. 2014).

I focus on olfaction because it persuades yet draws scant attention in rhetorical scholarship. Thus, taking up Parrish's call from the chapter epigraph, I analyze olfactory persuasiveness and the affiliated behaviors as argument. I use olfactory rhetoric as a conceptual apparatus to consider how environmental crises, from local pollution to regional drought to global climate change, are structurally embedded in the economic and institutional oppression of marginalized populations. To single out olfaction and how people discuss its a/effects reveals environmental justice issues. For example, tracing what stinks can lead to toxins dumped in a poor neighborhood or other noxious health hazards. Later in the chapter, I provide a four-stage process (a procedural method) to analyze and evaluate composite sensations, or clusters of sensuous activity, that emerge through "visceral publics'" environmental experiences with persuasive scent events (Johnson 2016, 2–3). Scent events inform mediated artifacts that circulate in the public sphere. Examples of mediated artifacts include social media posts, policy documents, news stories and broadcasts, public meeting minutes, videos, protest signage, and more. I argue that deploying the four-stage process helps us evaluate how people make sense of changes in environmental conditions and makes plain efforts to persuade policy makers to address environmental risks. As I show, this process allows rhetoricians and others attuned to social justice exigencies to uncover environmental injustices that emerge from olfactive experiences and shows how olfactory rhetorical analysis can prime more sensitive responses to people whose lives are routinely elided in public discourse about environmental hazards (Bullard and Wright 2012).

The Rhetorical Energy of Olfactory Persuasion

Olfactory persuasion exhibits rhetorical energy that translates into words and actions. Olfactory persuasion and how we use and communicate that information helps us understand, evaluate, and redress specific forms of environmental injustice. I focus on mediated artifacts circulating in the public sphere that deploy olfactory rhetoric as a persuasive device. Featuring examples of how people use olfactory rhetoric in the mediated public sphere is also "activist archival work," which Julie Collins Bates (2020, 211) describes as "a critical form of community engagement" that involves evaluating and "archiving activist interventions and positions the archival researcher in an activist role." It is not boots-on-the-ground activism, yet the work is designed to call attention to and rectify environmental injustices enmeshed with sensations as embodied, multifaceted experiences.

As we interact with different environments, a sensory spectrum helps us navigate those environments and assess whether they are hospitable and safe. Digital sniffing tools augment our senses and measure things like air pollution, soil contamination, and more. Often, the tools are given more credence than our natural senses are, particularly in legal contexts, where dominant risk assessment paradigms involving test tubes, labs, science, and rationality are privileged (Valverde 2019, 329). Yet people usually note the impact of environmental hazards and risks on and through bodily sensations that are "physical, . . . tangible and felt" and informed by prior experiences and perceptions (DeVasto et al. 2016, 139). Our sense of smell has a unique intimacy with our emotions and memories because it is so closely connected to our flight-or-fight responses. Odors violate boundaries, defy containment, and index the material presence of other entities in our midst. Circulating scents are "involved in just about every aspect of [nature] culture," from forming personal identity to judging social status and group affiliation, conveying traditions, and evaluating environmental health (Drobnick 2006, 1).

Ultimately, this chapter considers how people interpret and describe their olfactive inputs as they perceive changes in their environment and what triggers that sense-making, particularly in historically excluded and marginalized communities. Bodies in these communities routinely incur the most damage because they are disproportionately exposed to environmental hazards (human engineered and natural) over longer periods of time, at higher exposure rates, and in closer proximity (Banzhaf et al. 2019). Rob Nixon (2011, 2) names the results "slow violence" or "violence that occurs gradually and out of sight. . . . [And the results are] incremental and accretive." Specifically, slow violence incurs material and sensorial effects on bodies and is a matter for human memory and rhetorical inquiry. One example with which readers may be familiar is the lead contamination crisis in Flint, Michigan, which disproportionately impacted BIPOC and poor communities exposed to lead in the municipal water supply after the city switched from treated water outsourced from Lake Huron and the Detroit River to the Flint River to save money (Sadler et al. 2017). Municipal officials failed to add a corrosion inhibitor to the new water supply, causing lead to leach from old pipes; as a result, thousands of people were exposed to elevated lead levels (Bellinger 2016). After the switch, many residents noted that their municipal water smelled, tasted, and looked strange. Not long thereafter, residents reported feeling sick. City officials dismissed residents' embodied sensory claims and neglected to act promptly.

Overlapping ecological casualties that emerge from toxic aftermaths and slow violence are difficult to assess because they are complex and embedded in systemic injustices, but people who contend with an aftermath usually describe the impact it has on their bodies and on their loved ones via sensory rhetoric—how the affects feel, smell, taste, look, and sound—as Flint, Michigan, residents noted. The qualitative references people make to their sensory experiences inform how people understand and communicate about their environments and what circulates in those environments. Simply put, people contextualize aspects of environmental conditions through what they smell, feel, taste, hear, see, or otherwise sense. Public officials often dismiss sensory-rhetorical information or are skeptical when it first appears in the public sphere both because of the expense involved in cleaning up environmental hazards and because they devalue lived experiences as evidence. However, early action is less expensive in the long term, and it builds trust and can save lives.

When sensory transfer moves from the characterization of a more proximal sense like smell, taste, or touch to a distal category like vision, then the result can eclipse "nonvisual senses by rendering them unreliable, irrational, unable to contain or capture truth and, ergo, unsuited to serious study" (Smith 2021, 19). While no sense perception exists in isolation, when "we shift our focus to consider how our senses are entwined, then we need to consider the distribution of sensory attention" and how one sense perception may be culturally imbued with more credibility than another (Phillips 2015, 39). Our olfactive sense has an undeserved ethos problem, though its influence ripples throughout the body. Jude Stewart (2021, xiv) notes, "We smell with our entire bodies, and what we detect influences our lives more than we realize" because olfactory receptors are present not only in our noses but also in our skin, muscles, and major organs. Photoreceptors, by contrast, go no further than the retina, though our visual sense has ethos aplenty.

The fastest sensory process most humans have is olfaction. Our sense of smell is both speedy and shrewd. A groundbreaking 2014 study published in the journal *Science* asserts that humans can distinguish at least one *trillion* different odors, a finding that challenges the decades-long-held assumption that humans can only distinguish about ten thousand different odors (Bushdid et al. 2014, 1372, 1370). The speed with which we process odor experiences can help save a life or lives when seconds matter. One's body can react to a scent before one has a chance to do so cognitively. Our response to such stimuli affects our choices and emotions both consciously and subconsciously (Han et al. 2019). In *Rhetoric in Tooth and Claw*, Debra Hawhee (2016, 7) discusses the "intensities and capacities for dispositional transformation the [olfactive] moment entails" and how such moments can "emphasize the importance of the *other than rational* to rhetoric and rhetorical processes." The extradiscursive, or material beyond words, informs when a visceral public emerges and how and why it circulates mediated artifacts as evidence of a perceived environmental problem that ought to be addressed.

The next section provides a procedural method to understand how extradiscursive aspects of olfaction result in olfactory rhetoric used in the mediated public sphere and how that can shape policy making. Informed by an intersectional ecofeminist approach, all stages of the process must involve historically excluded or marginalized communities' concerns to work toward socioenvironmental justice goals.

A Four-Stage Process for Evaluating and Acting on Reeking Revelations

Stage 1: Sensing Emergent Problems
In stage 1, an environmental problem must be sensible, sensed, or readily perceived. Humans, nonhuman entities like dogs, birds, plants, and insects, or machine sensing technologies like e-noses, pressure sensors, or other apparatus all make up potential stage 1 sensors. For example, silkworms sense earthquake tremors long before humans do and exhibit behavior that forecasts the event (Ikeya et al 1998). Likewise, seismometers register tremor swarms that humans may not notice prior to a volcanic eruption (Einarsson 2018). In stage 1, humans may smell smoke or an unfamiliar odor and seek the source to decide if it is a threat. Targeted study of physiological sensation present in human and nonhuman living entities is a good starting point

for the four-stage process because no expensive equipment is needed, and it directs attention to changes in environmental conditions.

An example makes the abstract more concrete. For at least three decades, the majority-Black community of Brunswick, Georgia, has gone through multiple iterations of the four-stage process in its efforts to address environmental injustices. Brunswick has seventeen known hazardous waste sites, four major polluting industries, and four Superfund sites. The US Environmental Protection Agency (EPA; 2023) defines Superfund sites as locations so polluted with hazardous materials that they need long-term response and cleanup. In 1990, the community formed the Glynn Environmental Coalition (GEC). The nonprofit organization consists of residents from a range of backgrounds. Several have scientific training and provide "technical assistance," and all focus on "governmental oversight and environmental justice" (Glynn Environmental Coalition 2023b), which includes help administering EPA technical assistance grants related to the Superfund sites. The grant funding provides the "community with answers and an independent review and analysis of [Superfund] site documents" (Glynn Environmental Coalition 2023b). The GEC also assists residents with air quality improvement initiatives that include pollution compliance enforcement and supports residents' efforts to report sensory-based air quality data (Glynn Environmental Coalition 2023a). Although dedicated to improving community health outcomes, the GEC is a small group with limited power.

Stage 1 events happen frequently in Brunswick because of the proximity to four active polluting industries, which include a paper mill, a resin factory, a water sanitation plant, and a waste and recycling facility. Stage 1 scent events shift with the wind direction, the heat of the day, and the pollution produced, which is tied to the intensity of residents' lived experiences of these events and their exposures to airborne toxins.

Stage 2: Articulating Group-Based Sensory Experiences to Publics
Bearing in mind that "nothing is in the intellect that is not first in the senses," in the second stage, an environmental problem must be sensed and then perceived in intellection with others to gain traction and circulate in a sensory-rhetorical ecology (Cory 2018, 101). If someone, something, or a multitude senses something amiss within an environment or social scene and does *not* communicate that sensual experience, then composite sensations fail to emerge in the public sphere or circulate in the form of mediated artifacts. The reverse is also accurate. When people do communicate sensual

experiences, then composite sensations will emerge in the public sphere and circulate in the form of mediated artifacts. If people choose not to communicate about composite sensory experiences, it is often related to economic interests like concerns about property value, time to converse, access to the mediated public sphere, and other issues tied to capitalism.

Returning to the Brunswick example, in 2019, frustrated Brunswick residents created a Facebook group named Smell Something, Tell Something! Residents who experience a stage 1 scent event report their experiences to others in stage 2 communication in the group and help one another determine how and to whom they should report their concerns. In other words, they informally collaborate and often use olfactory rhetoric. The "About" page of the group provides a salient illustration:

> Trying to track down the source of the noxious middle of the night horrible smells? . . . It used to be only occasionally and now it seems like it [happens] every week. Let [us] know if you smell it at night. And the date, time and location. Whatever it is cannot be good for us to breathe. . . . In order for the EPD [Environmental Protection Division] to investigate potential air quality violations, an official complaint must be filed. . . . TIME, WIND DIRECTION, AND WIND SPEED are a must! The EPD will be better able to investigate the situation if you have these details. (Smell Something, Tell Something! 2019)

The olfactory rhetoric that Brunswick residents engage in transmits personal sensory experiences to the group, and residents often share data that corroborates their lived experiences using scientific data to warrant their embodied claims. For example, on January 10, 2023, one resident explained their difficulty breathing and attributed it to exposure to odors from a nearby paper mill; to corroborate their bodily experience, the resident then checked the air quality index data on a local weather app. The resident wrote, "I was awoken this morning . . . with uncontrollable coughing, postnasal drip, difficulty breathing and a headache. I checked my weather app to see that Brunswick's 'Air Quality Index' was at the dangerous unhealthy level of 154. The toxic odor fumes, from the Georgia Pulp Mill, were also present." Another resident conferred with the original poster on the same thread: "They [city officials] know the worst [pollution emission] is happening 'off hours' and those in-the-know know impacts of this type of business." A third poster argues that residents must "call out" mill owners and other polluters, "for trespassing on our health." Yet another declares, "I don't understand why 'odor' is not pollution? What chemicals are in the odor? Whatever it is goes into your lungs and bloodstream; this is just a medical fact. Who wrote the law that says it is not? The law needs to be changed" (Smell Something, Tell Something! 2023). The group members also share ways to report their experiences to the authorities, logging the effects of "slow violence" over time and working to elicit action to address myriad environmental problems (Nixon 2011).

Stage 3: A Visceral Public Broadcasts Sensory Experiences to Elicit Action
In stage 3, an environmental problem must be acted on and broadcast into the mediated public sphere by a visceral public to address an environmental problem. It differs from stage 2 communication because it has broader reach and circulation. Sensitized people and nonhumans need to have focused energy to address a problem, and that involves affect and emotion, time, and access to resources. Stage 3 is where we may see mediated responses to composite sensations fizzle out because people with the power to address an emergent environmental problem may ignore or suppress the situation out of ignorance or for a host of unethical reasons (e.g., financial, racist, sexist, ableist, and classist).

Let us return to Brunswick, Georgia for a stage 3 example. A January 10, 2023, Smell Something, Tell Something! post involved one Brunswick resident reminding other residents how, why, when, and where to officially report odor nuisances to regulatory agencies. To officially complain to state and local environmental protection and regulatory agencies in the Brunswick area requires residents to log in to an online portal that contains a form designed to capture the location, intensity, duration, and description of an odor and its embodied impact. The poster makes clear that odor nuisance reporting alone is an insufficient report category because, as the poster explains, public officials lump "all of [the] community complaints in an 'odor' category which requires NO action" (Smell Something, Tell Something! 2023). Subsequently, the poster explains that residents need to file a "health" complaint and provides additional guidance for doing so. An earlier, February 19, 2022, post features stage 3 news coverage that circulated broadly in the community. *The Brunswick News* ran a story about air quality concerns and a public meeting notice for a "drop-in event" hosted by a spokesperson for the Georgia-Pacific paper mill. The stage 3 event emerged due to formal complaints residents consistently filed with the Georgia EPA. Stage 2 communication on the social media site "became a central hub for comments about the issue" in late 2020, which led to stage 3 communication and community forum events designed to address residents' concerns (McDonald 2022).

Stage 4: Broadcasted Sensations Transform Policy

Finally, in stage 4, a visceral public's broadcast sensations must transform or move policy makers to redress the concerns of said public, and this also involves intersecting axes of power that impact who or what receives a more immediate response. The last step often involves different kinds of genres based in quantitative analysis and scientific and/or legal inquiry. For example, the Georgia Environmental Protection Division acted on air quality complaints that "began to pour in" to the local office in 2020 (McDonald 2022). In the Brunswick example, stage 4 is incremental and iterative. Clearly, a visceral public is present and active in Brunswick, but olfactory rhetoric has not fully persuaded public officials to resolve the health complaints that stem from scent events. Moreover, the results are tied to overlapping axes of oppression that have historically impacted mitigation measures in BIPOC communities (Chavis and Lee 1987). Local laws impact how odor nuisances are treated or left untreated. The environmental justice advocates Robert Bullard and Beverly Wright (2012, 178–80) explain how communities create anticipatory nuisance laws and policies to circumvent new problems before they arise, but that does not help communities address preexisting racist siting policies that put the majority-minoritized communities in harm's way originally. In Brunswick, the Glynn Environmental Coalition supports residents and local government agents to build antinuisance clauses and preventive measures into any new business development or expansion plans for existing industry settings.

Ultimately, the four-stage process can prove useful to rhetoricians who want to evaluate how, when, where, and why people use sensory rhetorics to redress environmental issues that emerge in their communities, as the procedural approach provides a practical method we can use to find emergent environmental issues, track visceral publics' sensational efforts, look for mediated artifacts that circulate in response, and evaluate policy response. The process can also help policy makers or risk communicators understand when, where, and why sensory rhetoric might be deemed insufficient evidence of environmental risk and how to address community health concerns respectfully, ethically, and effectively. Human sensory rhetoric can commingle with nonhuman and machine sensing technologies to triangulate data in legal cases. Additionally, the process could inform the design and implementation of anticipatory language built into permitting processes to prevent different forms of environmental hazards from taking place or gaining traction due to inadequate policies. For example, if we apply the procedural method to multiple sites across a geographical locale, then patterns may emerge tied to the region's dominant ideologies and power structures.

In short, the four-stage process supplies evidence and analysis of patterns of environmental injustice. Knowledge of the patterns will lead to better arguments for rectifying environmental injustices. Imagine how a community could include language in new building permits that address odor nuisances, eyesores, excessive noise, or other environmental impacts associated with different types of businesses that the applied four-stage process reveals are associated with environmental harm. A community would have the legal authority to nip problems in the bud. Granted, responsive stakeholders can account for implicit biases that sway who or what is considered a nuisance when drafting permit language. The process could also be useful to help different grassroots environmental justice groups understand when the four-stage process communication breaks down or when it would be useful to merge human sensory responses with machine sensing technologies to help a community address health and other socioeconomic and environmental concerns.

Connecting Transdisciplinary Aims and Olfactory Rhetoric to Environmental Justice Projects

My transdisciplinary aim in this chapter connects our bodies and sensations to what circulates in the material environment and examines how people articulate extradiscursive or other-than-rational olfactory experiences in the mediated public sphere to address perceived environmental risks. The guiding socioenvironmental justice principles are not new endeavors for rhetoric, composition, or technical communication scholars. Scholars in these fields often theorize sensation or examine interesting case studies without offering practical solutions or methods that could prove useful to the public or for public-facing advocacy work. The dearth of practical methods developed to help risk communication practitioners, communities, and environmental justice advocates to assess environmental injustice scenarios, understand how they unfold, and analyze whether policy makers deliberate and equitably redress concerns drives my approach. Thus, the process I have outlined above propels sensory rhetorics in a direction that provides a useful step-by-step method to analyze environmental risk communication and interrogate policy making. I argue that sensation, bodies, materiality, and mediated visceral publics are (in)formed by the environmental conditions in which they are enmeshed, and because environmental injustices disproportionately impact some bodies more than others, we also need to consider the power dynamics at work in different places/spaces and sense perceptions and collaboratively work to address them. I purposefully unite conversation clusters that combat human-made messes through transdisciplinary inquiry, drawing from sensory studies, intersectional ecofeminism, biology, philosophy, anthropology, and rhetoric. "What distinguishes transdisciplinarity," Debra Hawhee (2012, 3) writes, "is its effort to suspend—however temporarily—one's own disciplinary terms and values in favor of a broad, open, multilevel inquiry." This type of inquiry is "marked by a shared interest in a particular matter or problem but often draws together radically different approaches" with the holistic goal of examining "broad thematic areas" such as "food, animals, language, climate, and . . . bodies" (6). "Nowhere is the need for transdisciplinary perspectives more obvious than in a consideration of bodies and materiality," Hawhee notes (6). Sensate bodies in environmental injustice zones deserve more consideration, reciprocity, and more-than-theoretical concern.

As I have illustrated, a reeking revelation has both embodied and rhetorical a/effects, persuading people to find and redress the source of contamination, move upwind, or otherwise escape the stench. This chapter demonstrates how visceral publics use sensations like olfactory perception to identify and address environmental problems that then circulate in the mediated public sphere. Olfaction and olfactory rhetoric help to shape both communities' perceptions of environmental health and the ability to improve it. Applying the four-stage process to assess the emergence of scent events or other physically sensed concerns empowers people to recognize and confront environmental injustices. It also allows people to discern patterns in policy makers' actions, distinguishing when policy makers address environmental injustice and when inaction contributes to the problem. Evaluating olfactory rhetoric using the four-stage process illuminates how theory can inform analysis and showcases how people take action to improve environmental conditions. I encourage environmental rhetoricians, policy makers, activists, advocates, students, and teacher-scholars to evaluate examples of what olfactory rhetoric involves when we sniff it out and use it to shape public policy around environmental risk.[2]

Notes

1. The Great Chain of Being is an enduring concept that originated in medieval Christian doctrine. Visual representations of the hierarchical structure place the Christian God at the apex, place a human male figure just beneath God, and situate women, beasts, birds, plants, and so forth in layers underneath. I also intentionally used lowercase *w* in "western culture" to deemphasize hegemonic constructs.

2. I have also developed a more detailed heuristic for rhetoricians interested in evaluating olfactory persuasion in a book project from which this chapter draws (Phillips 2025).

References

Banzhaf, Spencer, Lala Ma, and Christopher Timmins. 2019. "Environmental Justice: The Economics of Race, Place, and Pollution." *Journal of Economic Perspectives* 33 (1): 185–208.

Bates, Julie Collins. 2020. "Activist Archival Research, Environmental Intervention, and the Flint Water Crisis." *Reflections* 19 (2): 208–39.

Bellinger, David C. 2016. "Lead Contamination in Flint—an Abject Failure to Protect Public Health." *New England Journal of Medicine* 374 (12): 1101–103.

Bullard, Robert D., and Beverly Wright. 2012. *The Wrong Complexion for Protection: How the Government Response to Disaster Endangers African American Communities*. New York: New York University Press.

Bushdid, C., M. O. Magnasco, L. B. Vosshall, and A. Keller. 2014. "Humans Can Discriminate More than 1 Trillion Olfactory Stimuli." *Science* (American Association for the Advancement of Science) 343 (6177): 1370–72.

Chavis, Benjamin J., Jr., and Charles Lee. 1987. "Toxic Wastes and Race in the United States: A National Report on the Racial and Socio-Economic Characteristics of Communities with Hazardous Waste Sites." Commission for Racial Justice, United Church of Christ, 1–79.

Cory, Therese Scarpelli. 2018. "Is Anything in the Intellect That Was Not First in Sense? Empiricism and Knowledge of the Incorporeal in Aquinas." *Oxford Studies in Medieval Philosophy* 6 (1): 100–144.

Crenshaw, Kimberlé. 2020. "She Coined the Term 'Intersectionality' over 30 Years Ago. Here's What It Means to Her Today." Interview by Katy Steinmetz. *Time*, February 20. https://time.com/5786710/kimberle-crenshaw-intersectionality/.

DeVasto, Danielle, S. Scott Graham, and Louise Zamparutti. 2016. "Statis and Matters of Concern: The Conviction of the L'Aquila Seven." *Journal of Business and Technical Communication* 20 (2): 131–64.

Drobnick, Jim. 2006. "Introduction: Olfactocentrism." In *The Smell Culture Reader*, edited by Jim Drobnick, 1–9. Oxford, UK: Berg.

Einarsson, Páll. 2018. "Short-Term Seismic Precursors to Icelandic Eruptions, 1973–2014." *Frontiers in Earth Science* 6 (45): 1–15.

Glynn Environmental Coalition. 2023a. "Air Quality." Last modified April 4. https://www.glynnenvironmental.org/airquality.

———. 2023b. "Who We Are." Last modified April 4. https://www.glynnenvironmental.org/about.

Han, Pengfei, Thomas Hummel, Claudia Raue, and Ilona Croy. 2019. "Olfactory Loss Is Associated with Reduced Hippocampal Activation in Response to Emotional Pictures." *NeuroImage* 188:84–91.

Hawhee, Debra. 2012. *Moving Bodies: Kenneth Burke at the Edges of Language*. Columbia: University of South Carolina Press.

———. 2016. *Rhetoric in Tooth and Claw: Animals, Language, Sensation*. Chicago: University of Chicago Press.

Ikeya, Motoji, Hiroshi Matsumoto, and Qing-Hua Huang. 1998. "Alignment Silkworms as Seismic Animal Anomalous Behavior (SAAB) and Electromagnetic Model of a Fault: A Theory and Laboratory Experiment." *Acta Seismological Sinica* 11:365–74.

Johnson, Jenell. 2016. "'A Man's Mouth Is His Castle': The Midcentury Fluoridation Controversy and the Visceral Public." *Quarterly Journal of Speech* 102 (1): 1–20.

Kerr, Thomas, Iain McAlpine, and Michael Grant. 2014. "The One-Eyed King: Positioning Universal Design Within Learning and Teaching at a Tertiary Institution." In *Rhetoric and Reality: Critical Perspectives on Educational Technology*, edited by Bronwyn Hegarty, Jenny McDonald, and S. K. Loke, 698–702. Tugan, Australia: Ascilite.

Mayo Clinic. 2023. "Chronic Stress Puts Your Health at Risk." Last modified June 20. https://www.mayoclinic.org/healthy-lifestyle/stress-management/in-depth/stress/art-20046037.

McDonald, Lauren. 2022. "Georgia-Pacific, JWSC to Host Event to Discuss Air Quality Concerns." *Brunswick News*, February 19. https://thebrunswicknews.com/news/local_news/georgia-pacific-jwsc-to-host-event-to-discuss-air-quality-concerns/article_d18043e2-dfe0-5c81-a45d-cd18222c5362.html.

Nixon, Rob. 2011. *Slow Violence and the Environmentalism of the Poor*. Cambridge, MA: Harvard University Press.

Parrish, Alex C. 2014. *Adaptive Rhetoric: Evolution, Culture, and the Art of Persuasion*. New York: Routledge.

Phillips, Lisa L. 2015. "Smellscapes, Social Justice, and Olfactory Perception." In *Rhetoric Across Borders*, edited by Anne T. Demo, 35–44. Anderson, SC: Parlor.

———. 2025. *Olfactory Rhetoric: Sniffing Out Environmental Problems*. Columbus: The Ohio State University Press.

Roberts, S. Craig, Jan Havlíček, and Benoist Schaal. 2020. "Human Olfactory Communication: Current Challenges and Future Prospects." *Philosophical Transactions of the Royal Society B: Biological Sciences* 375 (1800).

Sadler, Richard C., Jenny LaChance, and Mona Hanna-Attisha. 2017. "Social and Built Environmental Correlates of Predicted Blood Lead Levels in the Flint Water Crisis." *American Journal of Public Health* 107 (5): 763–69.

Singer, Ross N. 2020. "Toward Intersectional Ecofeminist Communication Studies." *Communication Theory* 30 (3): 268–89.

Smell Something, Tell Something! 2019. "Brunswick, Georgia, Community Group." Facebook, January 5. https://www.facebook.com/groups/1852807574805035.

———. 2023. "I Was Awoken." Facebook, January 10. https://www.facebook.com/groups/1852807574805035/posts/5721722004580220.

Smith, Mark M. 2021. *A Sensory History Manifesto*. University Park: Pennsylvania State University Press.

Stewart, Jude. 2021. *Revelations in Air: A Guidebook to Smell*. New York: Penguin.

US Environmental Protection Agency. 2023. "What Is Superfund?" Last modified October 30. https://epa.gov/superfund/what-superfund.

Valverde, Mariana. 2019. "The Law of Bad Smells: Making and Adjudicating Offensiveness Claims in Contemporary Local Law." *Canadian Journal of Law and Society* 34 (2): 327–41.

4

The Sense of Soil

Antiracism and the Community
Soil Collection Project

NATALIE BENNIE AND KELLY WILLIAMS NAGEL

In this soil, there is the sweat of the enslaved. In the soil there is the blood of victims of racial violence and lynching. There are tears in the soil from all those who labored under the indignation and humiliation of segregation. But in the soil there is also the opportunity for new life, a chance to grow something hopeful and healing for the future.

—Bryan Stevenson, in Equal Justice Initiative, "Community Remembrance Project"

Content warning: This chapter contains material of a highly sensitive nature, including racial violence, death, and torture, which may be distressing to some readers.

The early autumn humidity that overstays its welcome in Washington, DC, had broken as we crossed the Potomac and arrived at Market Square outside Alexandria, Virginia's City Hall. It was suddenly chilly and overcast, and while there were more people than we expected, Market Square was quiet and solemn as we collected ceremony pamphlets and tentatively took our seats. What we were about to witness was a moving experiment of efforts to reckon with the United States' history of racial violence. On September 24, 2022, the Alexandria Community Remembrance Project (ACRP), in conjunction with the Equal Justice Initiative (EJI), hosted a soil collection ceremony. Open to the public, this ceremony was part of a broader vision, called the Community Soil Collection Project, for communities across the United States to collect soil at known lynching sites.

The soil collection ceremony centered on the lynchings of Joseph H. McCoy and Benjamin Thomas. In April 1897, McCoy, an eighteen-year-old Black man, was accused by his white employer, Richard Lacy, of allegedly assaulting Lacy's two young daughters (James Madison University 2023). He was quickly arrested and put in jail, but white Alexandrians broke in and forcibly apprehended McCoy from his cell. They "shot him, bludgeoned him, and hanged him from the lamppost on the southeast corner of Cameron and Lee Streets" (ACRP Research Committee 2020b). McCoy's lynching represented racial tensions locally and across the United States at the end of the nineteenth century. Two years later, white Alexandrians would participate in another lynching.

In August 1899, a sixteen-year-old Black teenager named Benjamin Thomas was accused of a crime similar to McCoy's and many Black Americans throughout this time period: allegedly assaulting a white woman. This act was never proven, but Black community leaders that night warned local law enforcement and the mayor that a lynching would probably occur. White locals attacked the city jail, and Thomas "was dragged half a mile to the southwest corner of King and Fairfax streets, opposite Market Square" (ACRP Research Committee 2020a). The mob of over two thousand people dragged him over rough cobblestones for several blocks, threw stones, iron, and knives at him, and shot him for the entire distance. They hung Thomas from a lamppost, and the coroner later pronounced him dead from a gunshot wound to the heart (ACRP Research Committee 2020a). While these two stories are local to Alexandria, systemic racial violence and decades of willful community forgetting prompted the EJI to urge a different mode of remembrance through the Community Soil Collection Project.

Established in 1989 under the leadership of Bryan Stevenson, the EJI is a nonprofit organization dedicated to confronting the United States' history of racial injustice. Among its current initiatives, the EJI has begun creating physical spaces of remembrance through markers, memorials, and Community Soil Collection Projects that acknowledge the legacies of slavery, lynching, and racial segregation (EJI 2023a). This chapter examines one such project: a collaborative soil collection ceremony between the EJI and the Alexandria Community Remembrance Project.

Over the course of ninety minutes, the soil collection ceremony honoring Joseph McCoy and Benjamin Thomas led the audience through a meditative and somber set of memorial activities. Alexandria's mayor, Justin Wilson, welcomed the audience and read an official city proclamation that acknowledged the extrajudicial murders of both men, committed the city to reconciliation, and memorialized the lives of McCoy and Thomas. After this proclamation, two young Black men from the local high school performed fictionalized firsthand narratives from the perspectives of McCoy and Thomas. The descendants of the McCoy and Thomas families, present at the ceremony in the first rows, were recognized. Each of these elements of the ceremony set the stage for the main event: the act of communal soil collection. Audience members queued in two lines and used either trowels or their hands to place soil in jars labeled with McCoy's and Thomas's names, which would be taken on a pilgrimage to the EJI's Legacy Museum in Montgomery, Alabama, the following month for public display.

In the summer of 2022, members of the ACRP and city archaeologists consulted on notable sites from which to unearth soil for the ceremony. In August, they collected soil from not only where the lynching occurred but also places of significance in Alexandria's civil rights history. The soil was placed in two vessels, one for McCoy and one for Thomas. Gretchen Bulova of the ACRP called this soil "sacred" during her presentation at the ceremony. Later, her codirector, Audrey Davis, likened the jars to urns filled with soil and "souls no longer with us" (HistoricAlexandriaVA 2022). Before any hands at the ceremony touched the soil, it was anointed as a sacred object that contains far more than dirt. This sacred soil holds souls and the memories of generations. It is alive, requiring only the interaction of the audience to reveal itself. In this way, the soil is an archive—holding the past within, asking to be uncovered—though the materials in this archive are not physical but rather affective and memorial. Dubravka Sekulić, Milica Tomić, and Philipp Sattler (2020, para. 9) summarize how viewing soil as an archive can reveal memories: "The memory of the historical event which the local community wants to forget, grows out of the soil, but to be read as such, the soil has to be understood as an archive and the memorialisation as an active investigation, a process of assembling knowledge and simultaneously creating an intervention in both the existing and the new public sphere, by bringing the knowledge to interpret the event into the public realm."

We argue that this soil functions as a multisensorial agent of public memory. The truth-telling of the ceremony and the gathering of soil are an act of antiracism, as participants rethink the foundations of our nation's history, offering "healing for the future" (EJI 2023b). To support our argument, we draw on a methodology of rhetorical fieldwork that focuses on the sensorial elements of the collection ceremony and how meaning-making of antiracist activism comes to life. This chapter reads soil through the lens of sensory rhetoric by attending to elements of performance, activism, and memorialization and is thus of interest to both scholars and community organizers alike. Seeing, smelling, and touching soil that represents lynching victims in the present engages "sensory public memory," in which multisensory experiences bring forth opportunities to interrogate, engage, and reckon with our problematic pasts.

There is no such thing as senseless violence. While certain events may defy explanation, this is not the same as being senseless. Rather, we argue that such acts are rife with sensory elements and communicated through appeals to the senses, which are passed down to future generations and can perpetuate violence by and toward others. It is necessary to interrogate how the senses move bodies toward violence and consider how sensory rhetorics can play a role in antiracist activism. Meeting the violence of lynchings in sensorially appropriate ways can destabilize the status quo and help Americans confront the country's history of racial injustice. To do so, we engage first with scholarship concerning the rhetorical construction of lynchings, with attention to the sensory components of racial violence in American public memory. Second, we provide a short genealogy of fieldwork as a method and discuss how our positionalities as white women impact our analysis and presence at the soil ceremony. Last, we describe chronologically, in sensory detail, our experience of the soil collection ceremony and the impacts it will have on the community, rhetorical fieldwork, and antiracist scholarship and activism.

Race, Memory, and the Senses

In what follows, we attend to the roles that sensation plays in the creation, maintenance, and deliberation of Alexandria's public memory of racial terror. In so doing, we focus on the corporeal and affective means by which public memory is communicated. It is one thing to organize public speeches in memory of Joseph McCoy and Benjamin Thomas; it is altogether another to ask community members to participate in the act of remembrance through the tactile act of soil collection from lynching sites. We suggest that these acts—orations from a stage and the soil collection—are equally rhetorical in nature in that they seek to constitute a coherent memory of the past that is relevant to a present community. Touching the soil, witnessing poetic performances of McCoy and Thomas, sitting in Market Square, and other moments both destabilize and reinforce moments of American public memory. These sensory experiences undercut arguments that racism is a moment from the past and arguments that the present-day neo-Confederate movements are about heritage and not hate.

The history of the senses is not neutral. Indeed, the senses have always been culturally and politically mediated. E. Cram (2016, 116) describes sensation and feelings as "landscapes entangled within sociality and power, necessitating that critics apprehend the political and historical conditions that organize the visceral." Specifically, white American southerners constructed race in part through sensation. As Sachi Sekimoto (2018, 92–93) puts it, white southerners and slaveholders "literally sensed—smelled, touched, heard, felt, and saw—blackness and black inferiority into existence." Indeed, racial violence, including lynching, was justified using appeals to assumed sensory difference, such as the belief that Black skin is thicker and less sensitive to physical pain compared to white skin. Senses were—and are—a vehicle through which cultural discourses are mapped onto bodies. To exclude the senses would be to avoid a formative component of how racial violence has been perpetuated for centuries in the United States.

Lynching was a common way for white Americans to handle racist fears about newly freed slaves and Black Americans' proposed integration into white society after Reconstruction. Under slavery, the murder of Black individuals was considered an economic loss and a destruction of property. With emancipation, the unowned Black body now constituted a "threat" to uninterrogated white supremacy and sociopolitical power. One outgrowth of this perceived threat was to both physically and symbolically destroy the emancipated Black body through lynching. Spectacle lynching, defined as "murder endorsed by community, regardless of how many . . . actually committed the crime," became a foundational aspect of white supremacist reactions to newly freed Black Americans (Apel 2004, 14). The communal aspect in this definition is key. Spectacle lynchings were not isolated events by one or two people. Rather, these were performances that could and often did include the entire community as a way to constitute a unified white identity and collective of citizenry (Ore 2019, 52).

Spectacle lynching, according to Kirk Fuoss (1999), was a performance that mutually reinforced the validation of violent actions and racist ideologies. This form of lynching followed a standard set of practices. First would be an accusation. Sometimes it would be a crime, and other times it would involve the accused not following the rules of decorum placed on them by whites (Eatman 2017, 157). Typically, the accusations levied against Black Americans would be sexual assault against a white woman, which was the case for McCoy and Thomas. Though these accusations were often falsified, they created prevalent, unfounded myths of Black men as sexual predators (White 2005, 43–61). Once there was an accusation, a mob would form and capture the individual and then kill them either in a public place or at the scene of the crime. Lynchings in civic spaces were strategic, as "highly public spaces such as courthouse lawns, jailhouse grounds, and town squares placed lynching spectacles at the center of civic life" (Ore 2019, 53). Indeed, spectacle lynchings strengthened the legitimacy of racial violence despite its extralegality. White citizenship supported and required anti-Black violence to survive.

Spectacle lynchings operated as a rhetorical form that garnered power through white audiences using their senses to create notions of "community" by their terms. While the lynchings created civic connections for whites, such public murders also enabled a "climate of intimidation" for Black Americans (Apel 2007, 44). Because they were not to be included in white civic spaces, spectacle lynchings reinforced the material consequences of breaching decorum. Lynching attendees would stab, beat, and drag lynching victims, creating tactile dominance through violence. They would later cut off body parts and sell them as souvenirs. Smells of food like popcorn would intermingle with the smell of burning flesh as lynched bodies were frequently set on fire by white men. These sensorial moments worked together with the visual nature of whites watching lynchings to assuage fears and create unfounded arguments about civility and dominance in public spaces (Bostwick 2023). Public memories of lynchings have been passed down through white and Black communities through photographs, body part souvenirs, oral histories, and other sensorial ephemera. Few whites ever faced repercussions for their crimes, and today there is often hesitation in offering official apologies for actions taken by white ancestors (EJI 2024). This fact remains true for McCoy's and Thomas's murders. All white Alexandrians with ancestors present in the late nineteenth century are potential culprits, thus generating a need to plan and attend the soil ceremony. Its public nature and connections to the past create a climate of atonement for these crimes.

Making Sense of Rhetorical Field Methods

This chapter relies wholly on our physical presence at the soil collection ceremony, thus positioning our method as rhetorical fieldwork. In the past thirty years, the role of the rhetorical critic has expanded to include a more direct involvement with the "field" where rhetorical action takes place (McKerrow 2018, 217). The field can be defined as "the nexus where rhetoric is produced, where it is enacted, where it circulates, and consequently, where it is audienced" (McKinnon et al. 2016, 4). Fieldwork allows for researchers to visit the live, in situ space where rhetoric is "actually happening" and can entail "interviews, focus groups, observation, personal narrative, ethnography, autoethnography, oral history interviews, performance, thematic analysis, iterative analysis, grounded theory, and many other forms of data collection and analysis" (McKinnon et al. 2016, 5). Fieldwork can be a methodological option for scholars who may or may not belong to the community, movement, or culture they are researching, and it can last for any duration of time—from a few hours to years of study (Pezzullo and de Onís 2017, 107). Engaging in fieldwork can reveal complex interrelations of rhetoric by attending to the dynamics and movement of space/place, vernacular and official perspectives, affects, the more-than-human, and performances. Being there matters—embodied contexts can reveal dimensions and relationships that are not apparent through text alone (Druschke 2018, 30). Being in the "field" can resist the flattening of a text and the populations we study by creating embodied descriptions of experiences, which has the potential to make cultural rhetorics matter to readers (Blair 2001, 275–76).

The idea of fieldwork "conjures the tradition of ethnography," which in its early iterations involved scholars traveling to their destination and creating hierarchical space between themselves and their "subjects," thus forwarding opportunities to center colonial and racist ideas (McKinnon et al. 2016, 4). However, over time, critics have reconceptualized what it means to engage in field methods, considering things like when to foreground the researcher and when the researcher should step back and attune themselves to the field itself (McKinnon et al. 2016, 4). Engaging in fieldwork is a delicate balance that requires care and intention: It is imperative to consider the power structures that stratify the field and the bodies of those present. As Karma R. Chávez (2018, 242–43) argues, "if rhetorical studies commits to resisting forms of dominance such as white supremacy and misogyny, then analyses must grapple with bodies—the subjects we study, the scholars we are and depend on, and the perspectives far removed from taken-for-granted values." Fieldwork offers space to witness and enact moments of resistance against hegemonic rhetorical practices; it also involves an attentiveness to all the bodies present (including the researcher's body). One way to pay attention to the embodied aspects of research is to focus on sensation: how seeing, hearing, smelling, and touching all work together to create presence and expand the insights gained beyond secondary research into the text.

The body is a productive site of epistemological sense-making for field researchers. Writing to an interdisciplinary audience, Sarah Pink (2015) suggests that the sensory elements of the body are integral to knowledge production and ethnographic projects in general. By turning to the sensory instead of only the cognitive, field researchers activate an embodied imagination that can lead to novel ways of understanding and communicating their findings to various audiences. Attention to the body as a legitimate epistemological source does present methodological difficulties. It is easy to take a photograph of a monument—it is much harder to describe the feeling of hunger, the sensation of guilt, the heat of the sun, the smell of nearby construction, or the touch of an embrace. Yet sensorial elements are always present, whether or not they are documented by a researcher. It is important to attend to them as valuable sources of knowledge. Simply put, feelings matter.

This is true in the realm of public memory studies as well. Connecting sensory studies, rhetorical theory, and archival research, E. Cram (2016, 125) describes the act of feeling archival materials as a sensation that "evokes imagination and inventive potential." But a researcher noting their feelings or senses *in situ* does not a critical scholar make. Rather, "a transformative relation to the past requires feeling remains in ways that generate capacious historical imaginations reflexive of the losses we might create otherwise" (Cram 2016, 125). At the soil collection ceremony, it was integral that each person use their body to physically place the soil in the collection urns, but the transformative potential of this act per se is mediated through the rhetorical construction of antiracist reckoning that occurred throughout the ceremony's speeches and performances.

Our bodies as researchers and those present at the soil collection ceremony are important to assess. Our white, female, able bodies interact in spaces in a particular way—we feel the sensory effects of a phenomenon differently than others and from each other. We represent normative sensory abilities; thus, we did not experience difficulties traveling to, witnessing, or participating in the ceremony. While we represent a wide swath of populations, we acknowledge that our analyses do not showcase the totality of experiences and conclusions that could be drawn; however, we do offer a lens with which to approach sensory fieldwork as white scholars engaging in antiracist work.

One challenge of rhetorical fieldwork is extrapolating beyond each individual researcher. Given how whiteness developed as an "embodied sensory subjectivity that assumes itself as the normative, standard, human, sensory experience," we are especially conscious of our position as two white women writing a chapter based in part on our own embodied experiences (Sekimoto 2018, 94). The very sensations we reported in our notebooks and conversations are not neutral but culturally informed. Yet to generate the "capacious historical imagination" necessary to enable a transformative public memory of the past, we must bring a balanced awareness to these senses—we must become curious about sensation's capacity to either uphold whiteness or beget an antiracist orientation. Specifically, the tactile sensation of touch is a heavily racialized sensation. But as Sekimoto suggests, "If we take a moment to reflect on our bodily experience of touching/being touched and how the world becomes knowable through touch, the false sense of racializing touch will be disrupted.... It is the return to the embodied experience of the tactile world with phenomenological curiosity that can open our senses beyond the apparatus of racialized touch" (96). It is our hope that the following case study helps make the case that rhetorical fieldwork can enable this "return to the embodied experience of the tactile world" among rhetorical critics dedicated to reckoning, justice, and antiracist work (96).

Soil Collection Ceremony

We approached the heart of historic Alexandria on the afternoon of September 24, 2022, where Market Square had been prepared for the occasion. We were tentative and sincerely felt uncomfortable walking into a ceremony without knowledge of how many people would be there and what would be asked of us. Near the front of the square was a table run by EJI volunteers, who chatted with us about their excitement and reverence for the ceremony. They let us take as many free booklets as we wanted, so we took all of them. They included a calendar of important events in Black history, information on the EJI, a ceremony program with a map of important places relevant to the soil collection process and important places in McCoy's and Thomas's lives, including the sites of their murders, and a booklet on lynching in the United States. These booklets became a significant resource in our fieldwork in Alexandria, as well as our research and writing process.

Over a hundred chairs were arranged in front of an empty stage. The names of Joseph McCoy and Benjamin Thomas loomed large on a banner underneath the words, "Remembering Alexandria's Lynching Victims." At least fifty people were already milling around the square—some took their seats early; others engaged in conversation with friends, family, and colleagues. We took our seats rather quickly. We sat two rows back on the aisle, leaving space for city employees and participants in the ceremony but being close enough to the stage to be part of an immersive experience. Details such as the location of the event (held on a permanent stage in front of Alexandria City Hall) and the slate of prominent speakers on the program make it clear that the Alexandria Community Remembrance Project is deeply tied to the city's political administration first and citizens second. We witnessed an awkward moment before the ceremony started, when a Black female pastor was asked by a white woman working the event to move to the second row so that the (mostly white) city council members could take their seats in the front row. The pastor said, "Of course, move the Black people to the back like always!" The white woman looked uncomfortable and laughed it off before retreating to a "new" task. The pastor moved, but the relegation of citizens and clergy to a second tier (below mostly white city council members) felt particularly unfitting of the purpose of the ceremony to right wrongs in favor of recognizing the equality of Black citizens.

The ceremony opened with a short performance of the gospel song "Take My Hand, Precious Lord" by the minister Siera Grace. She performed the song a cappella, and the lack of background music or additional singers allowed us to put our sole focus on listening to her set the tone for the ceremony. The lyrics "take my hands / lead me on / help me stand" and "through the storm / through the night / lead me to the light / take my hands, precious Lord" evoked the tactile nature of the ceremony but also allowed the audience to visually imagine the trials and tribulations of McCoy, Thomas, their families, and the millions of Black Americans who have suffered under white supremacy. After Grace's performance, Mayor Justin Wilson acknowledged those individuals who put the event together, and before long, the ceremony was under way.

Perhaps the most affectively powerful moment in the ceremony came in the middle. For over sixteen minutes, two local high school students—both young Black men around the same ages as McCoy and Thomas—performed a first-person narrative of the events of each man's last days in Alexandria. The narratives were a combination of facts ("We were on King and stopped at the lamppost at Fairfax") and fictionalized performances of each man's perspectives and feelings at the time ("My mom's hand tightened around my arm as if her holding me would anchor me in place"). Both narratives ended with phrases that evoked a contemporary resonance. The narrative of Joseph McCoy closed with the performer stating an all-too-familiar refrain after the 2020 murder of George Floyd: "I can't breathe. I can't breathe." Benjamin Thomas's narrative, too, ended with words that have unfortunately been repeated at the scenes of twenty-first-century murders of Black men by police: He begged for his mother and stated his innocence.

As audience members listening to this performance, we were captivated and, for those sixteen minutes, unable to sense the temporal distance between the nineteenth century and the present day. The use of first person situated the audience as witnesses to the boys' testimony, obligating them to listen as the boys described the violence inflicted on their bodies, took breaths to collect themselves, and pled their innocence to a crowd on the very site where the bodies of Benjamin Thomas and Joseph McCoy were beaten and murdered over a century ago. We shifted uneasily in our seats as the speakers scanned the audience, making eye contact with their mayor, their sheriff, tourist bystanders, and ourselves. There was an uncanny sense to their speech, the truth of their words being declared in a public hearing that was denied to the men they sought to embody. This tension was not resolved but rather left to a breathless audience to feel for themselves. As the speakers transported the audience to the nineteenth century, we no longer felt like researchers detached from this place and the lynchings of McCoy and Thomas. We were folded into history as witnesses. While we, of course, were not culpable in the murders, we felt a connection to our ancestors who may have participated in spectacle lynchings. This ancestral bond connected us to generations of racial trauma and the events in Alexandria in surprising ways. We expected a comfortable distance but instead felt the synecdochical connection between these lynchings and the over four thousand documented lynchings across the United States. This connection helped us feel the magnitude of the event and underscored the necessity of soil ceremonies that overwhelm the senses to collapse temporal distances and make present-day Americans understand the effects of lynching felt to this day.

The young men's performances engaged the senses in a few different ways. First, the narratives' truth-telling utilized the senses, making the live performances distinct from the historical narratives of the lynchings that can be found on the Alexandria Community Remembrance Project website and in the printed materials given to attendees. Whereas the material published by the ACRP used newspaper accounts and court records to report the course of events, the performances relied on sensory detail. The young men described the sounds of voices outside the jail, the "boom" of weapons being fired, doors clanging shut, and keys scraping metal. Visual appeals further closed the distance between performer and audience as we heard the performer for Joseph McCoy describe the sweat, blood, and tears running together to obstruct his vision. Their narratives evoked the olfactory as well, drawing attention to the barrel of fish in the basement of the jail in which Benjamin Thomas spent his last moments before the lynch mob murdered him. The tactile descriptions seemed to be an especially effective means of collapsing the distance between past and present. The young men described in detail the haptics of their final moments. Descriptions such as "a million white hands closed on my shoulders, tore my clothes, pulled my hair," "the cobblestones battered me," and "something cold and heavy pressed against my chest" made the bodily, sensory experience of violence extremely vivid.

The narrative choice to draw on the senses begets the second way the performances engaged the senses, which is through activating the audience's own embodied sensations. Toward the beginning of the performance, as the young man speaking as Benjamin Thomas described being arrested while at home with his mother, he noted, "My mother's hand tightened around my arm as if her holding me would anchor me in place." As he said this, one author could feel the pressure on her own arm, constricting the flow of blood to her hands, before realizing that the tension she felt was her own doing. She had her arms crossed over her body, her hands trying to ball themselves into fists around her arms, and the awareness of this sensation prompted by the description of a murdered man's last touch with his mother unsettled her. The performances left us both with discomfort and tension, both physically and emotionally. When we went to collect the soil, it was with those sensations of disgust, horror, and sorrow pulsing through our bodies.

After these performances, the Reverend Quardicos Driskell, a local faith leader, invited the audience to come up to the vessels near the stage to put the soil in the jars designated for the two young men. Driskell asked that the descendants of Joseph McCoy initiate the collection process, followed by faith leaders, and then the general public in attendance. We were asked to add only a small amount of soil to the jar so that everyone who wished to partake could do so.

After McCoy's descendants and the faith leaders took their turns, we joined the line to gather the soil into vessels. The outside of each clear jar stated McCoy's or Thomas's name, the date they were murdered, and the location of their lynching.

We approached Thomas's soil vessel first (see fig. 4.1), where we each used small trowels to collect soil. Digging into the soil was an especially sobering experience, amplified by the cello soloist who played music during the soil collection. Digging into the soil and listening to the music—while still feeling connected to and moved by the teenage boys' sensory-rich narratives—created a heightened sensorial experience. At times, the experience felt more surreal than anything. "How did we end up at a soil ceremony in Alexandria, a place neither of us had visited before? How do we feel so intimately connected to this history after only about an hour?" In part, the

FIG. 4.1 Benjamin Thomas's soil collection vessel, September 24, 2022, Alexandria, Virginia. Photo: Kelly Williams Nagel.

constant supply of tactile, visual, and auditory components of the ceremony tied us to the ceremony in ways we did not expect.

Despite the constant movement of audience members (see fig. 4.2), we were encouraged to take a reflective moment for McCoy and Thomas. For McCoy's vessel, one of us used our hands to collect the soil (instead of the trowel). McCoy's soil felt incredibly dry and brittle—like the soil of an unyieldingly brutal summer in the South. This does not mean there was a sense of unwelcome in the soil but rather that the soil was almost unflinchingly honest. There was no warmth or comfort to be found, no sense of idle complacency or hope for its potential to bear new life. While we wish to reiterate our commitment to the equality of senses as sources of meaning-making, it is the tactile components of the ceremony that remain with us years after the fact—specifically the soil itself.

As we dug into the soil, whether by hand or trowel, a literal unearthing took place: an uncovering of the lower layers of soil alongside a rhetorical unearthing in which the violence of the past is acknowledged and felt in the

The Sense of Soil

FIG. 4.2 Participants collecting soil, September 24, 2022, Alexandria, Virginia. Photo: Kelly Williams Nagel.

present. Yet the dirt passed quickly through our hands as we placed it in the waiting receptacles, evoking the act of a burial, with each visitor throwing a small handful of dirt into a grave. The moment of collection is thus one of simultaneous uncovering and recovering. Touching the soil offered what felt like a direct link to the past. It is a rare opportunity to touch the past, and the tactile experiences of the soil—along with other sensorial moments from the ceremony—evoked the presence of McCoy and Thomas. The soil was a visceral reminder that these teenagers were once very much alive, that their brutal murders represent wider experiences associated with over four thousand lynchings in the United States. McCoy's and Thomas's presence within the ceremony and our ability to witness and touch their remnants created moments of radical empathy that did not absolve us or our ancestors of racist wrongs but allowed us to acknowledge their embodied memories and carry them forward into antiracist scholarship, quotidian actions, and everyday relationships in our communities.

The soil collection in total lasted about twenty minutes. Once the jars filled completely, the ceremony closed with a final song before we were released. We stayed behind to watch as local community members talked to one another and other members took photos of the vessels. Some of those who stayed behind (from the city council, ACRP, faith leaders, and general public) hugged one another, talked about the ceremony, and noted a sense of reckoning and accomplishment in achieving the goals they set out to achieve. With the echoes of singing in our ears and soil beneath our fingernails, we silently walked away from Market Square.

Applying Sensory Rhetorics Within and Beyond the Academy

We hope we have offered some insight into how sensory rhetorics can enrich fieldwork. Traditional notions of text as static ignore corporeal, embodied, and sensory ways of meaning-making that are necessary for understanding a performed text in situ and for recognizing the body as a valuable epistemological source. We utilized a fieldwork methodology to analyze Alexandria's soil collection ceremony through the lens of sensory public memory, performance, and the legacy of racial terror. In addition to laying bare the violent foundations of this community, the narrativized performance of two Black students further collapsed the temporal distance between past and present. The embodied presence of the speakers alongside the contemporary resonances of their speech (e.g., "I can't breathe") placed the burden of witnessing onto the community audience, thereby involving each person in the memory work. In this context, tactile interaction with the sacralized soil transformed the sensory experiences of the audience.

We conceive of soil as both universal and particular. It is ubiquitous in the sense that it is always underfoot. If you are on land, you are either on soil or in a structure built atop it. Yet soil is also particular, reflecting the chemical and biological registers of its unique location. Take a handful of soil in one location and it will be distinct from a handful anywhere else. This distinction, however, is only apparent when one's senses are attuned to it. You can smell the difference in pH levels; the acid that causes sweet corn and blueberries to flourish is poison to a fig tree. With your hands, you can tell if the soil is dense with clay or dry and rocky.

Soil's fundamentally universal and particular nature makes it a fitting material of remembrance for victims of racial violence in the United States, individuals who suffered particular violence within a universal system of anti-Black racism. As Dave Tell (2019, 27) reminds us, "racism and commemoration have, from the very beginning, been entangled with the natural, cultural and built environments." The flat and fecund land of river watersheds in the South, for example, influenced the creation of plantation economies that profited off stolen Black labor, whereas the marsh topography of the Potomac River near Old Town Alexandria informed the city's reliance on shipping and railways, with rail companies enslaving Black men to build the necessary infrastructure (University of Nebraska–Lincoln 2023). The plantation and shipping economies functioned within a universal system of white supremacy but with instantiations of anti-Black racism. As soil determined the shape of the structure of white supremacy, the Soil Collection Project showed how soil can also be a vehicle for its destruction. In the act of uncovering soil and filling the ceremonial vessels, audience members began to reckon with not only the city's past but their own positionalities as citizens in the twenty-first century. Soil is thus an especially effective material to use in displays of contemporary remembrance for the victims of anti-Black violence.

While there are certainly a variety of ways for scholars to build on this academic research in the future, this chapter also highlights how people can create a collaborative local coalition with the EJI to organize a soil collection ceremony. There remain thousands of untapped locations that must reckon with their past and present. Scholars could engage in this form of activism, but this project goes beyond academia and is open to anyone interested in righting wrongs in their own communities.

References

ACRP Research Committee. (Alexandria Community Remembrance Project Research Committee). 2020a. "The Lynching of Benjamin Thomas, August 8, 1899." Alexandria Community Remembrance Project. https://media.alexandriava.gov/docs-archives/historic/info/blackhistory/benjaminthomashistoricalnarrative.pdf.

———. 2020b. "The Lynching of Joseph H. McCoy, April 23, 1897." Alexandria Community Remembrance Project. https://www.alexandriava.gov/sites/default/files/2022-04/McCoy-Lynching-Narrative.pdf.

Apel, Dora. 2004. *Imagery of Lynching: Black Men, White Women, and the Mob*. New Brunswick: Rutgers University Press.

———. 2007. "Lynching Photographs and Public Shaming." In *Lynching Photographs*, edited by Dora Apel and Shawn Michelle Smith, 42–78. Berkeley: University of California Press.

Blair, Carole. 2001. "Reflection on Criticism and Bodies: Parables from Public Places." *Western Journal of Communication* 65 (3): 271–94.

Bostwick, Will. 2023. "Inside the Decades-Long Effort to Commemorate a Notorious Waco Lynching." *Texas Monthly*, February 23. https://www.texasmonthly.com/being-texan/waco-historical-marker-saga-jesse-washington-lynching/.

Chávez, Karma R. 2018. "The Body: An Abstract and Actual Rhetorical Concept." *Rhetoric Society Quarterly* 48 (3): 242–50.

Cram, E. 2016. "Archival Ambience and Sensory Memory: Generating Queer Intimacies in the Settler Colonial Archive." *Communication and Critical/Cultural Studies* 13 (2): 109–29.

Druschke, Caroline Gottschalk. 2018. "Agonistic Methodology: A Rhetorical Case Study in Agricultural Stewardship." In *Field Rhetoric:*

Ethnography, Ecology, and Engagement in the Places of Persuasion, edited by Candice Rai and Caroline Gottschalk Druschke, 22–42. Tuscaloosa: University of Alabama Press.

Eatman, Megan. 2017. "Loss and Lived Memory at the Moore's Ford Lynching Reenactment." *Advances in the History of Rhetoric* 20 (2): 153–66.

EJI (Equal Justice Initiative). 2023a. "About." https://eji.org/about/.

———. 2023b. "Community Remembrance Project." https://eji.org/projects/community-remembrance-project/.

———. 2024. *Lynching in America: Confronting the Legacy of Racial Terror*. 3rd ed. https://lynchinginamerica.eji.org/report/.

Fuoss, Kirk. 1999. "Lynching Performances, Theaters of Violence." *Text and Performance Quarterly* 19 (1): 1–37.

HistoricAlexandriaVA. 2022. "Soil Collection Ceremony." YouTube, October 7. https://www.youtube.com/watch?v=BVuQftHwa1Q.

James Madison University. 2023. "Joseph McCoy in Alexandria." Racial Terror: Lynching in Virginia. https://sites.lib.jmu.edu/valynchings/va1897042301/.

McKerrow, Raymie E. 2018. "Text + Field: Innovations in Rhetorical Method." *Quarterly Journal of Speech* 104 (2): 216–20.

McKinnon, Sara L., Robert Asen, Karma R. Chávez, and Robert Glenn Howard. 2016. Introduction to *Text + Field: Innovations in Rhetorical Method*, edited by Sara L. McKinnon, Robert Asen, Karma R. Chávez, and Robert Glenn Howard. University Park: Pennsylvania State University Press.

Ore, Ersula J. 2019. *Lynching: Violence, Rhetoric, and American Identity*. Jackson: University Press of Mississippi.

Pezzullo, Phaedra C., and Cataline M. de Onís. 2017. "Rethinking Rhetorical Field Methods on a Precarious Planet." *Communication Monographs* 85 (1): 103–22.

Pink, Sarah. 2015. *Doing Sensory Ethnography*. London: Sage.

Sekimoto, Sachi. 2018. "Race and the Senses: Toward Articulating the Sensory Apparatus of Race." *Critical Philosophy of Race* 6 (1): 82–100.

Sekulić, Dubravka, Milica Tomić, and Philipp Sattler. 2020. "Digging Up the Past: Soil as Archive." *Architectural Review*, February 12. https://www.architectural-review.com/essays/digging-up-the-past-soil-as-archive.

Tell, Dave. 2019. *Remembering Emmett Till*. Chicago: University of Chicago Press.

University of Nebraska–Lincoln. 2023. "The Growth of Slavery and Southern Railroad Development." Railroads and the Making of Modern America. Accessed July 29. https://railroads.unl.edu/views/item/slavery_rr.

White, Lisa A. 2005. "The Curve Lynchings: Violence, Politics, Economics, and Race Rhetoric in 1890s Memphis." *Tennessee Historical Quarterly* 64 (1): 43–61.

5

Feeling Through Numbness, Healing with Awe

Not-Knowing as a Methodology for Sensory Rhetorics

AMES HAWKINS

It was a deliberate act—or rather a series of acts that accumulated over the course of years—for me to (re)make sense of my life and (re)align my embodied experience by choosing to have gender-affirming top surgery. Throughout the years-long process of coming to this decision, I made sense of what I was doing by negotiating a self in relationship to narratives controlled by Western medicine, ones that pathologize the individual through diagnoses of gender dysphoria and maintain a series of gatekeeping requirements that an individual must satisfy prior to surgery. I had to reconcile a long-standing hesitation-refusal to be diagnosed with gender dysphoria with a desire-need to transform the contour of my chest in a way that would make living my life as the-me-I-feel-I-am possible. I did so both through therapy and in the company of narratives by other trans and gender-nonconforming folx, stories offered through scholarship, memoir, television, film, and social media, that not only challenged and critiqued dominant narratives but allowed me to feel comfortable with my decision and less alone.[1]

In preparation for surgery, I was invested in the specifics of the procedure itself, both as told to me by my medical providers and those I accessed on social media. In other words, most of my sense-making was conducted through acts of self-reflection and information gathering prior to surgery (i.e., research), all of which were an attempt to prepare for (and perhaps even control) the experience through deliberate acts of learning, the pathway I knew best to access what it felt like to *know*: what would happen, when, and why.

However, my journey to and through top surgery—as is the case with most journeys we take as human beings—could not only happen in the mind. As much as I may have tried, I could not gather all the information necessary to anticipate the feelings and sensations—the sense-making—that would be necessary, despite my intense desire for the shift, to move from a body with breasts to one without them. While sense-making may be the result of deliberate acts—conscious deliberation of information, data, and so on—we can't assume that sense-making is only ever related to data we can (or just have yet) to gather, information that's just waiting to be (can ever be) known. Moreover, it isn't only that I wouldn't know what would happen until it did. What I learned—through-and-with my body—is that sense-making also happens in and as a result of a capacity to feel, recognize, and understand a state of *not-knowing*.

Not-knowing is not the same as nonknowledge, as the lack or absence of knowledge waiting to be discovered or found. Not-knowing, as I describe it in a piece about my friendship with the poet Sam Ace, "is a phenomenological state in which we become open to the possibilities of what it means to know without needing to know, a state beyond Cartesian, dualistic thought. Not-knowing is paraknowing, preknowing, embodied knowing, a knowing that has nowhere to land until it takes up residence in a yet-to-be-discovered, ever-latent connection, detail, forgotten note, fragment, sensorium, impulse, or event. Not-knowing is a generative, reflexive, empathic, affective force offering a way through that which can never be known. Not-knowing is a kind of queer knowing, a yet-will-be potential realization that defies time and space" (Hawkins 2021, 151).

In asserting not-knowing as a kind of queer knowing, I am thinking about Jonathan Alexander and Jackie Rhodes's 2011 aphoristic assertion that "queerness exceeds the composed self" (181). Queerness, in its excessiveness,[2] pushes against-beyond normative narrative structures that present the/a story of when and how we come to know something, to make sense of something: as dependable, logical, disciplined, and contained. Indeed, composed. Consider the motivation, as well as the unacknowledged privilege, behind asking when someone knew they were gay, trans, lesbian, queer, or whatever. Questions that assume (1) the inquiry deserves an answer (composed or otherwise) and (2) there is knowledge to discover, an answer to give.

When did I *know* that I was nonbinary/gender-nonconforming/trans? Was it when I refused to wear a dress at eighteen months old or when I consciously chose to wear female drag in high school to "blend in"? Was it when I was screamed at when I was in the "wrong bathroom" (even though that's where my mother told me to go) when I was three or nearly punched for the same reason when I was thirty-six? Was it when I was scolded for taking my shirt off in "public" (the backyard) at age nine even though my chest looked the same as my brother's or when I was ignored (blissfully so) for doing so post top surgery at a beach in St. Martin when I was fifty-four? Even more, do I need to figure all of this out and come up with a neat and tidy story just so I can explain it to anyone who asks?

Again, I turn to Rhodes and Alexander (2022, 1), who write, "confusion may be the most important offering of a queer rhetoric—that it leaves us troubled, perhaps incited, but delightfully and generatively so." Not-knowing is a kind of queer knowing because not-knowing presumes confusion, which, etymologically speaking, has to do with "mingling," "mixing," and "pouring together." Not-knowing is the accreted sum total of experience as con-fusion, being *with* that which is difficult, perhaps impossible, to pull apart: an embodied relationship with and to *bothand*. Not-knowing is not limited to queer folx, yet for many reasons, queers are more likely to have had more practice with sense-making that has to take not-knowing as a reality of human experience into account.

In this autoethnographic essay, I assert not-knowing as a potentially generative concept for sensory rhetorics by exploring how I made and (re) made sense of-through-with the feelings and experience of gender-affirming top surgery. Constructed as a creative-critical triptych, the format foregrounds the importance of juxtaposition, inviting a reader to engage in the work of making sense of the gap—the void—between.[3] Each section opens with a brief definitioning-experiment, a bit of exploratory writing produced with-through a kind of channeling process imagining a future of-for sensory rhetorics that is queerly not yet here. While I do a bit of work to unpack these definitioning-experiments, their purpose is to excite and invite your further engagement rather than offer definitive explanations. The remainder of each section begins with an image of a needlepoint I made from postoperative photos taken on weeks 1, 3, and 6 as my chest healed, followed by an example of how, when guided by my definition-experiments, I worked with *not-knowing*—as well as how *not-knowing* worked—to (re)make sense of my body and self in the days and weeks after alignment surgery.

The first section focuses on the idea of corporeal, affective, and emotional impact as expressed in writing and so offers a short piece of creative nonfiction consciously crafted with sensorially rich language, one that shares my experience of sense-making with respect to physical numbness, which unexpectedly and miraculously brought me to a moment of awe. Unlike many other personal narratives about top surgery, which often root themselves in a known *before* that articulates when, why, and how one came to make the decision and/or an informationally driven explanation of what happened in the context of current institutional affordances and constraints connected to access and care, this narrative expresses a sense of not-knowing as an expression of tensions between what I thought I knew and what I didn't yet know and between what I knew and what I could not know until it happened.

The second section offers both a rationale for and a boundary-pushing example of the importance of creative-critical scholarship to/for sensory rhetorics as an academic project. While this whole essay ought to be understood as a work of creative-critical scholarship, here I take particular joy in queering (i.e., fu*king with) form by using the structure of a segmented essay to foreground the creative practice of needlepointing to access a state of *not-knowing* and (re)make the phenomenological experience of what it meant to move from numbness to awe. I offer multiple examples simultaneously to reinforce the idea that sense-making is constantly (re)negotiated, that insights and new realizations occur both at once—in an instant—and through the processing of additional experiences and information over time.

The final section opens with thoughts on the recent explosion of research on awe and the ways this work frames the source of power and importance of this emotion. Refusing the expected form of a conclusion, the essay invites us to (re)making sense with alternate lines of inquiry: What if an ability to enter a state of not-knowing were the focus rather than the end result of awe itself? What if not-knowing were the key to ethically and equitably engaging with awe?[4]

One

Sensory rhetorics explore the impact of the premise that what *we* don't cognitively know our bodies affectively comprehend. Sensory rhetorics invite us to rethink and reposition ourselves with and to what we mean by "making sense," to look beyond dominant frames and normative structures and ask questions that have to do with when and how and where and why the sense that we make, the sensations we have that impact this *making of sense*, changes: our minds, our perception, our understanding of reality.

As scholars, in discussing processes and methods for sense-making, we need to become more attentive to how we craft these stories, how we evoke the senses and feelings and affect and emotion for others. While I do not specifically cite any scholarly work in this section, I write with Hélène Cixous (1993, 38) in my ear, who in Three Steps on the Ladder of Writing *explains, "The thing that is both known and unknown, the most unknown and the best unknown, this is what we are looking for when we write. We go toward the best unknown thing, where knowing and not knowing touch, where we hope we will know what is unknown. Where we hope we will not be afraid of understanding the incomprehensible, facing the invisible, hearing the inaudible, thinking the unthinkable, which is of course: thinking. Thinking is trying to think the unthinkable: the thinkable is not worth the effort." Though Cixous is talking about writing fiction, sensory rhetorics would do well to ground their methodological practices in identifying and articulating the space(s) "where knowing and not knowing touch," where we compose sensorially evocative investigations of those moments when meaning ruptures and we are challenged to move beyond normative, predictable narratives, thoughts, and conclusions—to recognize not-knowing as foundational to the process of (re)making sense. My approach to using sensorially rich language is simultaneously informed by a background in ethnographic writing, specifically Clifford Geertz's (1973) notion of "thick description" and Paul Stoller's (1989, 1997) attention to the senses. My language and syntax choices are influenced by creative writing research such as Francesca Rendel-Short's (2020) work on prepositional thinking and Joy Ladin's (2013) explanation of trans poetics. My theoretical positioning emerges in and through an embodied connection to the autotheory of Paul Preciado (2013) and McKenzie Wark (2020), writerly rites I locate as-with-in the pleasure of Barthes's seam (1973).*

Week 1—unwrap Ace bandages; remove drains.

On September 15, 2020, I had a double-incision mastectomy, a procedure also known as gender-affirming top surgery. First, my areolas were removed and set aside. Then two shallow-arced incisions were made above and below each breast, kind of like in an eye shape. A majority of breast tissue was removed and the remaining 10 percent or so recrafted into masculine-presenting pecs atop my chest wall. Each incision was closed by pulling the top piece of skin down to meet the bottom before suturing the edges together into side-by-side broad closed-mouth smile-scars. As part of this process, two small drains were inserted halfway down my rib cage

FIG. 5.1 Ames Hawkins, "Left Nipple, Week 1," 2020, needlepoint, 4.5 × 4.5 in., Ames Hawkins personal collection.

under my arms, a length of tubing running just under the surface of my skin up and over the top of the new pecs. Finally, using something described as a "kind of cookie-cutter," my areolas were cut down to "usual" masculine size (20–22 mm) and grafted back on in their new locations, perfect circles reaffixed with small black sutures held in place with mesh. "Nipple stickers" is what my partner and I called them.

Going into surgery, I thought I had as much information as I needed. I knew the steps and the process. I was well informed of the medical risks—most specifically hematoma and loss of sensation in my nipples.[5] As it turns out, there were some key facts I did not know. I did not know that to remove my breasts, the surgeon would have to sever and likely permanently damage three of the seven intercostal brachial nerves running from my spinal column around the rib cage and into and through the chest wall. I did not know that in cutting these major nerves and scraping away the majority of breast tissue, when I awoke in the recovery room, my entire chest would feel completely numb. While initially surprising, the numbness didn't cause me alarm. There was no sharpness, no burning, no throbbing. Without any additional data to counter my assumption, I made sense of the numbness as a temporary condition caused by the result of having three Ace bandages wrapped around my torso, extending from high under my armpits to my diaphragm, a sensation I had experienced on the occasions when I bound my breasts. Given what I thought I knew, I concluded that when the bandages were removed to withdraw the drains, the pressure would be relieved, and the numbness would dissipate. I settled into this numbness believing I knew its cause as well as how my body would respond when the bandages were removed, and I would be able to feel the surface of my skin and breathe again.

This is not what happened. A week later, I returned to the hospital to have my drains removed. The moment my physician's assistant Asa[6] began to unwind the long beige cloth, I noticed my heartbeat increase. I became diaphoretic, sweat instantly popping into discernable beads across my brow, down my back, behind my knees, on the palms of both hands. As Asa pulled away the second Ace bandage, my mind began to process what my body somatically understood. The bandages provided pressure necessary for healing, but they were not causing the numbness. I became nauseous. When the final bandage was removed, Asa told us how good everything looked—no infection, no hematomas. I sneaked a quick peek at myself sans mams and was overcome with panic. "I can't feel it. I can't feel anything," I said. "That's normal," Asa reassured me, adding that feeling would return—though not all of it—and I would know this was happening because I would feel pricking-poking-stinging pain as severed nerves reconnected in my chest.

Ten days later, I was able to resume the five-mile walk that my spouse, Jessica, and I took to and from Lake Michigan each weekend. I was still wearing two Ace bandages to support and protect the eighteen inches of incision (nine on each side) and the nipple stickers working to permanently adhere in place. Though I was tired of the constriction and feeling numb, I was as grateful for the temporary cloth-shield and thrilled to be able to take in the incredibly mild, end of September, slightly breezy, full-sunball day.

I remember exactly where I was on the sidewalk on the return leg of the trip a few blocks from home when I felt pricking on the right side of my chest for the first time. The pain was sudden, sharp, and far more intense than I anticipated. My mind raced to make sense of what was happening. It was a pain I both knew and did not know. This wasn't anything like the pulsing throb I experienced when I told people that "my crotch was on fire" after having a couple hundred stitches to mend my labia after giving birth. It didn't have the deep wound ache I recall after having my appendix out when I was nine. This was nothing like the process of getting a tattoo, what I've described to others as a surface-concentrated needle-pricking that ended up feeling "kind of like someone scraping a stick across your skin over and over," a pain that builds over time, one I somewhat enjoy.

What I felt in that moment was akin to what I had once experienced when shocked by an electrical outlet when I was young: an immediate, out-of-nowhere jolt that surged through the tip of the finger on my right hand so quickly and with such severity I thought I had been impaled by a spike, force that surged up my arm into my shoulder, where it seemed to "explode" into a whole-body tingle that made me unavoidably aware of every inch of my skin. The difference was that this time the source of the shock was internal rather than external and multiple rather than singular: a firecracking quick release of three or four ice picks erupting from the middle of my lungs piercing through muscle and ribs and skin and simultaneously emerging through a last quarter inch of the incision on my right side, the end closest to my armpit. Each "stab" held its intensity for fewer than ten seconds, but the explosion was so completely disconcerting, so severe, so sustained, I was terrified that it would never end. There was no blow to the midsection, but the wind was knocked out of me. My body seized, and I reminded myself, "Just breathe." In for four counts, out for eight. Again and again, as I felt another few rounds of neural detonations that lessened with intensity each time. My mind raced to make sense of this new-to-me sensation. A series of realizations thrust me into a new frame of mind. *This is what it feels like when nerves reconnect! I have electrical impulses—electricity itself!!!—in my body the same as in every atom! These tiniest fibers exploding in me are a micro-universe of shooting stars!* I was both fully in and-also beyond my body, an everywhere-rhizome of nerve(r)endings constellating as everything-stars. Fully present in my whole body for the first time, my mind raced to find language to describe this larger feeling, this overall sensation. This was and I was in: Awe.

Two

Sensory rhetorics encourage engagement with somatic methodologies and artistic and creative practice that involves not-knowing as method, thereby providing a potential pathway for scholars to explore and interrogate what we might understand as more "woo-woo" topics without disconnecting from their power and magic. As such, sensory rhetorics welcome and respect creative-critical scholarly contributions, including those that challenge traditional academic form.

Stated as simply as possible, creative-critical scholarship "engages creative practices/ processes as research method" (Hawkins 2025), the purpose of which is to "reimagine and revise, expand and extend, translate and transmogrify, traditional scholarly content and form" (Hawkins 2018, 161). While creative-critical scholarship can be argued to be inextricably linked to the field of composition and rhetoric via multimodal composing strategies and perspectives (Journet et al. 2012; Berry et al. 2016), it is important to note that creative-critical approaches cut across disciplinary boundaries and can be seen as powerful for other subfields in rhetoric, such as cultural rhetorics (Arola 2018; Soto Vega 2023), queer rhetorics (Bessette 2016; Morrison 1992), and sonic rhetorics (Hammer and Sieber 2020; Lambke 2013), as well as academic fields as far ranging as Black feminist studies (Gumbs 2018), education (Sameshima 2007), religious studies (Crawley 2020), and creative writing (Murray 2017). As a result, sensory rhetorics are poised to both benefit from and become a productive space for creative-critical scholarship, which, among other things, "grapples with that which is unexpressed, points toward that which is unrecognized, and strives to articulate the affective and ineffable knowledge with and through creative processes as they intersect with critical practice" (Hawkins 2025).

This grappling with that which is "unexpressed" sounds to me like "wrestling with angles," with keeping space open for topics and ways of making sense that may have been jettisoned in favor of post-Enlightenment epistemologies. A bold assertion, but here's where we might find space to discuss some of the "irrational" practices many rational folx (yes, academics, too!) consult and engage in for their own sense-making. Think tarot, astrology, alchemy, somatic practice, daily rituals, meditation, magic.

Week 3—remove mesh covering nipple grafts; begin wearing compression shirts.

In *Trans Care*, Hil Malatino (2020) recognizes his inability to eavesdrop—to recall something overheard—as a strategy his mind-body developed to protect him from transphobia in public spaces. He considers the implications of this sort of (dis)embodiment strategy by thinking seriously "about the different ways that trans subjects cultivate detachment, distance, and numbness in order to survive in and through inuring ourselves to the hostilities that surround us. How many of us have had to devise strategies for withdrawal and escape? How often do we strategically muffle our sensorium to get *through* a situation?" (50)

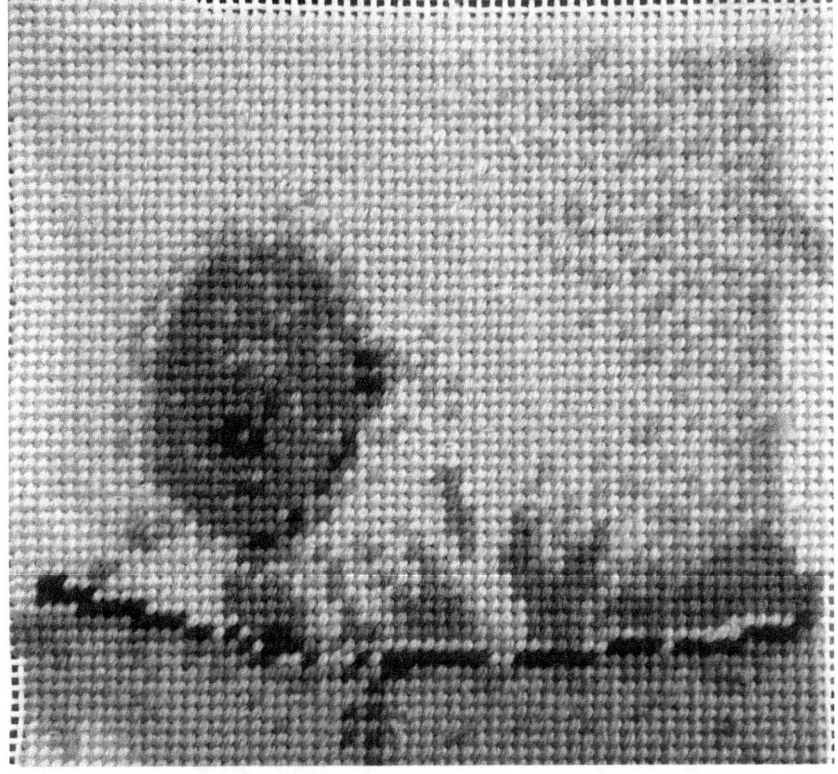

FIG. 5.2 Ames Hawkins, "Left Nipple, Week 3," 2020, needlepoint, 4.5 × 4.5 in., Ames Hawkins personal collection.

In reflecting upon my sense-making of postoperative numbness, I appreciate that over a lifetime of defending myself from external threats, I inadvertently atrophied pathways by which I might foster a cohesive and internally integrated sense of self. While Malatino wonders about the ways the distance is achieved, I am interested in the idea that this detachment isn't conscious, that his body and mine knew what to do without conscious input and without either of us realizing it. This is another way to describe the power of *not-knowing*: as-through the somatic wisdom of a body. Not-knowing as a resource, as something we affectively and somatically access—consciously or not—to shift perceptions and change our minds. Not-knowing as an affordance of the body that we might better examine when we pay closer attention to what and what lengths each of us goes to a-void.

pullthroughstabdownpulltaught**pokeuppullthroughstabdownpulltaught**pokeup pullthroughstabdownpulltaught**pokeuppullthroughstabdownpulltaught**pokeu ppullthro

Over the course of forty years, I developed a range of mind-body tactics that involved me doing whatever I could to keep myself from thinking about or looking at or otherwise acknowledging the existence of my breasts, small, daily, conscious and unconscious decisions that accreted over a lifetime, the impact of which I was unaware of until the pain of nerve regeneration began to course through my chest on a regular basis.

Each time I felt the intense stabbing, I closed my eyes and concentrated on visualizing the electrical impulse that was once hitting the "dead end" of a severed nerve now deftly making it across a newly (re)constructed bridge. It was magical to feel these electrical impulses and know that this meant that my body was regaining its ability to sense itself, a miracle to perceive light touch once again in my chest. It is nearly beyond my capacity to express in language how profound it was to realize that which the body not-knows: that the pain of healing physical numbness has the power to heal the shame and fear trapped in my heart, that the pain is intense and that awe can be the just reward.

ghstabdownpulltaught**pokeuppullthroughstabdownpulltaught**pokeuppullthro ughstabdownpulltaught**pokeuppullthroughstabdownpulltaught**pokeuppullthr oughstabd

I learned to needlepoint as a child and returned to it in 2016 to render images of violets for a piece called *Paper Violets, Vellum Prose*, a multimodal installation in which I considered the impact of my father's death from AIDS through the lens of weeks-old African violet plants that were left in his apartment when he died. The installation was the culmination of a years-long creative-critical project in which I constantly revised and remade the (meaning of the) story of his death.

My father was a visual and fiber artist who engaged with all kinds of materials and forms including but not limited to quilting, tatting, crochet, embroidery, and needlepoint. As a form of artistic homage, I translated images of the violets into seven small needlepoint pieces that were then quilted together and made into a cushion for a pew. In the installation, the cushion and pew sat adjacent to a window hanging from the ceiling, with images of violets on one side of each of the twelve panes and a paragraph of text on the other that collectively offered a narrative of his death. Participants could listen to me read the text through headphones when sitting on the pew. Curator Conor Moynihan (2017, 8) offers a satisfying summary: "Guiding us through a potentially uneasy death narrative, Hawkins paradoxically leads us to a pleasant, comfortable interior space."

My needlepoint practice offers "the kinds of gaps and opportunities that open up when phenomenological awareness of being in the world encounters uncomfortable spaces" (Kuppers 2022, 1). I didn't have that language immediately present when I decided, or more accurately felt compelled, to re-present the violets or to translate graphic postoperative images of my chest into small pieces of art. I was simply following a compulsion-as-desire, a sense-as-sensation that while I may have not known exactly why I wanted to make these things, this was the very right thing to do at this moment in time. In needlepointing the chest images with nerve pain in mind, I became aware of the relevance of physical making to sense-making, to the idea that needlepoint as an artistic practice allowed me both to access space for considering the relevance of *not-knowing* and to conceive of new and different ways of thinking about sense-making overall.

ownpulltaught**pokeuppullthroughstabdownpulltaught**pokeuppullthroughstab downpulltaught**pokeuppullthroughstabdownpulltaught**pokeuppullthroughsta bdownpullt

In *A to Z of Creative Writing Methods*, Juliette van Loon (2023, 114) invites the creative writer to push beyond an understanding of not-knowing as an imaginative state and argues for it as a "practice in its own right." Van Loon contends that "not-knowing as method privileges ways of doing research that recognize and value uncertainty, play and experimentation. Not-knowing as method facilitates uncertainty in our practice, deliberately extending productive states of doubt. This can require us to acknowledge and dwell with periods of practice replete with discomfort, failure and risk" (115).

In needlepointing these images, I am both engaging with not-knowing as method and reconnecting with the not-knowing of and in my body through making as/and a rhetorical act. I poke up through and reimagine the pricking pain I felt. I make without thinking, which opens space for different thoughts. Thoughts that have nothing to do with the needlepoint image and everything to do with the embodied process of gender-affirming top surgery begin to surface. The not-knowing of a body that has always been trans. The not-knowing of a body severing connection to the world and others to keep me safe. Feeling the pain as difficult but not the source of the trauma. Feeling the pain as important but not as the site of the most important healing. In this moment, I know nothing about the workings of trauma or the power of awe, other than this has something to do with not-knowing. It is knotted-knowing that I feel untangling with each stitch. Not-knowing, it turns out, isn't impossible to access. It can be done intentionally by-through creative practices of (re)making sense.

ught**pokeuppullthroughstabdownpulltaught**pokeuppullthroughstabdownpulltaught**pokeuppullthroughstabdownpulltaught**pokeuppullthroughstabdownpulltaught*

Needlepointing is a ritual of improvisational design choice and repetitive motion through which I enter liminal space. It has nothing to do with kits or predetermined patterns. It is a practice of translation. I first study the image, decide where and how my eye makes sense of distinct color contrasts, where and how shading might be achieved with variation in colors of yarn. I know exact color matching is unlikely, so I make decisions based on what I find to be the most "important" colors and from there build a cohesive palette. I begin by sketching key lines on the canvas in disappearing ink, marking approximate locations for important elements of the design. I use the simple basket-weave stitch. Singular small loops nestled side by side in neat symmetrical rows on the front. A crisscross weaving visible on the back.

The ritual's rhythm: Stare at the photograph. Choose a color. Thread the needle. Stare at the photograph. Select a space on the canvas.

*pokeuppullthroughstabdow npulltaught**pokeuppullthroughstabdownpulltaught*

Revisit the photograph. Translate. Hand and eye not-knowing where they are going.

*pokeuppullthroughstabdownpulltaught**pokeuppullthroughstabdownpulltaught*

Up and down and through over and over and over.

*pokeuppullthroughstabdownpulltaught**pokeuppullthroughstabdownpulltaught**pokeuppullthroughstabdownpulltaught**pokeuppullthroughstabdownpulltaught**pokeuppullthroughstabdownpulltaught*

I am here and not here. Making sense and-as stitching.

Stitching as thinking.

Stitching as not-knowing: as embodied mediative concentrated creative practice expertly engaged without any thought.

Not-knowing is-as a space of creative, somatic wonder, one that enables conscious, deliberate revisioning, reimagining, revising of the ways we make sense.

Three

Sensory rhetorics contend that when we engage in creating, uncovering, (re)discovering new pathways for sense-making, change is possible. Change of apocalyptic potential: to unveil unacknowledged causes, sites, and sources of systemic oppression. Revelations of not-knowing felt as relational revolution. New sense-making of relationality accreting in reparative paradigm shifts.

I wrote this statement striving to make the boldest, truest statement I could about the potential for sensory rhetorics. I wrote thinking about the fact that my story of top surgery is individual, but in feeling the sensation of awe as nerves connected in my chest, I felt inextricably connected to the universe. I wrote with José Esteban Muñoz (2009, 1) in my ear, reminding me that "queerness is the thing that lets us feel that this world is not enough, that indeed something is missing." Whatever that "something" is, it is a matter of and ever-always for-in the future. I knew I wanted top surgery. I now realize that as much as I knew it would be life changing, I was also connected to a sense of not-knowing, a deeply felt inarticulable awareness of a (queer) horizon, a future at which we never arrive, where-when we will all constantly be-come. This future as queerness, and here I would suggest as-also the sense of not-knowing, "is essentially about the rejection of a here and now and an insistence on potentiality or concrete possibility for another world" (1).

To reject the here and now and move us well beyond any logics that resort to settling for "it is what it is," we need to look to those who fall outside and beyond the usual bounds of academic engagement, specifically to artists, poets, writers, social justice workers, and activists, especially to those who identify as queer, trans, Black, Brown, Indigenous, crip, and/or any intersectional combination thereof. I know, for example, that I am not the only one in the academy who follows, reads, and personally engages with the work of folx such as adrienne maree brown (2017), Andrea Gibson (2021), Chani Nicholas (2020), Leah Lakshmi Piepzna-Samarasinha (2018), and Alok Vaid-Menon (2020), just to name some. But are we doing so only or most usually in ways that are immediately recognizable in the academy, through citational practices that establish recognizable lineages of logic?

Another way: What would it look like for us to bring our own admission and understandings of not-knowing into our scholarly methods and writerly practices? What do you, dear reader, expect of this academic essay? I have struggled to figure out how to make this piece usable, viable, quotable. Is it ever enough for me to share my awe experience via a seven-thousand-word effort to articulate the ineffable, affectively miraculous, awesome work of (re)making sense?

Week 6—remove any remaining sutures in grafts; resume normal activity.

While awe has been written about in multiple fields and cultures for thousands of years, what we might understand as research on awe is a phenomenon of the twenty-first century. Since 2003,[7] researchers across fields such as psychology, marketing, education, and neuroscience have found awe to, among other things, decrease aggression (Yang et al. 2016), trigger the release of oxytocin and dopamine to relieve stress (Keltner 2023), promote a sense of connectedness to other emotions (Nelson-Coffey et al. 2019), increase the desire for learning and experiential creation (Rudd et al. 2018), foster curiosity and the desire to learn (Anderson et al. 2020), and allow us to connect better with each other by reducing one's need to understand everything in terms of the self (Stellar 2021). I am fascinated by the near cultlike excitement and gold-rush energy driving research on awe,[8] which suggests that if we could just harness this emotion, we would be able to reduce violence, decrease stress, increase sales in experiential products, support academic success, and assist people in caring more about others. If we could just figure out how to manipulate openness (via awe), people could differently accommodate new ideas and information. Awe, it appears, is the magic elixir, a potential key to the future, to expanding people's perspectives and assisting them, in what might be the most seductive of the possibilities, to become willing and able to change their minds!

For me, the initial experience of awe following gender-affirming top surgery was indeed miraculous. One might argue that this was a result of the surgery—the fact I no longer had breasts. But while the "eureka" moment described earlier in this essay stands as crucial with respect to the sense making, this moment is a record of the beginning. In other words, the real revelation has less to do with a momentary flash of insight than the subsequent deep somatic re-membering of emotional pain endured over a lifetime of living while trans. The insight I felt was this: The intensity of the pain caused as

FIG. 5.3 Ames Hawkins, "Left Nipple, Week 6," 2020, needlepoint, 4.5 × 4.5 in., Ames Hawkins personal collection.

severed nerves reconnected in my chest revealed a deeply felt psychological, social, somatic trauma long held in my body, most notably my heart. Awestruck, I felt the numbness as simultaneously physical and emotional pain and cellularly understood this revelation as an opportunity to concurrently heal on both fronts. Not-knowing (how) drove my desire to needlepoint, and this embodied creative practice reminded me to let myself welcome and look forward to the pain of nerve regeneration every time it happened. Over the course of four months, my body for-with-by-through [itself] (re)made sense of a past and a possible future present. Five years later, I can tell you that, while truly relevant, the miracle is not that breastless Ames is happier and more able to feel connected—to joy, to others, to creativity: to literally everything and everyone. The miracle is that in the wake of these connections, in a reestablished relationship with and to the power of awe, my capacity for empathy continues to grow.

Recently, I have started thinking about my needlepoint triptych not simply as the representation of my personal story but in relationship to Ann Cvetkovich's (2003, 7) queer archive of feelings, an archive that considers "cultural texts as repositories for feelings and emotions, which are encoded not only in the content of the texts but in the practices that surround their production and reception." The discourse of trauma serves as the larger lens for her investigation, since this term invites accounts of pain both psychic and physical, as a space that "forges overt connections between politics and emotions" (7). But Cvetkovich is "interested not just in trauma survivors but in those whose experiences circulate in the vicinity of trauma and are marked by it" (7). She moves beyond individual therapy-centric conversations, as well as the critiques of "trauma culture," "by exploring how trauma can be a foundation for creating counterpublic spheres rather than evacuating them" (7). With this framing in mind, I assert that not only is the memory of trauma embedded in each needlepoint, but they are how I literally made meaning *through* (rather than of) my own "shock and injury" following top surgery. More importantly, not only is the trauma mine, but it is also ever-always connected to a "counterpublic sphere." Cvetkovich helps me understand that even though my needlepoints sit in my drawer, they are energetically connected to the queer archive of trans and nonbinary trauma, that even if you never knew anything about them, they are connected to a future world that values compassion, care, and equity over war, capitalism, and individual rights. They are the means by which I was able to articulate the ideas in this essay as scholarship. They are personal interventions in-of sense-making toward a different collective future for us all.

Notes

1. For an excellent overview of trans scholarship, see Patterson and Spencer 2020. Projects and publications taking up the medical rhetoric of gender-affirming surgery are noticeably absent and deserving of scholarly attention. Among the many books, shows, and YouTube videos I consumed in the years before my surgery, my favorite pieces of literary nonfiction are Coyote and Spoon 2014; and Bombardier 2020. If looking to YouTube for discussions regarding gender-affirming top surgery, especially one framed through a nonbinary perspective, I recommend the work of Ash Hardell.

2. Over the years, my writing has multiple times been described as "excessive," as in too dense, too intense, too much. The scene in the film *Amadeus* always comes to mind, when Salieri (F. Murray Abraham) critiques Mozart's (Tom Hulce) piece and then has no real reason to reject it other than there being "too many notes."

3. While I have crafted this essay to highlight for you the power of not-knowing, it is not lost on me that academics often skip over captions and images, moving to press into the place they feel they will glean the most information/knowledge. I'm also aware that they'll often skip over notes. Consider this both a clear statement of my intention and your fair warning. I appreciate you for coming here to take a look!

4. It is arguable that each section could/should be its own essay, that there is too much here, that the density, the excess, the

overabundance make it difficult for a reader to make sense of what's being said. Please know that the structure and content are purposeful. The goal is to (re)make a similar sense of overwhelm and the kind of sensory rhetorical work it takes to sift through and make sense of the multiple, conflicting, irrational, unavoidable not-knowings. As you read, I invite you to ask yourself, Where do you feel these ideas in your body? When and how has not-knowing been palpable for you?

5. In fact, my surgeon required me to sign a document titled "INFORMED CONSENT—MASTECTOMY (CHEST SURGERY FOR POSSIBLE NIPPLE GRAFT, POSSIBLE LIPOSUCTION) FOR GENDER CONFIRMATION." In addition to my signature, I was required to list three possible complications and write out in my own hand the following statement: "I have been educated on the risks, benefits, options and alternatives for my surgery and all my questions have been answered." I signed on August 16, 2020, believing this to be a true and accurate statement.

6. A pseudonym.

7. The explosion of research on awe can be traced to "Approaching Awe, a Moral, Spiritual, and Aesthetic Emotion" (2003), by Dacher Keltner and Jonathan Haidt, an admittedly "brief" literature review of the fields of religion, sociology, philosophy, and psychology that leads them to assert that awe has two consistent features: vastness and accommodation. Vastness has to do with perceiving oneself as insignificant, a sensation that may be brought about through comparison to something understood as greater and more powerful than the self. Accommodation involves challenges to ways of knowing and understanding that offer the opportunity for (re)making sense of reality. Simply put, awe is the sense(making) that there is something much bigger than ourselves, a new-to-us somatic experiential realization that causes us to recalibrate and realign our perception of reality, truth, and/or the way the world works. Keltner and Haidt end the paper with a call for "the empirical study of awe" and their final energizing assertion that "awe-inducing events may be one of the fastest and most powerful methods of personal change and growth." (312).

8. At the time of this writing, Google reports that Keltner and Haidt's article has been cited well over two thousand times.

Though beyond the scope of this essay, there's something worth exploring with regard to *why* this was the call that was heard. Hundreds of articles call for research. Few are this zealously answered.

References

Alexander, Jonathan, and Jaqueline Rhodes. 2011. "Queer: An Impossible Subject for Composition." *JAC* 31 (1): 177–206.

Anderson, Craig, Dante D. Dixson, Maria Monroy, and Dacher Keltner. 2020. "Are Awe-Prone People More Curious? The Relationship Between Dispositional Awe, Curiosity, and Academic Outcomes." *Journal of Personality* 88 (4):762–79.

Arola, Kristin. 2018. "A Land-Based Digital Design Rhetoric." In *The Routledge Handbook of Digital Writing and Rhetoric*, edited by Jonathan Alexander and Jacqueline Rhodes, 199–213. New York: Routledge.

Barthes. Roland. 1973. *The Pleasure of the Text*. New York: Hill and Wang.

Berry, Patrick W., Gail E. Hawisher, and Cynthia L. Selfe, eds. 2016. *Provocations: Reconstructing the Archive*. Featuring the work of Erin R. Anderson, Trisha N. Campbell, Alexandra Hidalgo, and Jody Shipka. Logan: Computers and Composition Digital Press / Utah State University Press. https://ccdigitalpress.org/reconstructingthearchive/.

Bessette, Jean. 2016. "Queer Rhetoric in Situ." *Rhetoric Review* 35 (2): 148–64.

Bombardier, Cooper Lee. 2020. *Pass with Care: Memoirs*. New York: Dottir.

brown, adrienne maree. 2017. *Emergent Strategy: Shaping Change, Changing Worlds*. Chico, CA: AK Press.

Cixous, Hélène. 1993. *Three Steps on the Ladder of Writing*. New York: Columbia University Press.

Coyote, Ivan E., and Rae Spoon. 2014. *Gender Failure*. Vancouver: Arsenal Pulp.

Crawley, Ashon T. 2020. *The Lonely Letters*. Durham: Duke University Press.

Cvetkovich, Ann. 2003. *An Archive of Feeling: Trauma Sexuality and Lesbian Public Cultures*. Durham: Duke University Press.

Geertz, Clifford. 1973. "Thick Description: Toward an Interpretive Theory of

Culture." In *The Interpretation of Cultures: Selected Essays*, 3–30. New York: Basic Books.

Gibson, Andrea. 2021. *You Better Be Lightening*. Minneapolis: Button Poetry.

Gumbs, Pauline. 2018. *M Archive: After the End of the World*. Durham: Duke University Press.

Hammer, Steven, and Greg Sieber. 2020. "Listening at the Seams: Curating a Relations-Based Narrative of the Schuykill River." *Journal of Multimodal Rhetorics* 3 (1). https://journalmultimodalrhetorics.com/4-1-issue-hammer-sieber.

Hawkins, Ames. 2018. "Why I Hate Times New Roman and Other Confessions of a Creative Critical Scholar." In *Type Matters: The Rhetoricity of Letterforms*, edited by Christopher Scott Wyatt and Danielle De Voss, 158–85. Anderson, SC: Parlor.

———. 2021. "Dear Sam; Dear Linda; Love Ames." *QED: A Journal in GLBTQ Worldmaking* 8 (3): 149–60.

———. 2025. "Creative-Critical Scholarship in Two Move(ment)s." In *Can I Ask You a Question? A Dialogue About Sonic Rhetorics, Professional Writing, and Creative-Critical Scholarship*, edited by Benjamin Lauren and Kyle D. Stedman. Intermezzo.

Journet, Debra, Cheryl Ball, and Ryan Trauman, eds. 2012. *The New Work of Composing*. Logan: Computers and Composition Digital Press / Utah State University Press. https://ccdigitalpress.org/nwc.

Keltner, Dacher. 2023. *Awe: The New Science of Everyday Wonder and How It Can Transform Your Life*. New York: Penguin.

Keltner, Dacher, and Jonathan Haidt. 2003. "Approaching Awe, a Moral, Spiritual, and Aesthetic Emotion." *Cognition and Emotion* 17 (2): 297–314.

Kuppers, Petra. 2022. *Eco Soma: Pain and Joy in Speculative Performance Encounters*. Minneapolis: University of Minnesota Press.

Ladin, Joy. 2013. "Trans Poetics Manifesto." In *Troubling the Line: Trans and Genderqueer Poetry and Poetics*, edited by Trace Peterson and T. C. Tolbert, 299–307. New York: Nightboat Books.

Lambke, Abigail. 2013. "The Oral Aural Walter Ong." In "Sonic Rhetorics." Special issue, *Harlot: A Revealing Look at the Arts of Persuasion* 9. https://pdxscholar.library.pdx.edu/harlot/vol9/iss9/9/.

Loon, Juliette van. 2023. "Not-knowing." In *A to Z of Creative Writing Methods*, edited by Deborah Wardle, Juliette Van loon, Stayci Taylor, Francesca Rendle-Short, Peta Murray, and David Carlin, 114–16. London: Bloomsbury Academic.

Malatino, Hil. 2020. *Trans Care*. Minneapolis: University of Minnesota Press.

Morrison, Margaret. 1992. "Laughing with Queers in My Eyes: Proposing 'Queer Rhetoric(s)' and Introducing a Queer Issue." In "Queer Rhetoric." Special issue, *Pre/Text: A Journal of Rhetorical Theory* 13 (3–4): 11–36.

Moynihan, Conor. 2017. "Ill Feeling, Feeling Ill." In *Ill at Ease: Dis-ease in Art*. Installation catalogue. Buffalo: University of Buffalo Center for the Arts.

Muñoz, José Esteban. 2009. *Cruising Utopia: The Then and There of Queer Futurity*. New York: New York University Press.

Murray, Peta. 2017. "essayesque dismemoir: w/rites of elder-flowering." PhD diss., RMIT University.

Nelson-Coffey, S. Katherine, Peter M. Ruberton, Joseph Changellor, Jessica E. Cornich, Jim Blascovich, and Sonja Lyubomirsky. 2019. "The Proximal Experience of Awe." *PloS One* 14 (5).

Nicholas, Chani. 2020. *You Were Born for This: Astrology for Radical Self-Acceptance*. San Francisco: HarperOne.

Patterson, GPat, and Leland G. Spencer. 2020. "Toward Trans Rhetorical Agency: A Critical Analysis of Trans Topics in Rhetoric and Composition and Communication Studies." *Peitho* 22 (4). https://cfshrc.org/article/toward-trans-rhetorical-agency-a-critical-analysis-of-trans-topics-in-rhetoric-composition-and-communication-scholarship/.

Piepzna-Samarasinha, Leah Lakshmi. 2018. *Care Work: Dreaming Disability Justice*. Vancouver: Arsenal Pulp.

Preciado, Paul. 2013. *Testo Junkie: Sex, Drugs, and Biopolitics in the Pharmacopornographic Era*. English-language ed. New York: Feminist Press at CUNY.

Rendle-Short, Francesca. 2020. "Preposition as Method: Creative Writing Research and Prepositional Thinking, Methodologically Speaking." *New Writing* 18 (1): 84–96.

Rhodes, Jaqueline, and Jonathan Alexander. 2022. *The Routledge Handbook of Queer Rhetoric*. New York: Routledge.

Rudd, Melanie, Christian Hildebrand, and Kathleen D. Vohs. 2018. "Inspired to Create: Awe Enhances Openness to Learning and the Desire for Experiential Creation," *Journal of Marketing Research* 55 (5): 766–81.

Sameshima, Pauline. 2007. *Seeing Red: A Pedagogy of Paralax: An Epistolary Bildungsroman on Artful Scholarly Inquiry*. Youngstown, NY: Cambria.

Soto Vega, Karrieann. 2023. "Amplifying Autogestión and Cultural Rhetorics of Resistance." *College Composition and Communication* 75 (1): 37–55.

Stellar, Jennifer E. 2021. "Awe Helps Us Remember Why It Is Important to Forget the Self." *Annals of the New York Academy of Sciences* 1501:81–84.

Stoller, Paul. 1989. *The Taste of Ethnographic Things: The Senses in Anthropology*. Philadelphia: University of Pennsylvania Press.

———. 1997. *Sensuous Scholarship*. Philadelphia: University of Pennsylvania Press.

Vaid-Menon, Alok. 2020. *Beyond the Gender Binary*. New York: Penguin Random House.

Wark, McKenzie. 2020. *Reverse Cowgirl*. Los Angeles: Semiotext(e).

Yang, Ying, Ziyan Yang, Taoxun Bao, Yunzhi Liu, and Holli-Anne Passmore. 2016. "Elicited Awe Decreases Aggression." *Journal of Pacific Rim Psychology* 10 (11).

6

Autokinesis and the Sense of Meaninglessness

BENJAMIN FIRGENS

A point of light shines in a pool of darkness. No clues about the light's identity exist anywhere but the light's luminosity. Scrutinize it, and it reveals only a steady shimmer. Stare at it longer—still your body, notice your heartbeat, narrow your eyes—and still, nothing. But stare one moment longer and something alarming happens: the light begins to dance.

This is an optical illusion called "autokinesis." A point of light appears to move if you stare at it in darkness (Levy 1972). Best known by pilots who must learn not to fixate on light sources at night or risk mistaking planets for oncoming air traffic, the illusion rarely impacts daily life. As a concept, however, autokinesis vexes. Its prefix, "auto," suggests self-direction and control but does not specify whether the "self" in question moves intentionally or whether it is capable of intention. The word's etymology performs the confusion it names: indistinction between meaning and meaninglessness regarding movements lacking self-evident subjectivity or purpose. And once met, this confusion lingers: To see movement of unclear significance is to notice the illusory foundations of our sensoria that we usually ignore in favor of our preferred sureties about the world. A pilot second-guessing whether a distant light is a star or an airliner can easily resolve their worry by scanning the cockpit before looking outside again—but they will not so easily shake the unease of having second-guessed the reality of what sensation seems to mean.

Illusions pose strange problems for rhetoricians writing about sense, not least the puzzle of how seriously to take them. Are they, as in the piloting example, a possibly dangerous problem to fix? Or are they mere disorientations, only risky when we take them seriously and thus not deserving of our attention? Are they all bad, or can they serve as little windows into alternate, and possibly generative, ways to view the world? The problem is that we cannot tell. Illusions draw out interest and anxiety precisely because they do not give any clear indication of what they mean. An illusion is a persuasive sensation at odds with otherwise-recalcitrant reality, a sensation that causes meaning and fact to smudge into gradients of dubious meaning and apparent fact. Illusions convince us, as they happen, that they are real, which makes them difficult to write about—especially as we recognize that visual sensation results from entwined material, social, and psychological relationships. Close attention to sensation, as Justin Eckstein (Eckstein 2021, 240–41) has written about sound, "redraws lines between subject/object, inside/outside, mind/body, and past/present/future." Any attempt to define what counts as illusory raises questions about what counts as sense and meaning in the first place and why.

Adopting "autokinesis" as a rhetorical term, this chapter insists that illusions do not represent a failure to make meaning out of sensation but instead name moments when we notice the usually transparent meaninglessness of all meaning-making processes. Illusions illustrate why rhetoricians must approach sensory rhetorics with awareness not only of the mutability of meaning and sense but also of the neurotypical forces that attempt to discipline that mutability. As M. Remi Yergeau (2018, 87) argues, invention occurs outside neurotypical notions of meaning, intentionality, and subjectivity, and perceiving how requires seeing movement mattering before it means anything. Following their lead, I illustrate the possibilities for neurodiverse vocabularies of invention that avoid assigning normative or instrumental value to meaning and meaninglessness. Autokinesis, a wandering concept about wavering eyes, points this chapter toward sensory rhetorics beyond the neurotypical and rhetorical invention beyond invention.

The following sections treat autokinesis as a material optical event, a metaphor for social responses to uncertainty, and a heuristic for rethinking neurotypical theories of rhetorical sense, appearance, and meaning. I begin by reviewing my argument's theoretical and sensorial context to theorize why we should not see meaninglessness as a problem to fix but instead as the basic condition of sensed movement prior to the social imposition of normative meaning. We as rhetoricians studying sense should learn to perceive both the risks common sense poses for bodies and the ways bodies sense potential beyond what anyone could define as their meaning.

Meaning and Sensation in Rhetorical Theory

Taking illusions seriously performs a sensorial return to perennial epistemological and ethical problems in rhetoric. Summarizing an Aristotelian line of thought, Thomas B. Farrell (1993, 31) writes that rhetoric exists to ensure "that the topography of appearances may be represented with sufficient clarity to yield prudent decision and conduct." According to this tradition, rhetoric, or practical communication involved in making decisions before "the facts are all in" (Lyne 2001, 5), must deal with the world as it appears in fleeting moments of contingent encounter. Historical and contemporary accounts of rhetoric resonate with Farrell's implication that consensus ("prudent decision"), if not harmony, is the ideal result of successfully meaningful rhetoric (Pernot 2005, 34).

The penchant for harmony hides a stubborn neurotypical premise that has outlived the consensus vision of rhetoric. "Consensus," literally "feeling together," names a normative assumption about the nature of sensoria disguised as a telos for rhetorical practice. As Jane Sutton and Mari Mifsud (2019, 11) write, in order to reach "a single resting place settled upon by all," consensus requires "turning down the other," foreclosing some possibilities in favor of resolving difference to a single decision. In the context of visual rhetorics and culture, consensus patches over alternate visions for meaningful political action, masking what Jacques Rancière (2011, 72) calls the "multiplicity of folds and gaps in the fabric of common experience that change the cartography of the perceptible, the thinkable and the feasible." Efforts to make sense shared, to put the "con-" in "consensus," can do much more harm than good.

Contemporary rhetoricians have critiqued the consensus ideal without questioning the ideal's root assumption that shared sense should be a default expectation of communicative exchange. Rhetorical scholarship on social movements began, for example, because of doubts over whether consensus was the right goal to impose on students protesting the Vietnam War on the scholars' own campuses (Benson and Johnson 1968; R. Scott 1969). Or, for more recent examples, critiques of rhetorical studies' pervasive whiteness have had to dissemble ideals of consensus, which effectively police racial hierarchies of citation, promotion, and publishing, to say nothing of dictating what counts as proper areas of study (Chávez 2015; Wanzer-Serrano 2019). As a general rule, since scholarship like this has focused—for good reason—on breaking down harmful practices and proposing paths for new scholarship, it spends little time interrogating what "sense" means or what sensing together looks like once "together" has been redefined, a quiet but consequential reification.

Exceptions to this rule exemplify another approach for critiquing the consensus ideal: attempting to center rhetorical theory around something other than meaning. Eric King Watts (2001), for example, shows how concepts of "voice" articulate a range of aesthetic and affective demands on hearers that are unintelligible within traditionally raced, gendered, and classed frames of meaning. Watts's work abuts a longer disciplinary conversation about aesthetics, meaning, and how to weigh their respective roles in rhetoric. Indeed, several of the discipline's most energetic ongoing theoretical developments share a common concern with relationship and communication mattering when they do not mean anything in a traditional (Western ontological) sense (Poole 2023; Rickert 2013). Summarizing these developments, Debra Hawhee (2015, 13) echoes contemporary commonplaces when she writes that "sensation needn't become encased in language to be known" and "needn't be so attached to meaning."

On the one hand, these two trends—to name and repair damage done by the consensus ideal and to theorize rhetoric beyond representation and meaning—represent successful efforts to keep rhetoric relevant in uncertain times. However, these modern theoretical developments tend to reify sensation and put it in a corner, to make it a taken-for-granted functionary that enables other, more complicated parts of the theory in question. Within the present collection's timely intervention into precisely this reification of sensation, my narrow focus is on that reification's neurotypical baggage.

Nearly all descriptions of sense to date fail to challenge a neurotypical assumption baked into rhetoric's historical fetishization of consensus: not just that shared feelings are desirable but that widely shared sensoria are possible. As Hawhee (2015, 12) notes, "one of the biggest challenges of rhetoric's sensorium" is how to write about sensation without "thinking in terms of communal sensation, without presuming sameness." The idea that practitioners of rhetoric can generalize about the substance of an entire audience's senses resembles what Ellen Samuels (2014, 213) calls "fantasies of identification," which function to "neatly categorize all bodies and identities." Writing about scientific attempts to sort bodies "delineated by race, gender, or ability status, and then to validate that placement through a verifiable, biological mark of identity," Samuels's work suggests how, through more heuristic and pedagogical means than scientific, rhetorical discipline has its own fantasies about how to sort bodies based on verifiable marks (2014, 2). That I can foresee how audiences will respond to me, how they will agree and disagree, build consensus and dissent—this, too, is a fantasy about bodies being readily identifiable, a fantasy about other bodies' senses.

Rhetorical theorists typically treat meaning and sensation like consistent mental attributes and not processes that vary within individuals and across encounters among unique minds, bodies, and environments. But sensation and meaning are not the kinds of processes that can be interpreted in universally applicable terms (Jack 2012). Instead, sense and meaning are each elements of what Charles Scott (1982, 24) calls the "vast depth of any given moment," the phenomenal profusion of the present's "discreteness forever blending into other discretenesses, in which there are vaguely shadowed reflections upon reflections upon reflections," a situation akin to the sight of a "disturbed sea on a bright day, or a prairie of grass." I quote Scott's imagistic language because I share his view that such imagery reaches, in a way that conceptual description cannot, toward the lived moment of sense and meaning, where theoretical parsing breaks down and calling experience "neurodiverse" feels like putting one more label on an enigmatic—meaningless?—present.

From the point of view I build out in this chapter, the problem of appearance is not how to build consensus from incomplete pictures of reality but how to unlearn damaging norms premised on assumptions about any pictures of reality being perfect or immutable. Put another way, questions of sensation and meaning resolve to questions of living in meaninglessness, not how to remove meaninglessness from life. To me, this is not an exercise in nihilism but an attempt to plot how to avoid causing harm out of the fear of nihilism—a reaching toward forms of scholarship that are "self-consciously flawed and intentionally hazy of telos," to borrow a phrase from Christa Olson (2021, 187).

Neurodivergence and neurodiversity, then, factor as necessary elements of rhetorical approaches to sense. Writing about sense with that in mind requires language that figures meaning not as the absence or solution or antithesis of meaninglessness but as the *result* of, or response to, meaninglessness. Illusions serve as good case studies for developing such language. To see an illusion is to notice the provisional and mutable process of social reality, to see the stability we impose on phenomena—selves, relations, senses—that have no stability. What would it mean to admit our sensoria contain multitudes, and therefore possibilities for political change, even absent the physical presence of intersubjective actors? A world of action and possibility exists not only between actors but within coconditioning sensoria. Finding ways to begin again is not only the necessary activity of a body politic moving through time but also the political activity of a body sensing something otherwise.

Two implications for how to consider sensory rhetorics generally, and autokinesis specifically, have come into view. The first is that the sensorium is a terrain of contestation, a dynamic place where dissensus can begin with the refusal to sense normally. In the context of rhetorical theory, rhetoricians do not face "the" problem of appearance (how to manage appearances as to lead to the best consensus) but problems of appearances (how to respond within the plurality of sensing what counts as "appearing" at all). We should strive toward rhetorics attuned to the latter question, looking not to prescriptive ideals but to the actually existing plethora of sensoria that constitute any group of people otherwise called an "audience."

The second implication is that meaninglessness is not an absence for invention to fill but a necessary condition of invention's possibility. Ordered by normative—race-based, class-based, gender-based, and neurotypical—assumptions about the motives, goals, and functions of rhetoric, rhetoricians have been quick to label nonnormative awareness as a fault or failure, a precondition for disappointment and persuasion gone sideways. In this, they have joined wider historical currents that have fetishized routinization as the path to efficient work, repetition as the practical method of self-mastery, and recognizability as the necessary precondition of appearing in public culture (Sloterdijk 2013, 322). And here is where even a small, situation-specific illusion like autokinesis poses irresolvable problems for received, fixed senses of meaning and where encounters with the sense of meaninglessness retain their power to unsettle the inevitability of any "normal" situation.

Autokinesis as Consequence of Retinal Fixation

Situations where our senses do not work as expected reveal the forces that condition our expectations. As Olson (2021, 18) argues, sensation (vision in her case) is "a matter of fleshy encounters" with social geographies of affect, scale, and power. Our feelings about how a sense should or could function are public feelings tangled with values about what counts as "normal." An illusion only seems delusive against assumptions about how a sense ought to work, assumptions that, by nature, are also assumptions about how bodies ought to relate to their worlds and each other. This section, which summarizes medical descriptions of the material optical event of autokinesis, not only describes a diagnosis but surveys the social phenomena that make that diagnosis thinkable. As we will see, the line between meaningful sensation and meaningless illusion is only brightly drawn by social norms, not any material necessity or bodily reality.

Autokinesis is disorientation caused by the absence of taken-for-granted frames of reference. Visual systems (eyes, brains, and the wiring that strings them together) struggle to continuously fixate on a focal point when they cannot rely on surrounding information to contextualize the point's location and distance. Avoiding autokinesis requires "a well-structured visual environment in which spatial orientation is unambiguous" (Gillingham and Previc 1993, 52). Most often, people experience autokinesis when staring at, or flying through, the night sky, because in that situation, curiosity about unknown aerial entities combines with a dearth of surrounding visual context.

Causing the autokinetic effect requires a stare to fixate for around fifteen seconds (Sannigrahi et al. 2020). As a term of art from the optical sciences, "fixation" describes a locked-in focus on a single object. The process is surprisingly complicated: Our eyes constantly jiggle with "saccades," rapid movements that drag the most detail-perceiving part of the retina over a wider field of view than stillness would capture. Because visual input during saccades is "masked"—not processed, so not perceived as happening at all—we are not distracted by movement constantly blurring our vision. But this also means we look at the world through the incorrect assumption that our eyes move and capture light in stable ways we can notice. In fact, what we "see" is mostly information processed by our visual systems in moments of fixation, not an accurate sense of all the light our eyes take in or of the movements our eyes make. Clear sight is its own kind of illusion.

More accurately, what we call "sight" is the illusion of the absence of process and diversity within the act of seeing. A brief example from another well-known optical puzzle helps illustrate this point. Scientists have been puzzled for years by "blindsight," or the phenomenon of people who report seeing nothing while being able to respond to visual stimuli. People with blindsight may self-consciously "see" nothing yet react reflexively to catch an object thrown at them. Of course, we will be puzzled by this only if we assume blindness and vision are binary opposites. Contemporary research into blindsight largely focuses on dispelling precisely that kind of ableist opposition, parsing instead the gradations among the variety of different experiences we label "vision" (Mazzi et al. 2016). Vision, like all senses, is neither a monolith that is the same thing for all people nor self-evident, in its process, as it seems to be in daily acts of looking. It is instead a self-masking process that dedicates significant mental resources to *seeming* self-evident, aided in this self-concealing by ableist cultures that define nonnormative seeing as unhealthy or disabled in contrast to the presumed health of the "normative body" (Alper 2018, 3564).

Scientists have debated the cause of autokinesis for over a century. The most recent consensus is this: Prolonged fixation creates a situation where we notice as movement the work our eyes do to fixate in the first place. Varieties of ocular movement—saccades and ocular drifts—that are necessary for fixation but masked from perception become perceptible under the duress of a lengthy and failing attempt at sense-making (Rucci and Poletti 2009). The eye's machinery leads the visual system to mistake its own labor for an object's motion. The only reason this does not happen more often is that the brain's visual systems are so good at masking their artifice and presenting a visual field that appears straightforward and indexical: reality, supposedly, as it is. Autokinesis witnesses the amount of instability required for cognitive processes to build apparently stable images.

We should pause to reflect on the situation that causes autokinesis to occur—namely, desperation to see in the dark. That desperation may be caused by a desire to know some feature in the night sky. It may instead be caused by the fearful need to ascertain whether the nature of a foreign light source could be harmless or dangerous. In any case, in autokinesis, fixation describes not only a specific movement of the eye but the rigidity of the observer's body. Autokinetic stares forget themselves and most of the world, like a more intense version of turning the car radio down to better see street signs. Collapsing all sensation to focus on a single point of light creates the perfect conditions to misperceive that light's movements.

Of course, that scene—turning the volume down to see better—also highlights how one of vision's illusions is its stability as a sense independent of other senses. Autokinetic illusions are a whole-body affair, and in their desperate attempt to overdetermine what one sense can "mean," they typify how no sense means anything on its own. This is true even at a definitional level: About the "intersecting histories" of "hearing techniques and blindness," Robert Stock (2023, 56, 61) writes that "each historical period frames specific understandings and knowledge of the senses in their normal and Other dimension," the intersensory relations of which "result from the unsettling mixtures and political materialities of scientific and everyday practices." Sight and hearing, vision and embodiment, norm and difference collide with historical and contemporary constructions of sense, all in the moment a point of light seems to wobble.

I can be disoriented and not know it. I can make meaning out of movements that are not there and make no meaning out of movements that are happening. If I do so in a tense moment, my awareness of the unknown laced with curiosity and fear, I set myself up to see any appearance at all, any movement of any nature, as meaningful insofar as I sense it happening, regardless of whether it happened in reality. Does the reality of its happening matter, in truth? How could I tell? And what does its possible happening mean for me? Does it entail risk? Delusion? Possibility? These questions turn us toward the complexities of sense, meaninglessness, and meaning at work in rhetorical invention.

Autokinesis as Metaphor for Public Disorientation

Autokinesis exemplifies the necessary role meaninglessness plays in the invention of meaning. I call this role the sense of meaninglessness, a paradoxical phrase for how encounters with the absence of received meaning impel us to sense something, *anything*, to affix with our prior knowledge, habits of evaluation, and/or sensory memories. Our discipline's long idealization of consensus is one reaction to the sense of meaninglessness; its long-running neurotypicality in theorizing sense is another. But the stakes of how we react to meaninglessness go much further than questions of academic interest. Instead, we can trace public reactions to sensed meaninglessness to better understand how and why publics overreact in times of confusion and paranoia.

Socially, the conditions in which autokinesis occurs—uncertainty, loss of frame of reference, unresolvable tension—are conditions that rhetoric, traditionally understood as a means for reaching consensus, exists to eradicate (Leff 2003). Autokinesis names a vision of rhetoric's failure, of traditions floundering and meanings failing to orient a stable social order, provided we understand rhetoric as a force for social cohesion alone. Yet the insistence that rhetoric means something definable, stable, and predictable masks the affective charge with which consensus appeals to publics—the felt need, as a condition of their ongoing existence, for truths and values, pasts and futures, to be fixed.

Do those truths, values, and temporalities need to be fixed? Recalling earlier insights into autokinesis (the danger of being desperate to see in the dark, the reality of clear sight being its own kind of illusion), we should not be surprised that contemporary scholarship is acutely attuned to how attempts to fix social life into rigid forms can foster violence, individual and systemic (Kang 2019; Squires 2002). Any normative fixation on a specific form of shared life, combined with a refusal to epistemically and/or materially recognize other forms, can turn toxic. In these circumstances, autokinesis and the vocabulary it allows—fixation, frame of reference, illusion, movement absent clear intentionality or reality—gives embodied language for understanding the sensory dynamics of consensus and dissensus.

After all, appearances, long understood as the destined material and subject of rhetorical practice, only matter in the ways we sense them. It follows that we get attached to ways of sensing appeared truths, to the frames of reference that offer assurances of stability. Any public can easily mistake the required means of sensing a given appearance as part of that appearance itself and thus also of the world so perceived. These are social processes of fixation, the overdetermination of certain meanings (and, through them, values, appearances, facts) caused by reliance on specific refusals of meaninglessness. Fixation in the body and body politic alike names a state of concerned stillness, the action of anxiously stabilizing a point of view in response to instability.

"Fixation" is an especially fitting term of art for describing how, in these bleak years of rising fascistic politics, swaths of the US electorate hold onto beliefs, values, and specific conspiratorial topoi to plainly self-destructive extremes (Crick 2022). The disconnect between how vaccine "skeptics" perceive public health measures and the reality of how those measures operate and are intended is one case in point. A list of the causal conditions of such antipublic cynicism looks like a holdover from the previous section: A loss of grounding frames of reference and a desperate search for meaning in a disoriented state produce a clear perception of meaningful movement where none exists. Seeing movement—perceiving threat and conspiracy *as material fact* embedded in vaccines—vaccine skeptics spy an illusory reality where healthy choices are seen as poisonous and vice versa.

Fixations also predominate around anxieties about failures to communicate or sense, which frequently amount to anxieties about being proximate to the subversive and nonnormative. Such anxieties express themselves in the common denial of agency of anyone deemed nonnormative through what Yergeau (2018, 46) calls "demi-rhetorical" framings, which see their subjects as only partly capable of rhetoric, with their "intentional capacities represented as matters of degree," a situation in which the "unlikeness in relation to the nondisabled supersedes any likeness." Cognitive gymnastics—such as separating the like from the unlike by any degree possible or believing that one's own capacities for action in the world of appearances are infallible because they are safely normal—result, in part, from anxiety about what proper sensation is and what it means to be the kind of person who has it.

When is precarity perceived, and when is it actual? Overfixation results in illusory situations where those questions cannot find answers and anxious searchers fabricate ever-new reasons for fear in response to the simple inability to determine whether fear is justified at all. And even "how we make sense of pain," Casey Ryan Kelly (2021, 210) reminds us, "is rhetorical." Perceiving precarity in loss of status and privilege, for example, white Americans frequently opt for the narrowness of whiteness's flattering but illusory stability rather than take an honest view of the world. Thus, affluent but nominally liberal whites who attempt to raise their children to be antiracist often find that their kids echo racist tropes that associate Blackness with poverty, mostly because the kids pay close attention to the choices their parents make for their schools. Even if parents place kids in predominantly white classrooms for putatively academic reasons, they send the message that their whiteness protects them from an economic precarity implied to exist in, and result from, nonwhite spaces (Hagerman 2018). Christina Sharpe (2023, 312) notes that "the machinery of whiteness constantly deploys violence" even as it "constantly manufactures wonder, surprise, and innocence in relation to that violence." For the white parent overfixated on the preservation of a privileged future, Blackness portends a violence that they themselves avoid seeing in their own actions.

Shared anxieties lead to public disorientations: public in the sense of a shared rhetorical space existing through the reflexive circulation of language; disorientation in the sense of containing illusorily stable meanings clung to in conditions of fear and desperation. As the eyes' fixation causes, in autokinesis, the opposite of its intent—as staring to still movement for proper perception instead invents unwanted movement—a public's fixation on unmovable norms causes disorientation as the values and truths clung to obscure other possible views of the world. Thus, for example, Phaedra Pezzulo (2023, 23) writes of "plastic culture," the widespread "fallacy that our more affordable, more convenient, more pliable futures are not limited by planetary limits but only our imagination." Only publics fixed in disorientation could persist with straightforwardly self-destructive patterns of transnational capitalism—as if green solutions are unrealistically ambitious and the current, truly physically impossible path were realistic.

We cannot begin to think through public cultures of disorientation if our basic concepts about meaning and invention presume some kind of stability in sense. And if it is true, as Isaac West (2014, 98–99) argues, that we need to shift our perspective from a "rarified understanding of the political" to a focus on "how the political is negotiated in our daily lives," then an appreciation for the impurity of sense (its fallibility, its grounding in no firm ground at all) like the one developed in this chapter goes along well with the "impure politics" that are called for by our current political moment. The impure sensation—the jitter of the eye, the brush between illusion and truth, the stare at something that may or may not be meaningful—occurs prior to the arrival of social convention and normative assumption and is therefore an unavoidable conditioning factor on conventions and norms. To write in this way is to pose autokinesis as neither an optical failure nor a social ill but simply a part of the process of meaning-making, a glimpse of meaningless at the heart of meaning.

Autokinesis as Possibility

Meaninglessness matters. Uncertainty in the face of meaninglessness drives varieties of rhetorical invention that create illusions seemingly preferential to absences, failures, or losses. Insofar as moments of contingence and difference constitute the very terrain of rhetoric, and thus make the sense of meaninglessness endemic to rhetoric as such, it is fair to say that we all enjoy illusory rhetorics from time to time. The danger of illusion is not illusion's occurrence but our denial, forgetting, or ignorance of it.

Rhetoricians should embrace illusion, or at least should get more comfortable with meaninglessness. Thinking back to examples offered in the previous section—vaccine skepticism, racist tropes, moral alibis for plastics pollution—each derives energy from fixed reactions to sensed meaninglessness. Simple changes of perspective or heart cannot solve those problems, of course. But as teachers and scholars of rhetoric trying to reckon with sense, we should model curiosity, openness, and a capacity to sit with meaninglessness. A discipline slightly more skeptical of its own certainties—its own illusions—would be, to that degree, more creative, empathetic, and neurodiverse.

Yergeau (2018, 211) writes that "a world without failure is a world without rhetoric." If it were possible to invent an infallible rhetoric, it would be possible to eventually invent everything that needs saying; if we lived in such a world, some scholastic mind would have finalized it by now. At least all such attempts are, like any other attempt toward perfection, creative in their shortcomings: The recurring failure of sense to make final meaning of the world is rhetorical invention's autocatalytic engine. It can be disturbing to look at a moving thing and wonder whether its movements are actual or imagined, disorienting to lose sense of how the world around relates to meaning, and disquieting to consider that, as Lorraine Daston and Peter Galison (2010, 371) write, "all epistemology begins in fear." But these experiences are encounters with the basic process of sense-making itself, not flawed derivations from that process.

To study an illusion is to study the other side of rhetoric's senses—to try to better understand sensory rhetorics by exploring where the normal processes, habits, and assumptions of sensation fail. This chapter may have been focused largely on an illusion that occurs under quite specific circumstances, but its general focal field (sensory illusions as such) is as wide as rhetoric itself. Rhetoricians should neither stigmatize uncertainty and meaninglessness as failures of mind nor treat them like problems to be resolved by reasonable rhetorical discourse. We should instead seek—as this chapter has sought—regenerative ways to pose anew old questions about what our shared lives mean in common, this time without neurotypical assumptions about how normal senses and rhetorics should resolve certainty and meaning out of sensation. After all, if illusions do not initially reveal whether they are harmless or dangerous, we cannot compose a sensible (much less empathetic) account of diverse ways of seeing and sensing if our account categorizes entire swaths of sensoria as defective in advance. Pilots do not learn about autokinesis as a flaw in their eyes that they must resist; they learn about it to remember, when staring, to blink. When is illusion, when is meaninglessness, a problem? When can it provide a generative reset? The point, for rhetoricians, might simply be to blink before answering.

What might this look like in practice? One answer, to borrow some vocabulary from Ariella Azoulay, is to distinguish between the sensed event and the event of sense. Azoulay (2015) uses a similar distinction between the "photographed event" and the "event of photograph" to dissociate the scene shown in an image from the civic and interpersonal power relations that were actually impacted by a photograph being taken. To her, reading through photographed events to the events of photography that they imperfectly archive is an act of "civic imagination" that fosters more self-aware and critical viewers of the body politic. Following her lead, if we learn to hold in mind that the sensed event (or what we think we sense, individually and collectively) and the event of sense (what interrelations of power, normativity, and so on serve as a condition of possibility for anything to count as "sense" and bear its assumptive qualities), then we can study sensory rhetorics while also paying attention to the unseen dynamics that complicate any easy sense of where meaning comes from.

This contrasts the most common response to autokinesis: the Federal Aviation Administration's attempts to teach all pilots what it is and why it happens so that no one angles an airplane in the wrong direction because of it. It makes sense to ensure pilots do not swerve into a mountain to evade Jupiter. But it makes less sense, taking autokinesis as a metaphor, to litigate the moral topography of its illusion in settings where "illusion" is inherently a normative label. The rhetorical response to social illusion needs instead to begin from a deep understanding of the vexing varieties of appearance—and needs to contain empathy, even, for the ways we all work too hard to sense meaning and motion where none exists.

Humility about how to respond to illusions gives us clarity about how to respond to cynical attempts to create ambiguity where there is none. On the day I write this—January 20, 2025—the richest man in the world performed, and then repeated, a Nazi salute to jubilant inauguration-day crowds in Washington, DC. To anyone paying attention to either the drift of Silicon Valley's politics or the habit of legacy media to "sanewash" or normalize far-right gestures into respectable guises, neither the salute nor the toothless reaction from the press is surprising. A white supremacist hides their dog whistle under bad-faith excuses of irony and/or innocence, and the gesture's "respectable" audience fails to muster the moral courage to name the gesture for what it is—and my sensory reaction to the event is the dull anger of being told I did not see something I did see, and I feel gaslit, and what else is new? Knowing what ambiguity, illusion, and meaninglessness look like helps us to distinguish them from their contrived doppelgangers and to find the moral clarity that does not take unserious ambiguity seriously.

At the very least, we should notice how some traditional vocabularies in rhetorical theory do not apply in the realm of illusions and thus fail to describe either prosaic or powerful encounters of sensory rhetorics. As Sutton and Mifsud remind us, a suspicion of difference and a penchant for denying the value of dissensus remain stubbornly present in many well-meaning visions of rhetoric's role in public life. In the big picture, one of the upshots of this work would be revising norms of rhetorical training that presume the nonnormative and nonneurotypical to be faults.

Raising these topics brings us back to the oldest tensions in rhetorical theory—reason and unreason, fact and appearance, trust and doubt—in an embodied sensorium that understands that we experience our worlds not through predictable sensations but with a variety of neurodiverse methods used to make uncertainty usable and meaninglessness meaningful. Here autokinesis offers a sense of theory—a way of seeing rhetoric—as movement, not construction, where what matters is not the generalizability of concepts but the freedoms of motion made possible.

References

Alper, Meryl. 2018. "Inclusive Sensory Ethnography: Studying New Media and Neurodiversity in Everyday Life." *New Media and Society* 20 (10): 3560–79.

Azoulay, Ariella. 2015. *Civil Imagination: A Political Ontology of Photography*. London: Verso.

Benson, Thomas W., and Bonnie Johnson. 1968. "The Rhetoric of Resistance: Confrontation with the Warmakers." *Today's Speech* 16 (3): 35–42.

Chávez, Karma R. 2015. "Beyond Inclusion: Rethinking Rhetoric's Historical Narrative." *Quarterly Journal of Speech* 101 (1): 162–72.

Crick, Nathan. 2022. *The Rhetoric of Fascism*. Tuscaloosa: University of Alabama Press.

Daston, Lorraine, and Peter Galison. 2010. *Objectivity*. New York: Zone Books.

Eckstein, Justin. 2021. "The Rhetoric of Sound Rhetoric." *Rhetoric Society Quarterly* 51 (3): 240–46.

Farrell, Thomas B. 1993. *Norms of Rhetorical Culture*. New Haven: Yale University Press.

Gillingham, Kent K., and Fred H. Previc. 1993. "Spatial Orientation in Flight." Armstrong Laboratory, Brooks Air Force Base, Texas.

Hagerman, Margaret A. 2018. *White Kids: Growing Up with Privilege in a Racially Divided America*. Critical Perspectives on Youth. New York: New York University Press.

Hawhee, Debra. 2015. "Rhetoric's Sensorium." *Quarterly Journal of Speech* 101 (1): 2–17.

Jack, Jordynn. 2012. "Gender Copia: Feminist Rhetorical Perspectives on an Autistic Concept of Sex/Gender." *Women's Studies in Communication* 35 (1): 1–17.

Kang, Jiyeon. 2019. "Call for Civil Inattention: 'RaceFail'09' and Counterpublics on the Internet." *Quarterly Journal of Speech* 105 (2): 133–55.

Kelly, Casey Ryan. 2021. "White Pain." *Quarterly Journal of Speech* 107 (2): 209–33.

Leff, Michael C. 2003. "Tradition and Agency in Humanistic Rhetoric." *Philosophy and Rhetoric* 36 (2): 135–47.

Levy, John. 1972. "Autokinetic Illusion: A Systematic Review of Theories, Measures, and Independent Variables." *Psychological Bulletin* 78 (6): 457–74.

Lyne, John. 2001. "Contours of Intervention: How Rhetoric Matters to Biomedicine." *Journal of Medical Humanities* 22 (1): 3–13.

Mazzi, Chiara, Chiara Bagattini, and Silvia Savazzi. 2016. "Blind-Sight vs. Degraded-Sight: Different Measures Tell a Different Story." *Frontiers in Psychology* 7:901.

Olson, Christa J. 2021. *American Magnitude: Hemispheric Vision and Public Feeling in the United States*. Columbus: The Ohio State University Press.

Pernot, Laurent. 2005. *Rhetoric in Antiquity*. Translated by W. E. Higgins. Washington, DC: CUA Press.

Pezzullo, Phaedra C. 2023. *Beyond Straw Men: Plastic Pollution and Networked Cultures of Care*. Environmental Communication, Power, and Culture 4. Oakland: University of California Press.

Poole, Megan. 2023. "Witnessing the Open Semiosis: A Method for Rhetorical Listening Beyond the Human." *Rhetoric Society Quarterly* 53 (1): 30–44.

Rancière, Jacques. 2011. *The Emancipated Spectator*. London: Verso.

Rickert, Thomas J. 2013. *Ambient Rhetoric: The Attunements of Rhetorical Being*. Pittsburgh: University of Pittsburgh Press.

Rucci, Michele, and Martina Poletti. 2009. "Fixational Eye Movements and the

Autokinetic Illusion." *Journal of Vision* 9 (8): art. 431.

Samuels, Ellen Jean. 2014. *Fantasies of Identification: Disability, Gender, Race*. New York: New York University Press.

Sannigrahi, P., Ajay Kumar, Saria Mishra, and M. S. Nataraja. 2020. "Autokinesis Illusion in Fighter Flying Revisited." *Indian Journal of Aerospace Medicine* 64 (2): 56–61.

Scott, Charles E. 1982. *Boundaries in Mind: A Study of Immediate Awareness Based on Psychotherapy*. New York: Crossroad.

Scott, Robert L. 1969. "The Rhetoric of Confrontation." *Quarterly Journal of Speech* 55 (1): 1–8.

Sharpe, Christina. 2023. *Ordinary Notes*. New York: Farrar, Straus and Giroux.

Sloterdijk, Peter. 2013. *You Must Change Your Life: On Anthropotechnics*. Cambridge, UK: Polity.

Squires, Catherine R. 2002. "Rethinking the Black Public Sphere: An Alternative Vocabulary for Multiple Public Spheres." *Communication Theory* 12 (4): 446–68.

Stock, Robert. 2023. "Hearing Echoes as an Audile Technique: From 'Facial Vision' to Experimental Psychology and Echolocation." In *Techniques of Hearing: History, Theory, and Practices*, edited by Michael Schillmeier, Robert Stock, and Beate Ochsner, 55–65. London: Routledge.

Sutton, Jane S., and Mari Lee Mifsud. 2019. *A Revolution in Tropes: Alloiostrophic Rhetoric*. Lanham, MD: Lexington Books.

Wanzer-Serrano, Darrel. 2019. "Rhetoric's Rac(e/ist) Problems." *Quarterly Journal of Speech* 105 (4): 465–76.

Watts, Eric King. 2001. "'Voice' and 'Voicelessness' in Rhetorical Studies." *Quarterly Journal of Speech* 87 (2): 179–96.

West, Isaac. 2014. *Transforming Citizenships: Transgender Articulations of the Law*. New York: New York University Press.

Yergeau, M. Remi. 2018. *Authoring Autism: On Rhetoric and Neurological Queerness*. Durham: Duke University Press.

7

Unsettling Colonized Sensory Archives

ROMEO GARCÍA AND KYLE S. BOND

We live amid archives. Anthony Giddens (1981, 173) claimed, "History is not retrievable as a human project; but neither is it comprehensible except as the outcome of human projects." One could interpret this passage as saying that history and power are an archive. Edward Said (1985, 101) would seem to support that position when he called for an "epistemological critique . . . of the connection between the development of a historicism" and the "actual practice of imperialism by which . . . the incorporation and homogenization of histories [is] maintained." In a different context, Pierce Lewis (1979) observed that people are not taught to deeply see, feel, and listen to landscapes. His claim that landscapes are cultural records or autobiographies of cultural meaning reflecting taste and values suggests landscapes are archives. Alan Pred (1984, 279, 292) gives credence to this by asserting that place in part "represents" a "human product." Additionally, James Baldwin (2012, 129) noted, "People are trapped in history and history is trapped in them," which is perhaps why Frantz Fanon (1986, 231) pleaded, "O my body, make of me always a man who questions!" This body is a rhetorical concept (Chávez 2018) and, importantly, an archive that can be examined, returned to, and carefully reckoned with. In the context of this chapter, we propose that if we unsettle the settled, we might be able to recognize colonized/colonizing structures of feeling and thought (Williams 1977) that mask how we live amid "death-spaces" (Taussig 1991, 133), imaginaries of "space[s] of death" (Holland 2000, 4), "discourse[s] of the dead" (Certeau 1992, 46), and textual death spaces—archives that have fundamental orientations toward the public. We can examine the senses and aesthetics themselves as an archive and thus a powerful medium for decolonizing agendas.

In this chapter, we investigate the sensory archive and aesthetic philosophy of the church-settler: Latter-day Saint (LDS) hymnody, and particularly the archival collection and use of hymns, as a modern/colonial and settlerizing technology. In this analysis, we take up the relationship between the way local coloniality senses and the colonization of both the senses and *aisthēsis*, or sense experience, which gives way to global coloniality. In other words, we approach coloniality as an epistemic and aesthetic issue (Mignolo and Walsh 2018, 125), one that church-settlers at the local scale used to build their *imperio* in Utah and beyond. Ultimately our case study on church-settlers of Utah and the senses functions in a tetrad of movements—unveiling, unsettling, delinking (coloniality and the senses), and reclaiming. It is our hope that this chapter offers insight on how to translate such movements in the context of sensory archives, whether religious (theo-politics) or secular (ego-politics).

Coloniality is understood as a structure of domination, management, and control of all human domains (Mignolo 2007; Quijano 2007). To gain a sense of coloniality, it is necessary to search for how coloniality senses. The relation between coloniality, the senses, and *aisthēsis* is understudied in the field of writing and rhetorical studies; thus, this chapter works to open up the conversation from a historical viewpoint. "Global coloniality," Madina Tlostanova (2015, 40) writes, "is always manifest in particular local forms and conditions." Here, the local and global begin with a settler colonialism at the start of the modern world in the Americas. We aim to make sense of how sense has been made since then in other locales and among other identity politics, such as that of the church-settlers of Utah. To do so, we treat the senses as some *thing* (re)written, or an archive, a prism by which to see both some *things* left behind and the inner workings of sense models and processes that enable epistemic control and obedience. Archives have fundamental orientations toward the public, so we initiate our investigation with the following question: *How are rhetoric, the senses (sound, sight, taste, touch, smell), place, archives, and designs (whether religious or secular) intertwined?*

The reason for this question is that coloniality is marked by specificities and particularities (Tuck and Yang 2012, 21; Mignolo 2007, 498). What this means is that we need critical methods that can contend with the "development of a historicism" and a theoretical apparatus that can address "incorporation and homogenization of histories" (Said 1985, 101). In this chapter, rhetorical, archival, and sonic methods of analysis take center stage as we advance a theory of archival impressions. It is a theory that begins from the premise that while coloniality is (re)written differently across various colonial contexts, coloniality is an *Archive*—an assemblage that can be traced back to a turning and nexus point in world history, a settler colonialism in the Americas that established coloniality. It is a theory that assumes the *Archive* is *in* assemblage with *smaller archives* that cohere as distinct sensory experiences and knowledge but nonetheless recirculate as the Same into the Same *Archive* (Yang 2017, 62). The result is *archival impression*, or the process by which coloniality contains and maintains influence by writing itself into the sensory, discursive, and material structures that govern historical and thus cultural systems. And this is why, ultimately, we argue that the sensory archive of the church-settlers of Utah is in fact a prism by which to see *designs* (*idea of Deseret* and *Mormon/ism*) refracted through the lens of *Americanity* and within the frame of modernity/coloniality. Writing and rhetorical studies is uniquely positioned to intervene in conversations about coloniality, and our emphasis on the sense models and processes of church-settlers-as-archive functions as one example.

Rhetoric and sensibility are components in the written and embodied archives of the senses. Sensory knowledge is inscribed in order that it may be passed along, transferred from body to body, discourse to discourse. Where there are archives, there is a writing of inheritance. Rhetorical inheritance and sensory inheritance are two ways that perception is constructed and then archived. "Inheritance" here means the way language and writing are used to shape the senses and educate the sense organs to receive stimuli in an approved manner, one that fits such frames as a cultural model, perceptual commons, value system, and moral design. Similarly, the idea of *rhetorical taste*, or the sensory preferences of content, ways of seeing, listening, and feeling, can be understood, to a degree, as culturally socialized through particular contexts and styles of valuation within knowledge systems. *Culture* can be understood as a unique form and fostering of sensate modes, each with its own heritage and locus. The idea of repentance and the practice of confession are general examples of Christian value whereby contrition, remorse, and sorrow make up an *affectual ecology* on which a collective sensibility is built.

Within the colonial context of Utah's church-settlers (officially members of the Church of Jesus Christ of Latter-day Saints but historically known as "Mormons"), this chapter inquires after how such *aisthēsis* make up the building blocks of collective sensibility and consequentially the modes and aims of socialization established within similar institutions. Here, we gravitate toward Walter Mignolo's (2011, 141) definition of institutions, which function to train "new (epistemically obedient) members" and control "who enters and what knowledge-making is allowed, disavowed, devalued, or celebrated." In other words, rhetorical taste is an endorsement of particular styles of valuation, embodied *aisthēsis*, and knowledge systems (see Black 1997, 2–3, 5).

The sensory archive of experiences housed in the body of the individual who turns to repentance and confession has rhetorically inherited sense-ideas such as contrition, remorse, and sorrow, which make up an affectual ecology valued by a particular religious community. Such an ecology, which we date to the arrival of the Spanish in the Americas in the fifteenth century and the rise of *Americanity* vis-à-vis settler colonialism and coloniality, is buttressed by friars and Jesuits such as Gerónimo de Mendieta, Bartolomé de Las Casas, José de Acosta, and Bernardino de Sahagún. More specific to this chapter, underscoring the local form and condition of coloniality and senses strengthens this ecology as Latter-day Saint scripture (Church of Jesus Christ of Latter-day Saints 1977) upholds the inevitability of the righteous as a "white and delightsome people" (2 Nephi 30:6, *The Book of Mormon*) or that the deserts of Utah, once settled, "shall blossom and rejoice as the rose" (Isaiah 35:1).[1]

Sensory archives are twofold. First, they refer to embodied memories, perceptions, and sensibilities aligned with, at, or against prescriptions of cultural normativity. Second, they are modes, materials, and events used as tools to pass on rhetorical inheritances, cultivate sensibility, reproduce a value system, and produce a way of knowing, feeling, and sensing the world. It bears repeating: We live amid archives. We have to be present and be a witness to archives otherwise to realize how much they actually "bleed" into our public memories and rhetorics (Edbauer 2005), including how they socialize collective sensibilities. Overall, we argue in this chapter that the sensory archive of Latter-day Saints, as a working part of the *Archive*, perpetuates a rubric of Truths that warrants domination elsewhere and otherwise and reveals the epistemological experiment of managing the senses, *aisthēsis*, and aesthetics.

Delinking the Senses

To ask, "How are the senses socialized?" is to inquire about both value and one's sensory inheritance. This question points to the task of "epistemic and emotional (and aesthetic) delinking" (Mignolo and Walsh 2018, 126).

Delinking the senses will require further scholarship that investigates aesthetic compositions, such as aesthetic theology, or the historical textures of Divine approval (i.e., how God wants people to feel toward and about events). Texture in this context refers to aesthetic cohesion and aesthetic coherence. Aesthetic cohesion refers to appeals at a local level, such as principles and doctrines, whereas aesthetic coherence refers to appeals at the level of narrative structure and cosmology. Settler-colonial sensibilities can thus be divided into two units of analysis: sense models and sense processes.

This sense model includes such features as a canon (scriptures and narratives), characters (models or figures who embody sensibility types), and instruction (living authority, handbooks, pamphlets, etc.). For example, consider how the Spirit acts as a compositional instrument within the LDS sense model, producing an internal monitor, or an affectual guide, which can work to negate plural sensibilities and thus establish the potential for a common sensibility. Sensorially, the Spirit acts as a confirming agent of spiritual truth through an embodied experience wherein one can "feel that it is right" (Church of Jesus Christ of Latter-day Saints 2025a, 9:8, see also Galatians 5:22–23). Teleologically, the Spirit aims its recipient toward immortality and eternal life (Moses 1:39, Church of Jesus Christ of Latter-day Saints 2025b), and the indexicality of epistemic obedience means adherence to an understanding of the correct sense model.

This sense process involves the achievement of an individual alignment through (1) associating positive experiences with the Spirit as God's approval; (2) changing act, behavior, setting; and (3) restoring harmony with the Divine through searching for emotional regulation that fits the rhetoric of harmony with the sense model. What we are identifying and naming with both a sense model and sense process is a coloniality of instruction-and-curriculum, a settler-centered instruction that colonizes the senses, enables epistemic control, and manages epistemic obedience. Decolonizing settler-colonial sense models and process(es) thus must include delinking positive sense experiences from totalizing religious frames and experiences. Insourcing sensibility requires a formal mode of thought, which is to say *sensing how we sense*. Sensing one's own sensibility has the potential for reconfiguring interaction.

Reconfiguring interaction from interpretations of the Spirit as totality toward a search for "a contact of minds" (Perelman and Olbrechts-Tyteca 1971, 17) refuses a hegemonic interaction where conversion of the *other* is the ultimate goal of interaction. It denies the either/or frame of classifying all as either a "potential investigator" or "anti-Mormon." These are a few ways that one might begin to investigate the sense predicate of church-settler coloniality. Precisely, we argue that sensing, like sound, is not outside the sphere of coloniality or the "rhetoric of modern salvation" (Mignolo and Walsh 2018, 129). The task of decolonization for sensate rhetoric is then as much about rhetorical reflection as it is about epistemological delinking and institutional critique.

Positioning Church-Settler Sensory Rhetoric: Sound and Decoloniality

We begin our case study with an examination of hymnody. Why is there so much music in church services? Hymns, hymn books, and the singing of hymns are often necessary tools for religious experiences and belief maintenance. Mormonism did not invent but rather inherited uses of hymnody from Christianity. Harmony, as early as Classical Greece (fifth and fourth centuries BCE), was used as a concept in pedagogical discussions concerning the leading of the soul (see Moss 2012). The "most musical" were those whose musical education served its true purpose: "the harmonious agreement of reason and spirit that produces control over appetite" (Nehamas 1999, 261). While there are many differences between church-settler hymnody and classical uses of music, the point here is that an instrument of perception can be found in many contexts, but so too can the senses, including that of memory and expression.

Noteworthy textual and musical technologies aiding belief production and maintenance during the European medieval period include neumes (Burkholder et al. 2014, 29–31) and chants (Burkholder et al. 2014, 32–38).[2] The Roman Liturgy rhetorically composed music pairing instruments, the human voice, and lyric to produce alignment in human subjects with the Catholic church (Burkholder et al. 2014, 46–52). In the early modern era, René Descartes's philosophical treatise *Les passions de l'ame* expanded on Plato's understanding of the role of emotions, passions, and actions. Cartesian-influenced poets, such as Pietro Metastasio, made an important rhetorical contribution to *opere serie*, a style elevating language over mathematically arranged sound (C. Smith 2017, 195). Again, what becomes evident is the role of sound and music as archive—an archive that involves all the senses, including those of memory and expression.

Mormonism, appearing at the tail end of the Enlightenment, inherited these European uses of music. Mormonism rejects, or believes itself to have escaped, the paradigmatic influence and rhetoric of the Enlightenment. Yet no Euro-American religion could have escaped the influence of the continent's philosophies. Eve Tuck and K. Wayne Yang (2012, 3) might refer to this rejection as a move toward innocence, which maintains church-settler futurity. The analysis of futurity begins with the past.

To understand what church-settlers were doing on the ground, we must first understand some of the epistemological and ontological tools they brought. We argue that a hymnody analytic helps reveal a "listening regime" aimed at "'settling' perception itself" (Robinson 2020, 40)—showing how particular uses of music had/have the ability to reorient and train perception and compose ontological worldviews. In this way, music and the senses function as *aisthēsis* (sense perception / way of knowing), and within an epistemological regime of modernity, the colonization of *aisthēseis* (sense perceptions / ways of knowing) means the domination, management, and control of epistemic obedience. In the church-settler context writ large, epistemic obedience is accompanied by the disavowal, erasure, or subsuming of other things, which at the local level manifests as a rigid dichotomy between the wicked Lamanite and the righteous Nephite. Within this framework, the Lamanite remains the absolute other, though both groups are linked to Indigenous peoples of the Americas as framed within the narrative. In the *Book of Mormon*, "Lamanite" designates the descendants of a once-righteous but later fallen branch of Israel, marked as dark-skinned and positioned in opposition to the Nephites, the supposed keepers of divine truth.

Like their church-settler doctrines, Latter-day Saint sensibilities and dispositions were formed as responses and extensions from the European continent. Musical composition and praxis in these contexts worked as rhetorical forces to settle perception itself. Mormon hymnody can therefore be read as aiming at reorienting the senses toward a perceptive taste and aesthetic, namely, focus management, including perceptual and behavioral reform of "coming to rest or becoming calm" (Robinson 2020, 40). Hymnody produces epistemic obedience. The task of delinking Mormon hymnody from coloniality means separating positive sensorial experiences from the idea of "the Spirit." Liberating music (from generating merely transcendental, ideal, sublime experiences), understood not as "something to be attained" but as "a process of letting something go" (Mignolo and Walsh 2018, 149), would open new possibilities for community and the possibility to hear Indigeneity on its own terms. Equally as important, it would open up room for new soundscapes. This will require questioning and unsettling the structural, epistemological, rhetorical, and ideological integrity of modern/colonial and settlerizing tools, instruments, and/or technologies that have a regulative function (e.g., the *Archive* and smaller archives). To delink, open, and reclaim music and the senses requires needed work in rewor(l)ding an-other aesthetic of music and senses.

According to David J. Whittaker (1991), the early twentieth-century Latter-day Saint efforts to curate a positive image included three tasks: acquiring historically significant land, establishing information bureaus, and founding the Tabernacle Choir. Here, writing, music, memory, and expression meet. To further explore the connections between music and coloniality, we note that the etymology of the English word "memory" comes from the word for "archives." Institutional memory and music work together as part of a sensory archive. Sensory archives are embodied and material networks that write and are written in the bodies, senses, and minds of their members. How the past happened (for whom) and how we feel are bound in the rhythms, tones, and attitudes of musical compositions.

Mormon musical compositions contain instrumentation (e.g., hymn-books, pianos, organs, voices) and material arrangements (e.g., churches, pews, bodies singing in a church) that contribute to cultural valuation and doctrinal maintenance. Below we explore one *design* in the compositions: the language of persecution. We use *organ* as an analytic thread to examine the connection between its biological and musical uses. The organ serves as a cultural conjunction, a place where music and bodies meet to gain a sense of perceptive unity.

Sense Organs and the Sonic Rhetorics of Church-Settler Hymnody

The skin is a surface rhetoric, the "border between exterior and interior fades away"; it is a site of exteroceptive induction, retaining "physiological importance" and "cultural significance," establishing "the very foundation of individual and collective identity" (Maurette 2018, 140). Though Paul Reeve (2015) reminds us that Mormons were racialized as *other*, they found a collective identity in a shared color: "We are white folks" (Kimball 1854, 224). Stephen Toulmin (1979, 7) nods to this individual-language-collective node in a different context, noting that "thought is interior language and interior language originates in outward language" and that inner speech is "both social and communal." The skin as a metaphor for a border—represented here with a slash—is a bridging of the surfaces/depths, interiority/exteriority, language/culture. On the other hand, each individual is a deep rhetoric. Each of us is a site where transcendence and the possibility of revealing being in language lie (Crosswhite 2013, 56) and where interoception and the inner life, the forming of opinions, ideas, and the processing of sense data, are not separate from "specific embodiments" (Maurette 2018, 129). Neither, we add, are we separate from cultural codes, or symbols and systems of meaning (see Hyatt and Simons 1999, 23).

The organ is a historic instrument in Mormonism. A connection exists between the Schoenstein Organ at the Salt Lake Tabernacle and European uses of music for coloniality's training/settling of the senses. As Jack Bethards, president of the Schoenstein & Co., puts it, "Organs, as do orchestras and singers, all have the accent and language of their country. . . . There is no pure American organ sound because . . . we borrow from the great cultures of Europe and England" (Barone 2005). The *design* of the Mormon hymnal, which features a black embossment of the Schoenstein pipe organ, reminds singers of the European and English rhetorical inheritances—from the very markings on the cover to the sounds printed inside.

Hymns were one of the first practices of settlement in Utah. The term "hymn" refers to both the songs contained in the official institutional canons (organizational hymns) and folksongs of LDS musical practice, some of which were transformed into the former. A history of hymnody is recorded on the Tabernacle Choir's website: "When Latter-day Saints moved to the Salt Lake Valley," Brigham Young saw that "a small choir was formed which first sang at a conference of the Church on August 22, 1847, just 29 days after the first pioneers arrived" (Church of Jesus Christ of Latter-day Saints 2015). The role of place and settlement can be seen in a number of organizational hymns. In "Israel, Israel, God is Calling," we hear of a supposedly promised people: "Now a glo-rious morn is break-ing / For the peo-ple of his choice" (Church of Jesus Christ of Latter-day Saints n.d.-b, 7). In "Holy Temples on Mount Zion," we hear of promised land: "Let the mountains shout for gladness / And the valleys joyful be" (Church of Jesus Christ of Latter-day Saints n.d.-b, 289). In "Israel, Israel, God is Calling," settlement is framed as a divine ultimatum: "Come to Zi-on, come to Zi-on Ere His floods of an-ger flow" (Church of Jesus Christ of Latter-day Saints n.d.-b, 7). Together, these hymns indicate a supposedly empty land—one of promise—and explicitly encourage European settlement. The very *idea* of Zion is predicated on the *ideas* of terra incognita, nullius, and arcadia to produce images of empty landscapes.

Consider further how the following church-settler music works to create the sound of religious persecution, depicting Mormons fleeing oppression and heading west to the "promised land" of Utah. The early Mormon folksong "Tittery-Irie-Aye" uses language of movement and forced exodus: "They've been driven from their homes and away from Nauvoo / For to seek another home in the wilderness anew" (Fife and Fife 1947, 46). Determinism can be heard in two early hymns. "A Song for the Elders" relates that "mobs have drove us" (Alford 2011, 3), and "For Strength of the Hills" recalls "At the hand of foul oppressors / We've borne and suffered long" (Alford 2011, 21–22). Similar imagery can be seen in "Ladies of Utah," where "cruel persecution" leads to being "Driven to the wilderness" (Alford 2011, 7). In an early version of the popular hymn "Come, Come Ye Saints," memory functions as a governing metaphor of this persecution/deliverance cycle: "Let's not forget the afflictions which we bore / . . . In Nauvoo,—in Far West / . . . For in this Valley of the West, there is none to molest" (Alford 2011, 3). The same rhetoric is maintained in the current version: "We'll find the place which God for us prepared / Far away in the West / Where none shall come to hurt or make afraid" (Church of Jesus Christ of Latter-day Saints n.d.-b, 30). The point is not whether Mormons were persecuted, nor is that a subject we aim to debate or discount in this chapter. Rather, we are interested in how the sounds of oppression and religious persecution through music set the stage for the image of a peaceful church-settler that covers up and over *designs* to maintain church-settler futurity.

The listening of modern/colonial and settlerizing music and sound involves a way(s) of listening. Here, we depart from Krista Ratcliffe's (2005) concept of rhetorical listening. While she proposes a rhetorical concept that underscores a way of doing-with others, what is required is a praxis that intentionally seeks out to unsettle the settled. While the intervention of rhetorical listening is attributed to a departure from acts of reading, it nonetheless remains committed to modes of subjectification and subjugation of the *other* vis-à-vis a gaze that renders, affirms, and thus (re)reads the (meaning of the) *other*. Never mind the epistemological crisis it portends to overcome, rhetorical listening has other inherent limitations, and thus, we reiterate that what is required is a listening that operates from the praxis of unsettling the settled. Dylan Robinson's (2020, 38) call for decolonial listening includes moving beyond *hungry listening*, or "prioritize[ing] the capture and certainty of information over the affective feel, timbre, touch, and texture of sound." He describes the settler position as a "starving person," trapped inside a mode of listening for a particular kind of knowledge (Robinson 2020, 38). Settled sound and listening utilize colonial tools. Now, whether rhetorical listening is entangled or complicit in all this is beyond the scope and breadth of this chapter, but once more, we are inclined to argue that the kind of listening demanded is one that intentionally unsettles the settled—a decolonizing (instead of a decolonial) listening. Of the Latter-day

Saint hymnal, the church writes the following: "It is designed for use by congregations, choirs, families, and individuals" (Church of Jesus Christ of Latter-day Saints, n.d.-a). The network of subjects and tools comes together in the technology of settler song, which uses hymnody to produce subjectivities that obey, aligning their wills with God's, acting together in institutional extension.

Members are given "tin ears," not allowing them to hear rhetorics elsewhere and otherwise because their tastes are managed and settled. As a part of the Latter-day Saint objectives to "live the gospel" and "perform the work of salvation and exaltation," the use(s) of music is connected to the curation of a particular rhetorical taste. From the *Book of Mormon* to the everyday practices of church-settlers, such tastes cohere in and around iniquities, where "Lamanites/Indians" retain both God's promise as a "remnant of the House of Israel (Church of Jesus Christ of Latter-day Saints 1977, title page) and the designation as a lost, fallen, and uncivilized race in need of salvation, reeducation, conversion, and restoration. Such tastes are encapsulated by a labor "to aid in the enlightenment of the world" (Wells 1861, 48).

To conclude this section, we want to reiterate an important point. Musical compositions function as a sensory archive. We can excavate this archive for the *idea* of *Deseret* and *Mormon/ism*. What we hope to have illustrated by now is a theologically and secularly structured psyche consciously documenting its existence, exhibiting a power to belong-to land by supplanting original inhabitants and legitimizing rights-to land via the projects of territorial and epistemological expropriation.[3] Such compositions are a prism by which to see *designs* (*idea of Deseret* and *Mormon/ism*) refracted through the lens of *Americanity* and within the frame of modernity/coloniality. This is to say, the *idea* returns us to the invention of the Americas (and the colonization of the senses) and, thus, the *Archive*. As we return to below, the *idea of Deseret* is but a smaller archive, a working part that, in the local context, covers up and over the name of the land, providing a fictitious portrait of the settler and renaming the people inhabiting the land. Overall, this smaller archive contributes to the palimpsestic narrative of the *Archive*, Western civilization.

Terms, Codes, Tropes

Mormonism is assembled through acts of literature, rhetoric, belief, faith, land acquisition, and song. Church-settlers spoke of Utah in two ways, first as a place that had not been "beheld" by a "man upon the face of the earth" (B. Young 1847, 144). They were confronted with the reality that Utah was not empty. They resorted to translate the *Book of Mormon* to their everyday: "We are here in the mountains with these Lamanites" (B. Young 1853, 106). "The American-Indian," invented and reduced by church-settlers to things of mere nature, was not considered man. So, when church-settlers questioned, "Why are these Lamanites living upon reptiles of the earth?" (Woodruff 1855, 198) or when they observed that "the Lamanite" lived in a natural state as "beasts of the field" (Pratt 1854, 97–98), they invented impressions of their supposed natural and animalistic propensities.

The second way church-settlers spoke of Utah was as a place "scientific men" and "travelers" had "declared worthless" (Smith 1854, 24). Indeed, one hymn confirms this outlook: "Oh, what a dreary place this was when first the Mormons found it" (Emrich 1952, 7). Church-settlers observed "dead grass" (Smith 1852, 44), "desolate waste" (B. Young 1857a, 344), a "parched and barren desert" (Woodruff 1873, 279), a place "nobody else would live upon" (Taylor 1857, 186). When church-settlers argued that no "civilized people" (B. Young 1855, 253) or "class of people" (B. Young 1857a, 344) had inhabited Utah, again, "the American-Indian" was not considered worth acknowledging. Utah as a "desolate waste" or "barren desert" relies on the ideas of terra incognita (nullius, arcadia), doctrines of discovery-rights to land, and divine and natural designs, while the invention of the other and reduction of the other to *things of mere nature* depends on epistemic (lesser knowers, knowing) and ontological differences (inferior, lesser beings). Both ways are necessary in the settler universe of Man-Human-Rights: first, to produce images of empty landscapes from which the inhabiting bodies of the other vanish or disappear; and second, to create the basis for staking claim to land not as intruders but per divine and natural designs.

As we wind down this chapter, we argue that with rhetorical, archival, and sonic methods of analysis, it becomes possible to conceive of an assemblage and relation of assemblages. Like other decolonialists, we turn to the start of the modern world—a turning and nexus point in world history—and argue that it is the backdrop for the materialization of a superstructure of written record we refer to as the *Archive*. In short, the *Archive* is in assemblage with smaller archives, or the working parts (Yang 2017, 62), which function to explain, rationalize, and justify the *idea*. The *idea of Utah* and *Mormon/ism*, for example, are imaginative and compositional designs, the rhetoricity behind archival impressions that ensure the *Archive* continues to be made. And the *Archive* feels that touch and sound by the hand and voice of Mormon/ism. The idea of Utah and Mormon/ism continues to be felt with the erection of 170 temples across the world over the past thirty years. This is not conjecture, as we have as evidence the historicity of (the palimpsestic narrative) and rhetoricity—the physical and figurative penetration—behind their archive. It is a prism by which to see *designs* refracted through the lens of *Americanity* and within the frame of modernity/coloniality. And in this way, their archive is but an archival impression entered into the *Archive*.

We recall Locke ([1689] 1821) to underscore this point: "bringing the elements into successful use for the benefit of man, and reclaiming a barren wilderness [desert], converting it into a fruitful field, making it to blossom as the rose [through industry and enterprise]; such a man I would call a financier, a benefactor of his fellow man" (Young 1877, 97). In this quote from the church-settler prophet Brigham Young are the undertones of Locke's ideas: images-signs-sounds and ends of and on labor, property, civilized (Man), and (Man) supporting (Human) life. Like Locke, Mormons saw (North and South) America as the space and place where the heavenly father "planted the Garden of Eden" (Young 1863, 222). The "American desert," or Utah, was to be redeemed per divine and natural *designs* by physical work (labor), from a waste place into the Garden of Eden (Pratt 1870, 299). Present church-settlers are not unalike from Locke or others who came after. Arthur de Gobineau (1915, 160) once wrote, "all Aryan societies began by exaggerating." The exaggeration of a crisis, whether theo- or ego- structured, always already stages the emergence of a penetration into the space, place, and time of an-other. The *Archive* and its smaller archives tell us that much. Each local place has its own micro archive working in assemblage with a much bigger archive, all of which speak to *ideas* that are haunted/haunting and that are an ongoing epistemological experiment.

That it is important to trace words from a rhetorical and archival standpoint is an understatement. The *idea of Deseret* and Mormon/ism rely on words and ideas. The church-settler is Nephite is Adam. Wasteland is choice; land is the Garden of Eden. Cultivation is tilling the earth (like Adam and Eve were to do) and replenishing it. It all comes into view in the *Book of Mormon*: "he will make her wilderness like Eden, and her desert like the garden of the Lord" (2 Nephi 8:3, Church of Jesus Christ of Latter-day Saints 1977). These are coded words of settler colonialism that transform the *idea of Deseret* and Mormon/ism into reality elsewhere and otherwise. Take, for example, the word "replenish" according to church-settlers: "In Latin, Re = repetition while plenus equals complete, and together, its means to re-complete" (Hyde 1854, 79). Now, church-settlers realize they cannot say for certain where the Garden of Eden was located. Here, the Latin word *alibi* becomes relevant, a logic to be elsewhere. Yang (2017, 14) tells us, "specific colonial apparatuses differ but similar technologies recirculate in them." The Garden of Eden trope is one such technology, a code for the *idea*, the *idea* of a replenishment of what can be seen across the whole face of the Earth. It is code for the idea that domination, management, and control are justifiable and rationalizable as the price of modernization and human progress.

Utah may just be a state name. Yet a careful rhetorical analysis of its origins—the Hive, Territory, State of Deseret—underscores Mignolo's (2005, 151) claim that words and ideas make "it possible to transform an invented idea into 'reality.'" "Deseret" is an invention, a wor(l)ding aspiration, rhetorical and affective through what Jennifer Wingard (2013) calls "assemblage" and "branding work." It is not inconsequential but an archival impression with structural underpinnings and material consequences: the Constitution and Law of Deseret, The University of Deseret (The University of Utah), the Deseret Alphabet, *The Deseret News*, the Valleys-Mountains of Deseret, and Citizens of Deseret. Today, the state is referred to as "Utah," but trace marks remain—the *idea* of *Deseret* and *Mormon/ism*. Utah is a case study of how what occurred in the Americas five hundred years ago continues to appear and be consequential—a smaller archive or the working parts of the *idea of the Americas* and a modus operandi of *designs*. That the images, myths, meanings, and rhetorics of place and citizen/ship remain associated in Utah with the church-settler is not coincidental. It is the by-product of settlerizing encounters and performances of visuality, branding, and ghosting. The *idea* of Utah—as an American place bolstering a model of hegemony vying for power, and place myth, a destined place and gathering space of and for the favored church-settlers—is an archival impression in the *Archive*.

Homesteading is always already a project of appropriation and exclusion. Neither "Zion" nor "the Lamanite" exists ontologically. Still, these knowledge fictions materialized as truths. Mignolo's view on modern/colonial situations comes into focus as "church-settlers" become associated with place, place with church-settlers. That is to say, the ways church-settlers spoke of Utah and the *other* ultimately impressed the *idea* of Utah as the "central place of gathering" (Pratt 1859, 312) and the "center stake of Zion" (Young 1857b, 46), a space and place to carry out the work of an absolute instruction of the *other*: "these natives should be looked to and sought after, for they are the seed of promise" (J. Young 1855, 230). After failed homesteading projects in Ohio and Illinois, church-settlers could at last claim that Zion could not have been established anywhere else but the mountains of Utah. Today, Utah remains a most haunted/haunting and wounded/wounding space and place (Till 2012). This can be attributed to how rhetoric, senses, place, archives, and designs are intertwined, underscoring that the colonization of the senses and thus *aisthēseis* (sense perceptions / ways of knowing) could mean the domination, management, and control of epistemic obedience in perpetuity. The *idea* of Utah and the church-settler ultimately situates us squarely on the demand both for decolonizing aesthetics and for unsettling moves toward issues of response and innocence and, thus, church-settler futurity. At the structural, epistemological, and ontological level, this is the unsettling work of a decolonial option.

Rewriting the Senses (Again)

Settlers can never be in control of the afterlife of what is produced. But it would be a mistake to chalk up the (re)writing of modern/colonial and settlerizing music, and thus the senses, as mere coincidence. We live under the yoke of the *Archive* that has a regulative function for smaller archives. Both a framework of rhetorical ecologies and a rhetorical framework of palimpsests encourage us to recontextualize the (re)writing in their historical, temporal, and lived contexts. When done, the *bleeding*, to return to Jenny Edbauer, of public rhetorics, memories, interactions, and forces is undeniable. We are more concerned both with the rhetorical phenomenon of (re)writing settler music and the senses as archival impressions additive to the *Archive* and how they exist *in* assemblage elsewhere and otherwise to make, unmake, and remake the *structures of feeling* (Williams 1977) and epistemic murk (Taussig 1991) that contaminate humanity. With William Benoit's (1996) notion of *discourse about actions*, we can approach the accumulation of settler music and senses elsewhere and otherwise as sites of *doing*, accounts that function to explain, justify, interpret, and/or rationalize certain actions through (re)writing. We argue that settler rhetorics of music and the senses, whether carried out by settlers, the posterity of settlers, or others who do work rhetorically to transmit such, reflect an awareness that impressions could be at the same time the domination of information, management of knowledge, and control of epistemic obedience. Our tetrad effort to unveil, unsettle, delink (coloniality and the senses), and reclaim the senses for everyone, open to anyone seeks new attunements, where "rhetoric stems from and is not imposed on the world" (Rickert 2013, 285).

Notes

1. The phrase "white and delightsome people" appeared in the *Book of Mormon* until the 1981 edition.
2. Neumes are early inscriptions of musical notation that joined pitch and text. Chants eventually became psalms and then hymns.
3. It is worth mentioning that theo- and ego-politics are two sides of the same coin (Mignolo 2011).

References

Alford, Kenneth. 2011. "Latter-day Saint Poetry and Songs of the Utah War." *Mormon Historical Studies* 12 (1): 1–28.

Baldwin, James. 2012. *Notes of a Native Son*. Boston: Beacon.

Barone, Michael. 2005. "Some Latter Day Sounds #0525." *Pipedreams*, June 20. https://www.pipedreams.org/episode/2005/06/20/some-latter-day-sounds.

Benoit, William. 1996. "A Note on Burke on 'Motive.'" *Rhetoric Society Quarterly* 26 (2): 67–79.

Black, Edwin. 1997. "The Aesthetics of Rhetoric, American Style." In *Rhetoric and Political Culture in Nineteenth-Century America*, edited by Thomas W. Benson, 1–14. East Lansing: Michigan State University Press.

Burkholder, J. Peter, Donald Jay Grout, and Claude V. Palisca. 2014. *A History of Western Music*. 9th ed. New York: Norton.

Certeau, Michael de. 1992. *The Writing of History*. Translated by Tom Conley. New York: Columbia University Press.

Chávez, Karma. 2018. "The Body: An Abstract and Actual Rhetorical Concept." *Rhetoric Society Quarterly* 48 (3): 242–50.

Church of Jesus Christ of Latter-day Saints. 1977. *The Book of Mormon*. Salt Lake City: Church of Jesus Christ of Latter-day Saints.

———. 2015. "Mormon Tabernacle Choir Inducted into the American Classical Music Hall of Fame." Newsroom. Accessed May 1, 2025. http://newsroom.churchofjesuschrist.org/article/mormon-tabernacle-choir-inducted-into-the-american-classical-music-hall-of-fame.

———. 2025a. *The Doctrine and Covenants*. Salt Lake City: Church of Jesus Christ of Latter-day Saints.

———. 2025b. *The Pearl of Great Price*. Salt Lake City: Church of Jesus Christ of Latter-day Saints.

———. N.d.-a. "19. Music." Accessed May 1, 2025. https://www.churchofjesuschrist.org/study/eng/manual/general-handbook/19-music.

———. N.d.-b. "Hymns of the Church of Jesus Christ of Latter-day Saints." Accessed May 1, 2025. https://www.churchofjesuschrist.org/study/manual/hymns?lang=eng.

Crosswhite, James. 2013. *Deep Rhetoric: Philosophy, Reason, Violence, Justice, Wisdom*. Chicago: University of Chicago Press.

Edbauer, Jenny. 2005. "Unframing Models of Public Distribution: From Rhetorical Situation to Rhetorical Ecologies." *Rhetoric Society Quarterly* 35 (4): 5–24.

Emrich, Duncan. 1952. *Songs of the Mormons and Songs of the West: From the Archive of Folk Song*. Washington, DC: Library of Congress.

Fanon, Frantz. 1986. *Black Skins / White Masks*. Translated by Charles Lam Markmann. London: Pluto.

Fife, Austin E., and Alta S. Fife. 1947. "Folk Songs of Mormon Inspiration." *Western Folklore* 6 (1): 42–52.

Giddens, Anthony. 1981. *A Contemporary Critique of Historical Materialism*. Vol. 1, *Power, Property, and the State*. Berkeley: University of California Press.

Gobineau, Arthur de. 1915. *The Inequality of Human Races*. Translated by Adrian Collins. New York: G. P. Putnam's Sons.

Holland, Sharon. 2000. *Raising the Dead: Readings of Death and (Black) Subjectivity*. Durham: Duke University.

Hyatt, Jenny, and Helen Simons. 1999. "Cultural Codes—Who Holds the Key? The Concept and Conduct of Evaluation in Central and Eastern Europe." *Evaluation* 5 (1): 23–41.

Hyde, Orson. 1854. "The Marriage Relations." In *Journal of Discourses*, vol. 2, edited by George Watt, 75–87. London: Church of Jesus Christ of Latter-day Saints.

Kimball, Heber C. 1854. "Obedience—The Spirit World—The Potter and the Clay." In *Journal of Discourses*, vol. 2, edited by

George Watt, 220–25. London: Church of Jesus Christ of Latter-day Saints.

Lewis, Pierce. 1979. "Axioms for Reading Landscape." In *The Interpretation of Ordinary Landscapes*, edited by D. W. Meinig, 11–32. New York: Oxford University Press.

Locke, John. (1689) 1821. *Two Treatises on Government*. London: R. Butler.

Maurette, Pablo. 2018. "Skin Deep." *The Forgotten Sense: Meditations on Touch*, 129–60. Chicago: University of Chicago Press.

Mignolo, Walter. 2005. *The Idea of Latin America*. Malden, MA: Blackwell.

———. 2007. "Delinking." *Cultural Studies* 21 (3): 449–514.

———. 2011. *The Darker Side of Western Modernity: Global Futures, Decolonial Options*. Durham: Duke University Press.

Mignolo, Walter, and Catherine Walsh. 2018. *On Decoloniality: Concepts, Analytics, Praxis*. Durham: Duke University Press.

Moss, Jessica. 2012. "Soul-Leading: The Unity of the Phaedrus, Again." In *Oxford Studies in Ancient Philosophy*, vol. 43, edited by Brad Inwood, 1–23. Oxford: Oxford University Press.

Nehamas, Alexander. 1999. "Plato on Imitation and Poetry in *Republic* X." In *Virtues of Authenticity: Essays on Plato and Socrates*, 251–78. Princeton: Princeton University Press.

Perelman, Chaïm, and Lucie Olbrechts-Tyteca. 1971. *The New Rhetoric: A Treatise on Argumentation*. Notre Dame: University of Notre Dame Press.

Pratt, Orson. 1854. "Language, or the Medium of Communication in the Future State, and the Increased Powers of Locomotion." In *Journal of Discourses*, vol. 3, edited by George Watt, 97–105. London: Church of Jesus Christ of Latter-day Saints.

———. 1859. "Privileges and Experience of the Saints, Etc." In *Journal of Discourses*, vol. 7, edited by George Watt, 308–13. London: Church of Jesus Christ of Latter-day Saints.

———. 1870. "The Restoration of the Gospel—Its First Principles—Accumulating Evidences of the Truth of the Book of Mormon." In *Journal of Discourses*, vol. 14, edited by George Watt, 289–99. London: Church of Jesus Christ of Latter-day Saints.

Pred, Allan. 1984. "Place as Historically Contingent Process: Structuration and the Time-Geography of Becoming Place." *Annals of the Association of American Geographers* 74 (2): 279–97.

Quijano, Aníbal. 2007. "Coloniality and Modernity/Rationality." *Cultural Studies* 21 (2–3): 168–78.

Ratcliffe, Krista. 2005. *Rhetorical Listening: Identification, Gender, Whiteness*. Carbondale: Southern Illinois University Press.

Reeve, Paul. 2015. *Religion of a Different Color: Race and the Mormon Struggle for Whiteness*. Oxford: Oxford University Press.

Rickert, Thomas. 2013. *Ambient Rhetoric: The Attunements of Rhetoric Being*. Pittsburgh: University of Pittsburgh Press.

Robinson, Dylan. 2020. *Hungry Listening: Resonant Theory for Indigenous Sound Studies*. Minneapolis: University of Minnesota Press.

Said, Edward. 1985. "Orientalism Reconsidered." *Cultural Critique*, no. 1 (Autumn): 89–107.

Smith, Craig R. 2017. *Rhetoric and Human Consciousness: A History*. Long Grove, IL: Waveland.

Smith, George A. 1852. "Liberty and Persecution—Conduct of the U.S. Government, Etc." In *Journal of Discourses*, vol. 1, edited by George Watt, 42–45. London: Church of Jesus Christ of Latter-day Saints.

———. 1854. "Reminiscences of the Jackson County Mob, the Evacuation of Nauvoo, and the Settlement of Great Salt Lake City." In *Journal of Discourses*, vol. 2, edited by George Watt, 22–24. London: Church of Jesus Christ of Latter-day Saints.

Taussig, Michael. 1991. *Shamanism, Colonialism, and the Wild Man: A Study in Terror and Healing*. Chicago: University of Chicago Press.

Taylor, John. 1857. "The Rights of Mormonism." In *Journal of Discourses*, vol. 5, edited by George Watt, 182–92. London: Church of Jesus Christ of Latter-day Saints.

Till, Karen. 2012. "Wounded Cities: Memory-Work and a Place-Based Ethics of Care." *Political Geography* 31 (1): 3–14.

Tlostanova, Madina. 2015. "Can the Post-Soviet Think? On Coloniality of Knowledge, External Imperial and Double Colonial Difference." *Intersections* 1 (2): 38–58.

Toulmin, Stephen. 1979. "The Inwardness of Mental Life." *Critical Inquiry* 6 (1): 1–16.

Tuck, Eve, and K. Wayne Yang. 2012. "Decolonization Is Not a Metaphor." *Decolonization: Indigeneity, Education and Society* 1 (1): 1–40.

Wells, Daniel H. 1861. "The Gospel of Salvation, &c." In *Journal of Discourses*, vol. 9, edited by George Watt, 43–50. London: Church of Jesus Christ of Latter-day Saints.

Whittaker, David J. 1991. "Foreword: Responding to the Critics." In *Tinkling Cymbals and Sounding Brass: The Art of Telling Tales About Joseph Smith and Brigham Young*, by Hugh Nibley, ix–xxi. Provo, UT: Maxwell Institute.

Williams, Raymond. 1977. *Marxism and Literature*. New York: Oxford University Press.

Wingard, Jennifer. 2013. *Branded Bodies, Rhetoric, and the Neoliberal Nation-State*. Lanham, MD: Lexington Books.

Woodruff, Wilford. 1855. "The Church and Kingdom of God, and the Churches and Kingdoms of Men." In *Journal of Discourses*, vol. 2, edited by George Watt, 191–202. London: Church of Jesus Christ of Latter-day Saints.

———. 1873. "The Signs of the Coming of the Son of Man—The Saints' Duties." In *Journal of Discourses*, vol. 15, edited by George Watt, 275–83. London: Church of Jesus Christ of Latter-day Saints.

Yang, K. Wayne (as la paperson). 2017. *A Third University Is Possible*. Minneapolis: University of Minnesota Press.

Young, Brigham. 1847. "The Pioneers—Capabilities and Settlement of the Great Basin—Exhortation to Faithfulness." In *Journal of Discourses*, vol. 1, edited by George Watt, 144–46. London: Church of Jesus Christ of Latter-day Saints.

———. 1853. "President B. Young's Journey South—Indian Difficulties—Walker—Watching and Prayer—Thieves and Their Deserts—Eastern Intelligence—Financial State of the Church—Gaining Knowledge, Etc." In *Journal of Discourses*, vol. 1, edited by George Watt, 103–11. London: Church of Jesus Christ of Latter-day Saints.

———. 1855. "Faithfulness and Apostasy." In *Journal of Discourses*, vol. 9, edited by George Watt, 248–58. London: Church of Jesus Christ of Latter-day Saints.

———. 1857a. "Practical Religion—Simplicity—Temporal Salvation—Advantages of Utah as a Settlement for the Saints—False Reports, Etc." In *Journal of Discourses*, vol. 4, edited by George Watt, 341–46. London: Church of Jesus Christ of Latter-day Saints.

———. 1857b. "Source of True Happiness—Prayer, Etc." In *Journal of Discourses*, vol. 6, edited by George Watt, 39–47. London: Church of Jesus Christ of Latter-day Saints.

———. 1863. "Instruction to the Latter-Day Saints, in the Settlements South of Great Salt Lake." In *Journal of Discourses*, vol. 10, edited by George Watt, 221–29. London: Church of Jesus Christ of Latter-day Saints.

———. 1877. "The Lord's Supper—a Word to Mothers—The Sacrament in Sabbath Schools—History of Some Things—Young Men to Preside—Home Manufactures." In *Journal of Discourses*, vol. 19, edited by George Watt, 91–97. London: Church of Jesus Christ of Latter-day Saints.

Young, Joseph. 1855. "Remarks on Behalf of the Indians." In *Journal of Discourses*, vol. 9, edited by George Watt, 229–33. London: Church of Jesus Christ of Latter-day Saints.

8

In*form*ing Rhetoric
Pluriversal Lessons on *Différance* and Rhetorical Energy

DAVID M. GRANT

Once upon a time, in some out of the way corner of that universe which is dispersed into numberless twinkling solar systems, there was a star upon which clever beasts invented knowing.
—Friedrich Nietzsche, "On Truth and Lies in a Non-Moral Sense"

Shhh. You don't have to worry about that here. Just be a rock.
—Daniel Kwan and Daniel Scheinert, *Everything Everywhere All at Once*

Sunlight shines on your body. Each second, a quadrillion photons radiate through the Earth's atmosphere to heat the surface of your skin. In response, your cells produce melanin. Your epidermis thickens. Blood vessels expand, transferring thermal energy through the body. The energy stimulates neurons whose ionic exchanges send electric currents to your brain, registering a feeling of warmth. In turn, bioelectric currents pass through the raphe nuclei of the brain stem to release serotonin, dopamine, and other neurotransmitters, which further relax blood vessels, muscles, and organs. These bioelectric currents also associate with memories and activate emotional responses alongside physical sensations. Among these currents, you are persuaded to linger, letting the energy of sunshine both envelop and saturate you.

Stay too long, though, and all this energy can overload your system. The longer, hotter wavelengths cause sunburn, pain, and perhaps heat stroke. The shorter wavelengths can kill skin cells, and still others will break molecules apart to produce free radicals in the skin. These bond with cell membranes, proteins, and genetic material to interfere with metabolism and cause cancers like melanoma. At the very least, with too much exposure to the sun, dilated blood vessels begin to deliver white blood cells, the skin reddens from capillary inflammation, and sites of overexposure switch the electrical current of nerve cells from pleasure to pain, and that switch persuades us to a very different end.

Bodies are complex systems, not simple machines; no two are alike. Some bodies can withstand far-longer periods of exposure and will react differently. A stone, for example, simply warms from the side facing the sun because it has no circulatory system to distribute the heat. How much radiation it absorbs depends on its molecular composition, coloring, the angle of the light, and the specific wavelengths reaching the stone. Excess heat or energy is simply radiated away, perhaps to enliven a small lizard after a particularly cool morning. The rock remains seemingly impassive to the energies around it. Yet, even so, with exposure to solar radiation, chemical bonds in the rock weaken. It may fade in color or flake in layers, depending on molecular composition and arrangement. While the stone's outer compounds may expand similarly to skin cells, they do so in what we understand as a purely mechanical process. The stone qua stone does not react. It has neither sensory nor muscular apparatus. It doesn't have to worry about the sense of its situation; it's just a rock. It would seem, then, that rocks figure as a kind of limit to sensory rhetorics, seemingly outside the bounds of what Debra Hawhee (2015, 4) calls "the senses *as such*."

This is not to say that a stone remains unaffected. Its body is woven into its environment differently. Rocks are affected differently by the sun compared to humans or plants because we are alive. But both living and nonliving bodies change in the presence of the sun, and we can perceive different responses with each. The issue is that we cannot theorize the response of the rock in the same way we theorize our own animal response or the responses of plants. John Muckelbauer (2016, 40) argues in his contribution to *Rhetoric, Through Everyday Things* that "plants turning toward the sun and audiences accepting an argument might well involve the same kind of action/motion." If they do, it is because both plants and audiences are capable of "sense." Biologically, light induces the production of auxin, a phytohormone that elongates plant cells. The living cells sense light and respond, a process that also forms a very basic conceptualization of how we tend to think about rhetoric; I say something, and you sense it and respond, preferably in the manner I envisioned.

If we shift the sensing thing from flower to rock, however, we cannot rely on such a model unless we can explain how rocks feel or come to judgment based on sense data. Rocks don't make sense; as far as we can tell, they sense nothing. Rocks remain impassive unless we physically move them by force. For all we know, they are impermeable to any rhetorical inducement, via either speech or sunlight. However, we may need a rhetoric of rocks if we heed those who have urged their inclusion into our ecological awareness. For instance, Ehren Pflugfelder (2022, 19) argues for a "geologic rhetoric" that might deal with "the immense, primordial geologic and atmospheric forces that have shaped and continue to shape the very ground we live on and the ontological grounds for our known ways of being." I also advocate for rocky rhetorics, but not along the lines of biological sensation.

Like Pflugfelder (2022, 22), I proceed by "refusing to align . . . with a specific ontological grounding." That is, Western minds don't need to think of rocks or geology as alive in order to bring them into a version of rhetoric; rather, Euro-Western approaches have to reconfigure their rhetorics in order to expand who and what they include. Instead of vitality or sensory stimulus and response as a basis for rhetoric, I look to the energy that constitutes the materiality of sensation. Such energy can hardly be considered separately from the body through which it flows, which it affects, and which is in*formed* by energy's flow. My approach removes rhetoric almost entirely from the epistemic and delinks it from the colonial epistemological matrix where sensation requires a sensing subject. We might say we can do away with the requirement that rhetoric implies *noesis*, a perception by a consciousness or thought in general. How might we think of rhetorical activity sans a being who perceives?

Ontology reinforces particular divisions in our theorizing between living and nonliving beings. Overall, Western ontology amounts to something of a biological imperialism in how we *approach* ideas like sensory rhetorics because we retain an image of what things can be so moved and what cannot. Even Pflugfelder (2022) points to Justine Wells et al.'s (2018) arguments grounded in a notion of "material life" and "the liveliness of the material." This, in turn, stems from Jane Bennett's (2009) vibrant materialism and her reenchantment of materiality through a reanimation of the mundane. But why reanimate what is not properly living? The trope of life runs deep, yet this trope is not universal.

Algonquin languages such as Sac and Fox (Meskwaki) grammatically mark nouns and verbs as either animate or inanimate. While largely similar to our own divisions of living and nonliving, there are exceptions, and I have been taught that pears are sometimes animate.[1] More importantly, the grammatical approach afforded by Meskwaki grammar is unlike anything we have in English or any European language. Perhaps more striking, among the Siouan-speaking Dakota and Lakota, stones are sometimes addressed as *tunka*, short for *tunkashila*, or grandfather-Creator.[2] They are believed to be "oldest" and worth paying attention to as animate beings in their own right and, like all things, have their own nonhuman order. They are not alive in the same sense that you and I or my dog are alive, but they are animate in a larger scheme of things. Rather than rejecting Western ontology or science, I think sensory rhetorics grounded in material energy can help unsettle Eurocentric rhetorical ontologies.

The line between living and nonliving may be foundational to ethics and rhetoric, but to say biology defines that line leaves out many non-Western ways. Because those of us raised in the Western mindset cannot simply appropriate other cultural ways to solve our own problems, we need to revise our own ontological story. Western science can be neither the only way to adjudicate existence nor entirely expelled from our thinking. As Romeo García, Damián Baca, and Ellen Cushman (2024, 5) affirm, decolonization is "not replacing or transplanting one knowing and knowledge-making path with another." While Muckelbauer's essay certainly expands the scope of rhetoric into nonhuman sensation, we must be cautious when extrapolating from it. I am not against taking our cues from plants, animals, or other creatures. Rather, I urge caution in sensory, creaturely, and comparative rhetorics regarding tacit assumptions about living and nonliving things. Must our theorizing of sensory rhetorics rely on paradigms of biological creatures? How might biological paradigms unwittingly replicate colonial perspectives and their "loci of enunciation" (Grosfoguel 2011)? Finally, how might an examination of such questions provide for and actively cultivate a more comparative dialogue within rhetorics of sense and sensation?

I move through these questions by first discussing decolonial perspectives and establishing solidarity with that ongoing work in rhetorics of science and literature. My main aim is to perform what Walter Mignolo (2022, 247) calls a "double translation" between ontological groundings of colonized and colonizer. Double translation is figured by Mignolo through the Zapatista spokesperson Subcomandante Marcos, a former urban intellectual who "realized that his Marxist ideology needed to be infected by Amerindian cosmology." My purpose, then, is similar to Marcos's. I mean to "infect" sensory rhetorical ontology with a pluriversal rather than universal cosmotechnics that is open to considering how rocks might have their own rhetoric. Double translation revises Western concepts by stripping the English words we use to talk about "abstract universal values" (Mignolo 2022, 257). Chief among these for my work here is the term "energy" and how it has been abstracted and universalized in rhetorical theory.

I then approach rhetorics of sense directly, noting a difference between uses of the term "energy" and the implication that has for rhetorical theory. I advocate for a particular road not taken, advancing my claims while still, to repeat Pflugfelder (2022, 22), refusing "to align . . . with a specific ontological grounding." That way forward is found, ironically, in the precepts of physical relativity, which holds that everything is in differential motion; there is no authoritative point of measurement, only relational options. Before deciding what *is*, one must decide how to sense what *might be*. Rhetorical movement is spatiotemporal in its effects, as Margaret Price (2024, 37) so clearly articulates with respect to her titular "crip spacetime," which "manifests beyond geometry" to include unavoidable harm in terms of space, time, cost, and accompaniment. Rather than a universal and universalizing construct, I double translate the term "energy" and its conceptual web so it becomes what Mignolo (2022, 257) calls a "connector," so "the primary meaning becomes one more among many, but with no claim to the privilege of being primary." My revision recenters relations at the heart of all that is.

I close with an example of how ontology is discursively policed in the case of the Thirty-Meter Telescope on Mauna Kea in Hawaiʻi. My aim is to show the duplicity in colonial discourses of science and their uptake into structures of settler colonial power so we can appreciate the difference my double translation offers. My conclusion holds colonial discourses to account and brings some potential consideration for rocks as literal rhetorical agents yet that lack "life" as we understand it. In short, through a double translation of rhetorical energy, I affirm the many different ways *"we are where we think"* (García et al. 2024, 15) but also where and how we sense.

From Universal Ontology to Pluriversal Ontologies

As the epigraphs to this chapter indicate, a rock may lie beyond "knowing" and lack any "sense," but we must, like Michelle Yeoh's character, Evelyn, in *Everything Everywhere All at Once*, be with the rock on its terms—not ours—if we are to survive the perilous time of the Anthropocene. Western ontology often posits a single world mediated by linguistic and cultural imaginaries, each of which is partial, useful, but relative to the single world. Kristin Arola helps make the point that Indigenous narratives about an animate natural world are not linguistically mediated "cultural imaginaries" but real perspectives on the world that hold powerful lessons (Schelly et al. 2021). Chelsey Schelly et al. argue that "emphasizing imaginaries without examining ontologies may obscure significant, tangible differences in how groups understand the very nature of reality, and these differences may be key to understanding who is involved and what decisions are made" (2). Clashes between Indigenous people and colonial powers often stem from a very fundamental cosmological difference about which worldly lessons make sense. Indigenous teachings and lessons about stones and water and many other things are *ways of being*, not just knowing. They are often lessons on how *to relate* to the world, not how *to understand* it. Approaching statements about how rocks sense and talk as a cultural imaginary insults and negates the very people we need to include.

While sensory rhetorics hold helpful insights, approaching sensation as strictly biological reinscribes a colonial ontology. To counter that colonial vision, and like Pflugfelder's "non-alignment," I refuse any binary that gathers the anticolonial into a totality. Posing rhetorics as alternative to a single canonical tradition "illustrates allegiance to the notion that a totalized reality of rhetoric already exists; therefore, alternatives to that reality are the only option for making rhetoric more representative and responsive to the lived realities of all people" (Cushman et al. 2019, 2). Both epigraphs to this chapter imagine that other worlds exist and that they hold lessons for our own. They point toward pluriversality—"a world of many worlds" (Cadena and Blaser 2018, 1) in which different ontologies can be affirmed.

Pluriversality recognizes diversity within solidarity and foregrounds a multiplicity of ontologies. For example, Nijah Cunningham (2023) explores a colonial heliocentrism in Franz Fanon's *The Wretched of the Earth*. He uses an analogy similar to Muckelbauer, but to different ends. Cunningham troubles the heliocentric metaphor for its enclosure of time and space along imperial lines—for establishing a horizon dividing what the sun can illuminate to our senses from what it cannot. This establishes and legitimizes what we can sense in "reality" from what we only perceive through a glass darkly, if at all. Cunningham's critique of Fanon comes from a stance of solidarity but points out an all-too-optimistic transcendence in Fanon's thinking. Attending to Fanon's inclusion of Keïta Fodéba's poem "African Dawn" within *The Wretched of the Earth*, Cunningham draws out what Fanon turns from. Cunningham names Fanon's interpretation of Fodéba's poem "heliology" or "how the sun functions as a form of expression, as metaphor, and . . . the narratives and imaginaries that its figurative meanings set into motion"

(46). Heliology and heliocentrism foreclose possibilities of the sun's absence, the lack of reference point, and the "uncertainty associated with anticolonial struggle by positing the 'crystallization' of a popular will" (50). This strikes at the very ego of any person—colonized or colonizer—who would valorize one form of consciousness above others or attempt to foreclose other forms of sensation: dreamtime, visions, spirits, faerie.

My method to theorize rhetorical energy works similarly to Cunningham's "contaminating" Fanon (2023, 50) with a "silencing . . . impossible for us to unhear." My provocation is to follow the sun's energy beyond its own horizon as a means to theorize sensations beyond the living. This can help move rhetoric away from problems with epistemological "making sense" without resorting to a singular naïve objectivism or intractable metadebates over ideological "false consciousness." I look to retain rhetoric's ethical (and existential) imperative without centering a Western "locus of enunciation," which Ramón Grosfoguel (2011) describes as "the geo-political and body-political location of the subject that speaks." To address this problem, to follow energies beyond the horizon of sun and enlightenment, to perhaps echo Christina V. Cedillo's (2022, 95) "smoke and mirrors" in "a shared subjectivity, matter contemplating itself from a location and perspective that deems itself human," I posit a sense of being (and a being-in-sensation) that does not hinge on the life-death binary of Western ontology. I hope to build from heliotropic metaphors treatments of energy in sensory rhetorics that hold potential to articulate new practices of being—be they non-Western, nonhuman, or perhaps some combination—that neither center the human nor abandon its relations and that might yet respond to wicked problems that Western reasoning, language, and sensibilities have gotten us into. While a full response is beyond the scope of this chapter, I hope to lay out some formulation of how rhetorical sensation can be differently energized to include all kinds of energies: solar, sensory, and otherwise.

Rhetorical Energies in Relative Systems

In Debra Hawhee's (2015) centenary article for *Quarterly Journal of Speech*, she shares L. S. Judson and D. E. Rodden's diagram of the rhetorical situation, which uses the image of electricity to theorize relations between speaker, audience, and context. Hawhee notes how "energy comes up repeatedly with discussions of sensation in the context of rhetoric" and argues that their diagram "attempts to encapsulate that which eludes encapsulation: the vast range of experiences, the infinite variety of ways that listeners might be 'keyed up'" (3). Our experiences condition rhetorical energy through memory, affecting it and its sensibility *to us*. Thus, Hawhee calls out the dangers of generalization and not paying attention to differences in sensation, such that contemporary theory "ought to resist presuming sameness across senses, even as it examines the pulses of existence that run through our media and—by extension—through us" (12). What one feels as worthy of admiration, another may feel as warranting disgust. These energetic pulses have political and ethical dimensions and are not just individual opinions. As she reasons, "If rhetorical theorists were to take seriously the participatory dimension of the sensorium, we might find more specific ways to think about political feeling that does not simply stall with the emotion/affect distinction" (12). There are larger and longer "waves" of sensation that motivate, persuade, and inform social bodies. Such energetic waves are temporally extensive, not simply zapped into a single moment.

George Kennedy also uses the metaphor of energy in another piece of landmark sensory rhetorics scholarship, "A Hoot in the Dark." He proclaims rhetoric as "in the most general sense . . . identified with the energy *inherent* in communication: the emotional energy that impels the speaker to speak, the physical energy expended in the utterance, the energy level coded in the message, and the energy experienced by the recipient in decoding the message" (Kennedy 1992, 2; emphasis added). Kennedy advances this same idea in *On Rhetoric: A Theory of Civic Discourse*. In the first edition, as in "Hoot," energy is "inherent" and "transmitted through a system of signs, including language, to others to influence their decisions or actions" (1991, 3). In the second edition, however, Kennedy writes that energy is "*imparted* to a communication to affect a situation in the interests of the speaker" (2006, 7; emphasis added). As something imparted, energy is separate from the subjects and objects who employ it and on which it acts. It is no longer within a particular sensorium but a component added to it from somewhere and by something else.

Kennedy follows Jacques Derrida that writing is prior to speech and "marking." Animals, according to Kennedy, expend energy through vocalization to mark space and social organization (1992, 14). He also states that "energy exists apart from living organisms and the energy of the life force, and thus rhetoric is perhaps a special case of the energy of all physics as known from subatomic particles" (13). Yet he cannot let go of the vitalism that might allow him to understand the rhetoric of rocks. Having already said that marking is not "prior to rhetoric among living creatures," Kennedy cannot undo his own conceptual knot to accept a nonmetaphorical marking that still persuades (14). That is, he cannot see how energy might itself be rhetorical, lacking correspondence to meaning yet always moving and on the move.

Or, perhaps more accurately, energy lacks any *single* correspondence to meaning because energy exists as multiple movements. Energy is a series of periodic amplitudes. It is interwoven with time. There is no need to "leave open the question of the qualities of being that made possible the evolution of both rhetoric and marking" (Kennedy 1992, 15) because rhetorical energy from its very outset is concerned with difference in time, with what changes from moment to moment and how to both sense and measure that change. Through concepts of energy expenditures and profitable markings by individual organisms, Kennedy reifies not only a European sense of being but a capitalist being who seeks to exploit and alienate rather than surrender and colabor.

We clearly need a different sense of rhetorical energy. While many cultural rhetorics pose a relativism among mental abstractions like imaginaries, ideologies, and representations, sensory rhetorics center on material bodies so that the rhetorics are "concerned with more than—and often something entirely other than—reason, rationality, or the symbolic work of language" (Hawhee 2015, 3). Bodies, then, provide a way to understand the energy of sensory rhetorics anew because it is not just epistemic frames that are relative to one another but bodies themselves. If we think of gravity through a rhetorical lens, we note that objects move relative to one another not because they sense the body of another but because of the inherent energy between them. It is not one body acting on another but the emergence of a change given a relation *between* bodies. Inherent relations in*form* bodies to the degree that, in the case of gravity, bodies not only move one another but also shape one another, just as the moon shapes tides.

Kennedy's imparted energy theorizes sensation as a Shannon-Weaver-type model of encoding and decoding messages—of energy as metaphor only (Shannon and Weaver 1949). But rhetorical energy can also be theorized like gravity, through an exposedness that Diane Davis (2010, 2) argues is "an originary (or preoriginary) rhetoricity—an affect*ability* or persuad*ability*—that is the condition for symbolic action." Relations come before symbolicity and subjectivity, or as Shawn Wilson (2008, 7) puts it, "relationships do not merely shape reality, they *are* reality." This is more like gravitational attraction and repulsion, where change happens *between* two bodies and in their mutual response-ability. Be it two planets or a rock and sunlight, change emerges in time and from a set of physically relative pathways within which energy contributes to the organization of a system. Energy works by weaving a *différance* of relations, to use Derrida's (1998) term for the continual marking yet deferral of sense.

If we follow the physics of energy, we soon hit upon how very queer it is.[3] From the energy that binds atoms into molecules to the very motion inherent in everything, energy is not only pervasive; it is also relative. Like *différance*, there is no authoritative or fundamental measure for energy's manifestations. Contemporary Western investigations of energy are at the basis of everything from speed to gravity to time. And there is an irony to how contemporary Western physics must work with two separate ontologies, the classical model and the quantum. While physicists try to combine these ontologies into a Grand Unified Theory, at this point at least, even Western reality cannot describe a single universe. That suggests a point with which to infect its discourse.

Dwelling on the Borders of Open and Closed Systems

Richard Coe's (1975) distinction between "open" and "closed" systems of rhetoric detailed something similar to rhetorical energy as *différance*. He describes how the energy input from an arm to pool stick to cue ball moves as a series of energy differences. Equations from mathematics can predict how matter and energy will move within the system because it is closed and the only energy of concern is kept within the system. As such, the system has a limited number of ways its elements can be arranged without altering it. It has low entropy.

However, if we make the same movement in an open system, such as striking a human being with the cue, then "the predictive process becomes more complex. Unlike a billiard ball, the person will respond not to the transfer of energy, but to the information which is carried by that energy. The energy for the response will come from that person's own energy system and the nature of the response will depend primarily on how that information is evaluated" (Coe 1975, 408). We can more fully understand Coe's description by adding that the energy of the pool cue moves through skin and muscle into the neuronal energy of sensation, just as I sketched out sunshine on skin. It transduces into other forms of energy and through various media. All this happens antecedent to meaning, *logos*, and subjectivity—under cover of darkness, as it were—because the arrangement of the system is affected by the movement of energy within it. The system has higher entropy, or more ways its parts can be arranged by the flow of energy.

For Coe, rhetoric is the work/play of difference in an ecologically thermodynamic system. As Coe (2001, 21) argues, "information is not matter, it is difference." Any difference is replete with information. As Coe sums pithily, "Information is in*form*ation only when it is in-formation" (15). The very *dispositio* of a body—its arrangement and disposition—is bound with its states of energy not as a subject or object of anything but coconstituted with them in multifarious and relational differences. We are not simply presented with an image when we see something; we are configured in a relation with it through a host of energetic pathways: light waves, bioelectricity, culture. Rhetorical energies flow and affect such pathways given our inherent capacities of response—an image of a loved one results in pupil dilation, color affects blood pressure. These are bodily responses only of a different, more complex mediation than sunlight on a rock because like data, sense is never given but made (Hong 2020).

Coe's (1974, 2) impetus is an attempt at "a movement from mechanistic to cybernetic thinking." However, he separates the epistemic from the ontological, replicating the anthropo- and biocentric divides of Western ontology. Helpfully, Derrida investigated such divides around the same time as Coe's eco-logic. Francesco Vitale (2014, 96) documents Derrida's 1975 seminar to retrace "*life* not only as one of the issues of deconstruction but as its very matrix, of thinking *différance* as the irreducible and structural condition of the life of the living and, thus, of *trace* and *text* as the structure of the stratified organization of life." Vitale distinguishes Derrida's overarching thesis, "there is no outside-text," to mean not, "in the wake of Heidegger and Gadamer, that only what is written in a book is the being that can be understood and, above all, that we can interpret everything as we interpret a book" but that "the trace is the condition of possibility of the living as well as the non-living, it structures the life of the living as a text" and "determines the relation of the living to the environment by responding to the laws of survival" (106). Derrida and Coe situate us in a relational and energetic *différance* of writing that saturates everything, not just biologic vitality.

Whereas Coe looks to follow cybernetics, Vitale (2014) shows Derrida's purpose in "deconstructing the very notion of model to point out the heuristic function ascribed to the cybernetic text as a model of the living is not only unable to account for the living itself but necessarily entails the reduction of what in the living escapes the hold of the cybernetic model while remaining the irreducible condition of the latter's structural possibility" (113). Similar to Barbara Biesecker's (1989, 112) understanding of provisional identities "of audience as effect-structure," there are not two different systems, one living and one not, both constituted by sensation or lack thereof. There is only a general system or economy of *différance*—a relational ontology in which nature's energy flow writes/marks both the living and the nonliving without intent. Writing is not just part of being human but a structuration of being-knowing-responding altogether because energy/matter is always in*form*ed through relations and any encounter presupposes in*form*ation. This is not a final ontology but the condition for ontologies and their lessons. *Différance* as the condition for rhetorical energy solves nothing but unsettles everything.

In understanding rhetoric as energy, sensory rhetorics have already begun tracing out *différance* as a flow of energy. Energy transduces across the living and nonliving, taking on various forms: kinetic, chemical, thermal, potential, and so on. Transduction has its own importance here. Casey Boyle, James Brown Jr., and Steph Ceraso (2018, 257) discuss digital transductivity, or "how a signal moves across disparate registers of relations: neural firings move to fingers to perform keystrokes that then transform into electrical charges that then become digital bits and are delivered to a screen by software or saved to a hard drive that becomes transcoded again whenever someone opens a file." However, transduction cannot be thought of separately from entropy since energies scatter and leak. Energy/difference is never separate from a body and its environment. Boyle (2018, 80) separately extends this idea of transduction to rhetoric as a posthuman practice in "the assumption that any given structure that exists only exists as a metastable identity momentarily taking place across multiple registers through a process of becoming." Beings and their identities are always multiple and capable of being affected by energies already inherent in their ecology—those energies on which their survival depends. We are what we relate.

Perhaps more accurately, we are *because* we relate. The rock is rock because it is in relation to the sun that shines upon it, the earth on which it rests, and the air that flows over it. It cannot be any other rock because that other body will have different relations and will be in*form*ed as such, not as a text to be read but as a textile woven with its environment. This is why the in*form*ation of colonized and Indigenous people is so vitally important. Not only have they been ripped from the weave of their places; they also are in dire need of restitching relations back together, and as they restitch, they may help lead others toward more sustainable options for their fellow humans. While my project here infects the Euro-Western tradition with its own incommensurabilities, it does so to open spaces to attend to non-Euro-Western lessons and ways of making sense.

Information and Thermodynamics of Epiphylogenesis

To exemplify a route I propose here, I turn to the protests over the building of the Thirty-Meter Telescope (TMT), the largest of thirteen already established atop Mauna Kea in Hawai'i. The siting of the telescope renewed attention to Indigenous Hawaiian claims that the mountain is "an ancestor to the Hawaiian people" (Yoshimura 2021) and an abode for spirits. The "discursive infrastructure" (Frith 2020, 401) of law and science composed the situation in ways that have excluded pluriversal options of relating to the mountain, thus blocking the rhetorical energy of Indigenous Hawaiians and their world from taking any in*form*ational role.[4] It is not simply the ability of Hawaiians to tell their stories and represent Mauna Kea in their own way that is at stake. It is, instead, the very fabric of the Hawaiian world and the constitution of that world through their relations with the mountain, each other, and colonial powers. They cannot *be* Hawaiian when their ways of relating to Mauna Kea are circumscribed by settler colonial power.

In 2015, David Ige, governor of Hawai'i, temporarily halted construction of the TMT, saying, "We have in many ways failed the mountain. Whether you see it from a cultural perspective or from a natural resource perspective, we have not done right by a very special place and we must act immediately to change that" (Hawai'i Office of the Governor 2015). The bifurcation of perspectives here is telling. Either the claims are cultural, grounded in epistemology, and relative to human beliefs, or they are natural, grounded in Western ontology, and relative to scientific verification. Beyond that, the term "resource" further underscores possessive and extractive ends, where nature ultimately serves capitalist society. The terministic screens of Governor Ige work to hide the relational dimension that Indigenous Hawaiians have with Mauna Kea, a relation that affects their own being *as* Hawaiians. Were Ige's call taken seriously, the mountain itself, irrespective of human use or resource, would be centered since it is the mountain that has been failed.

But Western science works rhetorically to define reality. What proceeds through environmental impact statements, zoning policies, engineering documentation, police reports, and courts of law tilts heavily toward knowledge as universal, nature as separate from human, and relations as secondary and subsequent to being. It is a colonial reality that erases Hawaiian reality to inscribe its own. In 2017, Hawai'i's Department of Land and Natural Resources (HDLNR) ruled that the TMT met eight important criteria outlined in Hawai'i Administrative Rule 13-5-30(c) and did so by restricting its finding to apply to a strict definition of "natural resources" as understood in

Western ontology. The finding reads, in part, "the TMT project will not cause substantial adverse impact to existing plants, aquatic life, and wildlife, cultural, historic, and archaeological sites, minerals, recreational sites, geologic sites, scenic areas, ecologically significant areas, and watersheds" (Hawai'i Board of Land and Natural Resources 2017, 221). Moreover, in HDLNR's findings for the criterion that "the proposed land use will not be materially detrimental to the public health, safety, and welfare," it dismissed testimony from Joseph Keawe'aimoku Kaholokua, associate professor and chair of the Department of Native Hawaiian Health at the University of Hawai'i at Manoa, because "he did not do any research directly relating to the TMT project, did not perform any clinical examinations of opponents of the TMT Project, and he was not aware of studies regarding partitioning the cause of stress allegedly from TMT and Mauna Kea from all other stress-causing factors for native Hawaiians, including poverty, single parenthood, and systemic diseases" (235). In short, cultural impacts were assessed by HDLNR through a narrow lens of Western medical diagnosis and treatment, neglecting any sense of relationality with the mountain as an important factor. Its diagnosis was not sufficiently in*form*ed through an incorporation of Hawaiian lessons about Mauna Kea that point to her own well-being as also constitutive of healthy Hawaiian identity. Instead, the rhetorical energy was channeled through white, Western bodies and for white, Western sensibilities.

Decisions that remove relationality like this deny more than claimants' systems of thought; they also deny claimants' own *technics of being*, where things like a sacred mountain may be necessary to make sense of one's world. In Coe's pool analogy, the resolution of the system depends on the relations between who is involved and how: a whole technics of attitude, historical circumstance, sensitivity, and other habitual and decisive *options* of being. Were there indications of ire or annoyance? Did the people involved have a history of joking, or were they rivals with short tempers? How hard was the strike of the cue on another body? Energy is always already present in the system, and the strike neither adds nor subtracts; it only in*form*s.

So it is not just that Hawaiians represent Mauna Kea but that their very interface with the world through stories, language, and practices—their cultural infrastructure (Read 2019)—has shaped both Mauna Kea and themselves. Non-Hawaiians may not be able to relate with the deep history of the mountain or how relations have both shaped and been shaped by Hawaiian people. Yet those aspects are still important for the ongoing survivance of Hawaiian people. Stories, languages, and practices of relating are threatened by the more powerful colonial structures of telescopic astronomy and

Enlightenment logocentric jurisprudence. Building more and larger telescopes threatens the very ability of Indigenous Hawaiians to be Hawaiian.

We can see this as an instance of Coe's "Information is in*form*ation only when it is in-formation." The being of the mountain engenders different representations but also different in*form*ation that is literally and materially responsive to how we make sense in relation. The very approach and orientation to what Mauna Kea is depends on where we are in the fabric of its weave. A warm rock affords a lizard the means to raise its metabolism while also affording a surface for a human to cook piki bread. In another arrangement of *différance*, the same rock affords shelter or perhaps a position of ambush to a spider. Its rough surface affords habitat for lichen and tardigrades. Entire worlds collide because the rock is all that it *relates*.

Toward Pluriversal Spacetimes

The rock scene from *Everything Everywhere All at Once* quoted in my epigraph takes place in "one of the universes where the conditions weren't right for life to form." The film is built around the idea of multiple universes inhabited by the same individuals with oddly different features or contexts. This is an imaginative adaptation of a scientific theory known as the "Everett interpretation" of quantum mechanics. According to this theory, quantum-level information exchange resolves in the creation of alternate universes. Hence, Everett's theory is sometimes called the "many-worlds interpretation." If a single rock is a set of differences depending on who perceives or engages with it on a material level and no privileged perception or engagement can grasp its totality and, further, if each perception or engagement transduces energy, thus implying temporal duration, then we can say that even according to the best scientific knowledge springing from the European Enlightenment, there cannot be a single universe but rather a pluriverse, or "a world of many worlds," as anticolonial scholars and activists have said. This, I submit, is our infecting agent—the self-contradiction that corrupts Western ontological biocentrism and that might help move some people to "turn away from cultural relativism through the expression of cultural rhetoric through whiteness's own representations" (Homer 2022, 5).

Thus, we might revise our understanding of sensory rhetorics and their energies. The energies are not relative to cultural imaginaries or to biological sense perception but are an ontological flow of *différance* that weaves worlds between the living and the nonliving. This brings ungeneralizable relations to the fore as distinct pathways for the transduction of rhetorical energy across multiple vectors. The conceptual affects the material and vice versa as energies flow through systems and in*form* them. As Margaret Price's (2024) work in disability rhetorics has shown, time, space, and environments are integral to our relational sense-making. If there is no absolute time, then time, space, and environments are not just encountered differently but are ontically different because we cannot help but in*form* them through our relations. Our emplacements make spacetime itself. Price also argues that while collective accountability to others "can be built through gathering of various kinds, we cannot ignore the fact that [accountability] occurs *through and because of* harm, not in spite of harm" (177). It is the electric zap of an energy differential that leads us to our creative, in*form*ational gatherings.

Perhaps most importantly, this flow of sensible energetic *différance* avoids the subjective cast of adjudicating between cultural "texts" as final resolutions of what is and moves us toward the larger project of asking which worlds and ways of being we support and want to be accountable to. It can act as a rhetorical frame check so that we look less at the preservation of identity for identity's sake and more at how our identity or identities shape the worlds we will bequeath to those who follow. As Joy recounts about the lifeless universe where she and Evelyn are rocks, "most of them are like this, actually." The film invites us to ask, Which worlds will we make possible and for whom?

Notes

1. Ke te bi—thank you—to Anita Kapayou and Wayne Pushetonequa of the Meskwaki Language Preservation program.
2. Pilamiya—many thanks—to so many elders for sharing their time and stories: Leksi James Reidy, Francis White Lance, and Danny Seaboy in particular.
3. I follow Karen Barad's (2015) notion of energy and/as queerness here.
4. I rely here solely on printed transcripts to discern the discursive infrastructure. For a more direct account, see Homer 2022.

References

Barad, Karen. 2015. "Transmaterialities: Trans*/Matter/Realities and Queer Political Imaginings." *GLQ* 21 (2–3): 387–422.

Bennett, Jane. 2009. *Vibrant Matter: A Political Ecology of Things*. Durham: Duke University Press.

Biesecker, Barbara. 1989. "Rethinking the Rhetorical Situation from Within the Thematic of Différance." *Philosophy and Rhetoric* 22 (2): 110–30.

Boyle, Casey. 2018. *Rhetoric as a Posthuman Practice*. Columbus: The Ohio State University Press.

Boyle, Casey, James Brown Jr., and Steph Ceraso. 2018. "The Digital: Rhetoric Behind and Beyond the Screen." *Rhetoric Society Quarterly* 48 (3): 251–59.

Cadena, Marisol de la, and Mario Blaser. 2018. *A World of Many Worlds*. Durham: Duke University Press.

Cedillo, Christina V. 2022. "Smoke and Mirrors: Re-Creating Material Relation(ship)s Through Mexica Story." In *Decolonial Conversations in Posthuman and New Material Rhetorics*, edited by Jennifer Clary-Lemon and David M. Grant, 92–114. Columbus: The Ohio State University Press.

Coe, Richard. 1974. "Rhetoric 2001." *Freshman English News* 3 (Spring): 1–3, 9–13.

———. 1975. "Closed System Composition." *ETC: A Review of General Semantics* 32 (December): 403–12.

———. 2001. "'Rhetoric 2001' in 2001." *Composition Studies* 29 (2): 11–35.

Cunningham, Nijah. 2023. "Heliology: On the Metaphor of Decolonization." *Representations* 162 (1): 44–55.

Cushman, Ellen, Rachel Jackson, Annie Nichols, Courtney Rivard, Amanda Moulder, Chelsea Murdock, David M. Grant, and Heather Brook Adams. 2019. "Decolonizing Projects: Creating Pluriversal Possibilities in Rhetoric." *Rhetoric Review* 38 (1): 1–22.

Davis, Diane. 2010. *Inessential Solidarity: Rhetoric and Foreigner Relations*. Pittsburgh: Pittsburgh University Press.

Derrida, Jacques. 1998. *Of Grammatology*. Translated by Gayatri Chakravorty Spivak. Baltimore: Johns Hopkins University Press.

Fanon, Frantz. 1967. *The Wretched of the Earth*. Harmondsworth, UK: Penguin.

Frith, Jordan. 2020. "Technical Standards and a Theory of Writing as Infrastructure." *Written Communication* 37 (3): 401–27.

García, Romeo, Damián Baca, and Ellen Cushman. 2024. "Practicing Pluriversal Literacies." In *Pluriversal Literacies: Tools for Perseverance and Livable Futures*, edited by Romeo García, Damián Baca, and Ellen Cushman, 3–27. Pittsburgh: University of Pittsburgh Press.

Grosfoguel, Ramón. 2011. "Decolonizing Post-Colonial Studies and Paradigms of Political-Economy: Transmodernity, Decolonial Thinking, and Global Coloniality." *Transmodernity: Journal of Peripheral Cultural Production of the Ludo-Hispanic World* 1 (1). https://dx.doi.org/10.5070/T411000004.

Hawai'i Board of Land and Natural Resources. 2017. "Findings of Fact, Conclusions of Law and Decision of Order." *Contested Case Hearing Re: Conservation District Use Application (CDUA) HA-3568 for the Thirty Meter Telescope at the Mauna Kea Science Preserve*. Case Number: BLNR-CC-16-002. https://dlnr.hawaii.gov/occl/tmt/.

Hawai'i Office of the Governor. 2015. "Governor Ige's Transcribed Mauna Kea Story." https://dlnr.hawaii.gov/mk/files/2016/10/B.01n-Gov-Iges-10-point-plan.pdf.

Hawhee, Debra. 2015. "Rhetoric's Sensorium." *Quarterly Journal of Speech* 101 (1): 2–17.

Homer, Matthew. 2022. "Towards a Decolonial Haole Rhetoric." PhD diss., Virginia Polytechnic Institute and State University.

Hong, Sun-ha. 2020. *Technologies of Speculation: The Limits of Knowledge in a Data-Driven Society*. New York: New York University Press.

Kennedy, George. 1991. *On Rhetoric: A Theory of Civic Discourse*. Oxford: Oxford University Press.

———. 1992. "A Hoot in the Dark." *Philosophy and Rhetoric* 25 (1): 1–21.

———. 2006. *On Rhetoric: A Theory of Civic Discourse*. 2nd ed. Oxford: Oxford University Press.

Kwan, Daniel, and Daniel Scheinert, dirs. 2022. *Everything Everywhere All at Once*. Film. IAC Films.

Mignolo, Walter. 2022. "The Zapatistas's Theoretical Revolution: Its Historical, Ethical, and Political Consequences." *Review* (Fernand Braudel Center) 25 (3): 245–75.

Muckelbauer, John. 2016. "Implicit Paradigms of Rhetoric: Aristotelian, Cultural, and Heliotropic." In *Rhetoric, Through Everyday Things*, edited by Scot Barnett and Casey Boyle, 30–41. Tuscaloosa: University of Alabama Press.

Nietzsche, Friedrich. 1990. "On Truth and Lies in a Nonmoral Sense." In *Philosophy and Truth, Selections from Nietzsche's Notebooks of the Early 1870s*, edited and translated by Daniel Breazeale, 79–191. Atlantic Highlands, NJ: Humanities Press.

Pflugfelder, Ehren. 2022. *Geoengineering, Persuasion, and the Climate Crisis: A Geologic Rhetoric*. Tuscaloosa: University of Alabama Press.

Price, Margaret. 2024. *Crip Spacetime: Access, Failure, and Accountability*. Durham: Duke University Press.

Read, Sarah. 2019. "The Infrastructural Function: A Relational Theory of Infrastructure for Writing Studies." *Journal of Business and Technical Communication* 33 (3): 233–67.

Schelly, Chelsey, Valerie Gagnon, Kristin Arola, Andrew Fiss, Marie Schaefer, and

Kathleen E. Halvorsen. 2021. "Cultural Imaginaries or Incommensurable Ontologies? Relationality and Sovereignty as Worldviews in Socio-Technological System Transitions." *Energy Research and Social Science* 80 (October): 1–7.

Shannon, Claude E. and Warren Weaver. 1949. *The Mathematical Theory of Communication*. Urbana: University of Illinois Press.

Vitale, Francesco. 2014. "The Text and the Living: Jacques Derrida Between Biology and Deconstruction." *Oxford Literary Review* 36 (1): 95–114.

Wells, Justine, Bridie McGreavy, Samantha Senda-Cook, and George F. McHendry Jr. 2018. "Introduction: Rhetoric's Ecologies." In *Tracing Rhetoric and Material Life: Ecological Approaches*, edited by Bridie McGreavy, Justine Wells, George F. McHendry Jr., and Samantha Senda-Cook, 1–36. London: Palgrave Macmillan.

Wilson, Shawn. 2008. *Research Is Ceremony: Indigenous Research Methods*. Halifax, NS: Fernwood.

Yoshimura, Kailee. 2021. "Astronomers Want the Thirty-Meter Telescope on a Sacred Hawaiʻian Summit. But Who Is It For?" *Massive Science*, June 20. https://massivesci.com/articles/opinion-hawaii-telescope-tmt-imperialism-astronomy/.

After(WORD)

JUSTIN ECKSTEIN

Text offers opportunities for sensory engagement—sensory knowledge flows through the act of reading—and has become so naturalized that we often forget that there are other ways of knowing and experiencing rhetorical force. John Mowitt (1992, 14) argues that the text became "irreducibly entangled in disciplinary politics" and lists a number of contingent pressures that produced the text. These pressures included the neoliberal restructuring of academic institutions that demanded new forms of scholarly legitimacy, an interdisciplinary crisis that pushed scholars to reconsider the foundations of cultural interpretation, and the influential work of the Tel Quel group, which included theorists like Roland Barthes, Jacques Derrida, and Julia Kristeva. The importance of the text spread throughout the academy in what we know as the linguistic turn. Famously, Clifford Geertz's influential method of "thick description" demonstrated how virtually any social phenomenon—from cockfights to ritual dances—could be "read" as a text.

The reliance on text as a master metaphor for sensation and experience imposes specific limitations that extend far beyond rhetoric into the humanities writ large. When we assume that cultural phenomena must function as text, we force them to follow grammatical logic; meaning becomes atomized into discrete parts that must be read. More than just reducing experience to language, textualism imposes an ordered sense of space: binary, linear, following single causal lines. The imagined consumer becomes a solitary reader reflecting on words, whether this assumption is explicit in our criticism or implicit in our theoretical models.

Against this backdrop, David Le Breton emerged as a crucial figure in sensory studies during a pivotal moment in French intellectual history. Working alongside Maurice Merleau-Ponty's phenomenology and Michel Foucault's cultural theory, Le Breton developed a unique approach to understanding how social and historical forces shape bodily experience and sensation. While Foucault analyzed how power disciplines bodies and Merleau-Ponty explored embodied perception, Le Breton investigated how different cultures create distinct sensory orders. His 1970s research in sensory anthropology challenged the notion of universal sensory experience, demonstrating instead how societies train bodies to perceive and respond in culturally specific ways. This work provided essential tools for understanding how cultures develop their own sensory hierarchies and distinct modes of feeling, perceiving, and knowing the world.

Consider how psychedelic ritual practices in a Peruvian coastal village demonstrate the complex interplay between material capacities, cultural frameworks, and enhanced forms of agency. The San Pedro cactus's material properties (containing mescaline) create specific physiological possibilities for altered perception. However, these material capacities only become meaningful through cultural cultivation. As Le Breton (2017, 15) writes, practitioners must "interiorize the code for deciphering the flood of images, acquiring a perception free from the scoria of everyday life and immersed in the spirit world." This training transforms raw sensory experience into meaningful clairvoyance, enabling practitioners to access and navigate spiritual realms. Crucially, this enhanced perceptual agency is not simply a natural result of the cactus's chemical properties. Rather, as Le Breton explains, "The emotional climate that binds the community is not natural; it is not the result of physiological processes inherent in the chemical properties of the drug. This emotional response is not a primary but a secondary effect. It is a symbolic process, that is to say, a learning process that is integral to the community members" (16). The example thus reveals how new forms of sensory agency emerge through the intersection of material possibilities (the cactus's chemical properties), cultural training (learning to interpret visions), and collective practice (the shared ceremonial context). Neither purely physical nor purely cultural, this form of sensing demonstrates how bodies can develop entirely new sensory capabilities when material and social forces are cultivated together.

Sensory frameworks are inherently rhetorical: They shape how communities understand and act on sensory experiences, creating shared vocabularies and interpretive frameworks that mediate our collective relationship with the sensory world. Understanding how these sensory regimes emerge and function becomes increasingly urgent as technological advancement accelerates the creation of new ways of sensing and knowing. We might even understand contemporary technological innovations as creating new forms of "technological clairvoyance," allowing us to "see" patterns in data or experience virtual worlds in ways that extend beyond ordinary perception. This suggests that as we develop new technologies, we must simultaneously develop cultural frameworks that help us meaningfully interpret and navigate these expanded sensory capabilities.

Unlike other approaches to the body as a stable entity, sensory rhetorics recognize the body as a historically contingent assemblage shaped by available technologies. From this perspective, we have a new way to understand bodies as a profusion of sensory experience as we emerge in materiality—vibrations, photons, odors, particles, and forces. The senses provide a limit of the world to each person; like a concentric circle, senses provide an embodied horizon of the knowable. Each new technological extension, from writing to microscopes to digital storage, reorganizes our entire sensory system and creates new possibilities for relating to the world. Writing externalized thought and enabled abstract reasoning, and wheels extended our capacity for movement; microscopes revealed previously invisible realms, and digital technologies transformed how we store and process information. These examples demonstrate how human capacities are not fixed but are continually reconfigured through their relationship with technological and material environments.

The relationship between sensation and rhetoric has long challenged scholars, from Plato's skepticism of sensory experience to contemporary methodological debates about embodied knowledge. This collection intervenes in that conversation by demonstrating how sensation demands rhetorical analysis precisely because it operates at the intersection of the subjective and objective, the material and the cultural. Through cases ranging from the political deployment of disgust to Indigenous ways of sensing place, from the transformative experiences of gender-affirming surgery to the sonic experience of colonial power in settler archives, these chapters reveal how communities develop distinct sensory orders that shape what can be felt, known, and communicated. In doing so, they advance our understanding of rhetoric as a material-semiotic force that works through multiple registers—tactile, sonic, olfactory, gustatory, visual—to structure both individual experience and collective action.

Sensory Rhetorics provides a vital framework for understanding how bodies, technologies, and cultural practices intersect to shape our collective experiences and capacities for action. This volume offers a rich understanding of rhetoric as a material-semiotic process that both constrains and enables new forms of sensing, knowing, and being in the world. The cases presented in this collection show how sensory frameworks are neither purely subjective nor purely objective but rather originate from the cultivation of material possibilities and cultural practices that create specific modes of perception and interpretation. *Sensory Rhetorics* illustrates that rhetoric is both a mode of power that structures sensory experience and a means of resistance that can create alternative ways of sensing and knowing—that the rhetorical process involves not just how we interpret sensations but how different assemblages of material forces, technological capabilities, and cultural practices create the very conditions for what can be sensed, known, and communicated in the first place.

A rhetorical approach to sensation necessarily begins from the recognition that bodies themselves are sites of contested meaning, shaped through ongoing interactions between material conditions and cultural interpretations. This is not simply to say that different cultures interpret bodily sensations differently but rather that the very capacity for sensation emerges through specific material-semiotic arrangements. The physical properties of sensation—whether sound waves, chemical reactions, or light patterns—gain meaning and force only through their embedding in cultural frameworks that determine what counts as meaningful perception. Yet these frameworks are neither singular nor stable. Multiple sensory regimes can and do coexist, each offering different possibilities for experiencing and interpreting the same material phenomena. This multiplicity reveals how sensory experience is fundamentally rhetorical—not because sensations are merely constructed through discourse but because they emerge through specific configurations of material forces and cultural practices that shape what can be felt, known, and communicated.

The body's instability and technological-cultural constitution becomes evident when we examine how sensory capabilities develop and transform over time. From basic perceptual processes to complex cultural practices, bodies demonstrate remarkable plasticity in developing new sensory capacities through engagement with both material and social forces. Regardless of whether they are ancient tools or modern digital systems, technologies do not simply extend existing bodily capacities but fundamentally reshape what bodies can sense and how those sensations are understood. Cultural frameworks determine not only how sensations are interpreted but what counts as sensation itself, what forms of perception are considered legitimate, and whose sensory experiences matter. It is worth repeating: This dynamic reveals sensation as neither purely subjective nor purely objective but rather as emerging through cultivated arrangements of material possibilities and cultural practices that create specific modes of perception and interpretation.

This collection uses case studies to demonstrate that sensory rhetorics are a powerful tool for understanding and addressing the complex issues of our time, particularly issues related to politics, technology, the environment, and social justice. The authors are not trying to deduce universal principles about rhetoric; rather, they are analyzing how sensory experiences shape our understanding of rhetoric in specific contexts. Thus, their writing is a form of practical reasoning, moving between sensory experiences (the smell of a paper mill, the feel of soil) and broader cultural patterns without attempting to abstract away from the embodied nature of these experiences. Each chapter operates through engagement with cases and concrete experiences rather than through abstract theoretical systems. The chapters collectively advance a practical philosophy grounded in sensation and embodied experience as sources of knowledge and judgment. They show how practical reasoning continues to operate through local, timely, and particular sensory engagements rather than abstract universal principles.

When we expand to a history of sensation, our basic understanding of the body and its capacity is recognized as contingent. Whether we consider artificial intelligence's ability to process vast amounts of data, virtual reality's creation of immersive digital environments, or various cultures' engagement with spiritual realms, we see similar patterns of new sensory possibilities being shaped by both material capabilities and cultural frameworks for judgment. Just as shamanic practices required cultural systems to make "sound" judgments about altered states, our engagement with artificial intelligence and immersive technologies requires frameworks for both experiencing and evaluating these expanded sensory capabilities. Each new sensory regime must develop its own criteria for what constitutes "sound" practice, with regard to both the material sensations it makes possible and the forms of judgment it enables (Eckstein 2025). The lessons from historical and contemporary sensory practices suggest that successful adaptation will depend on developing cultural systems that can meaningfully interpret and evaluate these expanded sensory capabilities while remaining attentive to questions of power, justice, and collective well-being.

To conclude, I want to point out two (among many) possible future directions for sensory rhetorics. First, we must examine how emerging technologies like artificial intelligence, virtual/augmented reality, and biomedical enhancements shift our understanding of individual sensations. Emerging technologies redefine agency, which challenges traditional notions of individual action and impact. Just as Le Breton's analysis of shamanic practices revealed how cultural frameworks shape the interpretation of altered states, we need theoretical tools to understand how communities develop frameworks for making sense of algorithmic perception, synthetic environments, and technologically augmented bodies. This includes investigating how different cultures and communities develop distinct approaches to integrating and evaluating these new sensory capabilities.

Second, we must deepen our understanding of how power operates through sensory frameworks in an increasingly globalized and technologically mediated world. As technological intervention and cultural contestation are unequally distributed, questions of justice and collective well-being become paramount. How do different communities resist or repurpose dominant sensory regimes? What kinds of cultural frameworks can help ensure that expanded sensory capabilities serve collective flourishing rather than intensifying existing inequalities? These questions demand that we consider specific cases and contexts while remaining cognizant of broader patterns in how sensation, technology, and power intersect to shape human experience and possibility.

References

Eckstein, Justin. 2025. *Sound Tactics: Auditory Power in Political Protests*. University Park: Pennsylvania State University Press.

Le Breton, David. 2017. *Sensing the World: An Anthropology of the Senses*. Translated by Carmen Ruschiensky. London: Bloomsbury.

Mowitt, John. 1992. *Text: The Genealogy of an Antidisciplinary Object*. Durham: Duke University Press.

Contributors

Kerry Banazek is an associate professor of rhetoric and professional communication and the director of the Creative Research Center at New Mexico State University. Her research explores the ways histories of description, visualization, and technology intersect.

Natalie Bennie is a PhD student in communication arts and sciences at Penn State University. She studies the broad linkages among memory, social change, and deliberation. Her current projects involve discussions of activism, performance, and memory conflicts in the US South.

Kyle S. Bond is a PhD candidate in rhetoric and composition at Florida State University. He has published scholarship in *English Journal*, *Thomas Hardy Journal*, and *Dialogue*. He is coauthor with Romeo García of two essays in the volume *Latter-day Eloquence: Two Centuries of Mormon Oratory* (forthcoming).

Justin Eckstein is an associate professor of communication, media, and design arts at Pacific Lutheran University and affiliated faculty in the Department of Communication at the University of Washington. He is the author of *Sound Tactics: Auditory Power in Political Protests* and coeditor of *Cookery: Food Rhetorics and Social Production*.

Margot Finn teaches undergraduate classes on food at the University of Michigan. Her 2017 book *Discriminating Taste: How Class Anxiety Created the American Food Revolution* investigates how social class has shaped popular US media narratives about food. Her writing has also been featured in the anthology *Food Fights: How History Matters to Contemporary Food Debates* and in *Breakthrough Journal*, *Slate*, and *Vox*.

Benjamin Firgens is an assistant professor of communication at Mount St. Mary's University. He studies how debates over technology allow publics to imagine and contest their futures and explores past developments in the social construction of technology to make sense of current trends in digital culture.

Romeo García is an assistant professor of writing and rhetoric studies at the University of Utah. His research appears in *College Composition and Communication*, *Rhetoric Society Quarterly*, *Across the Disciplines*, and *Rhetoric, Politics, and Culture*. He is coeditor of *Rhetorics Elsewhere and Otherwise: Contested Modernities, Decolonial Visions, Unsettling*

Archival Research: Engaging Critical, Communal, and Digital Archives, *Pluriversal Literacies: Tools for Perseverance and Livable Futures*, and *Community Listening: Stories, Hauntings, Possibilities*.

David M. Grant is a professor of technical communication at the University of Northern Iowa and coeditor of *Decolonial Conversations in Posthuman and New Material Rhetorics*. His most recent work appeared in *Rhetorical Ecologies*. He is the 2024 recipient of the CCCC Outstanding Teaching Award.

Ames Hawkins is a transgenre writer and the author of the award-winning work of literary nonfiction *These Are Love(d) Letters*. A professor of English and creative writing at Columbia College Chicago and director of the School of Communication and Culture, Hawkins also cohosted and coproduced the scholarly podcast *Masters of Text*.

Bryan W. Moe is an instructor in Southern California. His research focuses on the intersection of rhetoric, social movements, and food. His publications include chapters in *Handbook for Food and Popular Culture* and *Global Brooklyn: Designing Food Experiences in World Cities*.

Christa J. Olson is a professor of composition and rhetoric at the University of Wisconsin–Madison specializing in transamerican visual cultures, nationalism, and public life. She is the author of two books, *Constitutive Visions: Indigeneity and Commonplaces of National Identity in Republican Ecuador* and *American Magnitude: Hemispheric Vision and Public Feeling in the United States*, and coauthor of *On Visual Rhetoric* (forthcoming).

Lisa L. Phillips is an assistant professor of English at Texas Tech University in the Technical Communication and Rhetoric Program. Her 2025 book *Olfactory Rhetoric: Sniffing Out Environmental Problems* elaborates on ideas shared in this collection. She is also coeditor of *Grassroots Activisms: Public Rhetorics in Localized Contexts*.

Kellie Sharp-Hoskins is a professor of rhetoric and professional communication at New Mexico State University, where her research and teaching center rhetorical bodies and boundaries as well as methodologies designed to intervene in their differential mattering. She is the author of *Rhetoric in Debt*.

Kelly Williams Nagel is a lecturer in the Department of Communication at Baylor University in Waco, Texas. She is a scholar of public memory and visual rhetorics with a particular interest in how communities handle memory sites with controversial legacies.

Index

Page numbers in italics denote figures, and endnotes are indicated by "n" followed by the endnote number.

Abramowitz, Alan, 38
acceleration, logics of, 43, 44–49, 52–55
accumulation, logics of, 46–47, 48, 54, 55
Ace, Sam, 93
activist archival work, 64
    See also antiracist activism
Adams, Jonathan, 55
Adaptive Rhetoric (Parrish), 61
aesthetics
    aesthetic cohesion and coherence, 132
    coloniality as aesthetic, 128–31
    See also colonized sensory archives
affect, emotion and feeling vs., 6, 21n2
"African Dawn" (Fodéba), 151
agency, sensory, 165, 169
aisthēsis (sense experience), 129–31, 134, 142
Alexander, Jonathan, 93–94
Alexandria Community Remembrance Project (ACRP), 75, 76–77, 84, 85
Algonquin languages, 148–49
ambient rhetoric, 8
ambiguity. *See* not-knowing; uncertainty
Americanity, 130, 131, 138, 140
American Magnitude (Olson), 15
anthropology, 3, 12–13, 165
antiracist activism
    engaging sensory public memory, 77–78
    race, memory and the senses, 78–80
    rhetorical field methods, 80–83
    sensory rhetorics beyond academia, 89–90
    soil collection ceremony, 75–76, 83–89, *87*, *88*
archives
    activist archival work, 64
    archival impressions, 130, 141, 142
    landscapes as, 128
    music as sensory archive, 138
    See also colonized sensory archives
Aristotle, 7, 8, 9, 21n3
Arola, Kristin, 150–51
art, 97, 101, 102–5, 107, 108
artificial intelligence, 168, 169
A to Z of Creative Writing Methods (van Loon), 103
attention, digital marketplaces and, 50
augmented reality, 52, 169
autokinesis
    meaning and sensation, 114–17
    as metaphor for disorientation, 120–23
    normative theories of sense and, 117–20
    as possibility, 123–26
    rethinking meaninglessness, 112–14
awe
    not-knowing as space of, 99–105, *101*
    potential in, 105–8, *107*
    sense-making through not-knowing, 92–95, 109n7
    through numbness, 95–99, *97*
Azoulay, Ariella, 124

Baca, Damián, 149
Baldwin, James, 128
Barthes, Roland, 164
Bates, Julie Collins, 64
Beasley, Vanessa, 21n1
Bennett, Jane, 148
Benoit, William, 142
Bethards, Jack, 136
Biesecker, Barbara, 156–57
biocentrism, 148–49, 151, 160
Black communities
    antiracist activism, 75–76, 83–89, *87*, *88*
    race, memory and the senses, 78–80
    See also antiracist activism
Blaszczyk, Regina Lee, 49

blindsight, 118–19
bodies and embodiment
    the body as epistemological source, 81–83, 166–68
    embodiment of history, 128
    not-knowing as embodied knowing, 93, 100–101
    in rhetorical studies, 12
    seeing as embodied experience, 15–16
    somatic wonder, 99–105, *101*
Book of Mormon (Smith), 134, 139, 140
Bourdieu, Pierre, 31
Boyle, Casey, 44, 49, 55, 157
Bradshaw, Jonathan L., 46
Brilliat-Savarin, Jean Anthelme, 30
Brown, James, Jr., 157
Bullard, Robert, 70
Bulova, Gretchen, 77

Campbell, Colin, 36
Campbell, Karolyn Kohrs, 9
capitalism
    accumulation and, 46–47
    experience economy, 49–52
    proliferation and, 48–49
    See also digital sense-making
Ceraso, Steph, 157
Chávez, Karma R., 81
Christianity, use of music in, 133
Church of Jesus Christ of Latter-day Saint (LDS)
    church-settler hymnody, 135–38
    sense models and sense processes in, 132–33
    terms, codes and tropes, 138–42
    use of music, 133–34
    See also colonized sensory archives
Cicero, 7
Cixous, Hélène, 96
class, taste and, 31
Classen, Constance, 3
classical thought, sensory language in, 6–8
Clinton, Hillary, 33–34
Coe, Richard, 155–56, 159
collective sensory exchanges, 14–16, 21n3
colonialism
    biocentrism and, 149, 151
    coloniality as epistemic and aesthetic, 128–31
    countering colonial ontologies, 150–52
    sound and, 133–35
    See also colonized sensory archives; in*form*ing rhetoric
colonized sensory archives
    church-settler hymnody, 135–38

coloniality as epistemic and aesthetic, 128–31
    delinking the senses, 131–33
    rewriting the senses, 129–30, 142
    sound and decoloniality, 133–35
    terms, codes and tropes, 138–42
Community Soil Collection Project
    engaging sensory public memory, 77–78
    race, memory and the senses, 78–80
    rhetorical field methods, 80–83
    sensory rhetorics beyond academia, 89–90
    soil collection ceremony, 75–76, 83–89, *87*, *88*
"conflict cafés," 37–38
consensus, ideal of, 114–17, 120–21, 125
consumption and sensation. *See* digital sense-making
cosmologies, imaginaries vs., 150–51
COVID-19 pandemic, 1–2
Cracker Barrel restaurant, 26–27, 29–31
crafting, 97, *101*, 102–5, *107*, 108
Cram, E., 79, 82
creative-critical scholarship, 99–105, *101*
Crenshaw, Kimberlé, 62
Crowley, Sharon, 9
cultural-material intersectionality, 165–68
culture, rhetorically inherited, 130–31
Cunningham, Nijah, 151–52
Cushman, Ellen, 149
Cvetkovich, Ann, 108

Darwin, Charles, 28
Daston, Lorraine, 124
Davis, Audrey, 77
Davis, Diane, 154
death spaces, 128–29
decoloniality
    biocentrism and, 149, 151, 160
    pluriversal ontologies, 12, 150–52
    sound and, 133–35
    See also collective sensory exchanges; in*form*ing rhetoric
Deleuze, Gilles, 16
demi-rhetorical framings, 121
De oratore (Cicero), 7
Derrida, Jacques, 8, 153, 155, 156, 164
Descartes, René, 133
Deseret, idea of, 130, 138, 140, 141
DeVoss, Dànielle, 45
Dickson, Greg, 51, 58
différance, rhetorical energy as, 155–57, 160–61
digital sense-making
    acceleration, accumulation, and proliferation, 44–49

algorithmic logics and bias, 55–58
consumers and digital marketplaces, 42–44
the experience economy, 49–52
polysemy as agent of acceleration, 52–55
resensing digital marketplaces, 58–59
disability studies, 11, 12, 63, 161
"discourse about actions," 142
disgust in political rhetoric
conservative invocations of disgust, 31–34, 39n3
context, importance of, 28–31
Impossible sausage controversy, 26–27
liberal taste judgements, 35–37
sensual relations as social relations, 37–39
disorientation, public, 120–23
dissensus, 114–17, 120–21, 125
diversity and inclusion, 12
doctrine of discovery, 136, 139
Doing Sensory Ethnography (Pink), 3
double translation, 149–50
Douglas, Mary, 28
Driskell, Quardicos, 86
Druschke, Caroline Gottschalk, 4, 12–13

Eckstein, Justin, 4, 113
Edbauer, Jenny, 142
Edwards, Dustin, 56
electronic marketplaces. *See* digital sense-making
embodiment. *See* bodies and embodiment
emerging technologies, 166–69
emotion, feeling and affect vs., 6, 21n2
Encomium of Helen (Gorgias), 7
energy(ies), rhetorical
open and closed systems, 155–57
pluriversal ontologies, 150–52
relationality, removal of, 158–60
in relative systems, 152–55
revising ontological paradigms, 146–50
toward pluriversal spacetimes, 160–61
Engaging Ambience (McNely), 15–16
environmental injustice
intersectional ecofeminism, 62–63
olfactory persuasion and, 64–66
process for evaluation and action, 66–71
relationality and, 158–60
sensory hierarchies and, 61–62
transdisciplinary aims and, 71–72
Environmental Protection Agency (EPA), 66–67, 69
epideictic rhetoric, 21n3
epiphylogenesis, 158–60
Equal Justice Initiative (EJI), 75, 76–77, 83
Estes, Beth, 31

Eurocentric ontologies. *See under* ontology
"Everett interpretation" of quantum mechanics, 160
Everything Everywhere All at Once (2022), 146, 150, 160–61
Evins, Danny, 29
experience economy, 49–52
Expression of the Emotions in Man and Animals, The (Darwin), 28

Fanon, Frantz, 128, 151–52
fantasies of identification, 115–16
Farrell, Thomas B., 114
feeling, emotion and affect vs., 6, 21n2
feminist perspectives, 9, 12, 62–63, 66, 72
Finnegan, Ruth, 3
Fodéba, Keita, 151
Foucault, Michel, 165
Frosh, Paul, 54
Fuoss, Kirk, 79

Gadarian, Shana Kushner, 31
Galison, Peter, 124
García, Romeo, 149
gastrodiplomacy, 37–38
Geertz, Clifford, 96, 164
gender
exclusion based on, in ancient rhetoric, 9
fetishization of consensus and, 115
intersectional discrimination and, 62–63
queer knowing, 93–95, 105, 108
rhetorical scholarship and, 12
gender-affirming surgery. *See* not-knowing
geologic rhetoric, 148
Geurts, Kathryn, 3
Giddens, Anthony, 128
Gilmore, James, 50
global coloniality, 129
Glynn Environmental Coalition (GEC), 67, 70
Gobineau, Arthur de, 140
Gorgias (sophist), 7
Grace, Siera, 84
Great Chain of Being, 62, 73n1
Guo Jigzhi, 52

Hagedorn-Hatfield, Rebecca, viii
Haidt, Jonathan, 34, 109nn7–8
Harvey, David, 47
Hawai'i Department of Land and Natural Resources, 158–59
Hawhee, Debra
on consensus and meaning, 115
on differences in sensation, 17, 152–53
on olfaction and rhetoric, 66
on phantasia, 8

Hawhee, Debra (*continued*)
    on rhetorical power of feeling, 5, 14–15, 22n6
    "sensory rhetoric" concept and, 21n1
    "the sense as such," 147
    on transdisciplinarity, 72
hearing. *See* sound
Hege, Adam, viii
heliocentrism, 151–52
Hilton, Brandon, 27
historicism. *See* colonized sensory archives
homesteading, trope of, 141
homophobia, 29–30
Hood, Lanae, viii
"Hoot in the Dark, A" (Kennedy), 153
Howes, David, 3–4, 17, 22n4, 37, 49, 50
hymns, as settlerizing technology, 129, 133–38
hyperesthesia, 50–51

IBM (International Business Machines Co.), 44
Ige, David, 158
Illinois Environmental Protection Agency, 61
illusion. *See* autokinesis
imaginaries vs. ontologies, 150–51
Impossible Foods Inc., 26–27, 29–31
Indigenous peoples
    imaginaries vs. ontologies, 150–51
    Meskwaki grammar, 148–49
    relationality and, 157, 158–60
    settler-colonialism and sound, 134, 138
    settler-colonial tropes and, 139
in*form*ing rhetoric
    open and closed systems, 155–57
    pluriversal ontologies, 150–52
    relationality, removal of, 158–60
    revising ontological paradigms, 146–50
    rhetorical energies in relative systems, 152–55
    toward pluriversal spacetimes, 160–61
InfoWars website, 33
infrastructural rhetoric, 55–56
inheritance, rhetorical and sensory, 130–31, 136
Inscrutable Eating (LeMesurier), 13–14
interdisciplinary scholarship, 11–14, 164
interoception, 135–36
intersectionality
    cultural-material, 165–68
    intersectional ecofeminism, 62–63, 66, 72
    sensation and intersectional scholarship, 11–14

Jarratt, Susan, 9
Johnson, Benny, 36
Johnson, Steven, 33, 38, 39n3
Jones, Alex, 33, 37
Judson, L. S., 152

Kaholokua, Joseph Keawe'aimoku, 159
Kam, Cindy, 31
Kelly, Casey Ryan, 122
Keltner, Dacher, 109nn7–8
Kennedy, George, 153–54
knowledge-production, the body and, 81–83, 166–68
    See also not-knowing
Kristeva, Julia, 164
Kroonenberg, Salomon, 32
Kwan, Daniel, 146

Lacy, Richard, 76
Ladin, Joy, 96
land
    landscapes as archives, 128
    settler-colonial tropes, 136, 138–39
language
    animate and inanimate nouns, 148–49
    settler-colonial codes and tropes, 138–42
    textualism, 164–65
Lanham, Richard, 50
lead contamination, 65
Lebowitz, Fran, 35
Le Breton, David, 165
LeMesurier, Jennifer Lin, 13–14
Lewis, Pierce, 128
Lin Yutan, 30–31
listening, decolonial, 137–38
Locke, John, 140
Longinus, 8
Longman, Martin, 35
Lowe, Charles, 45
lynching
    of Joseph H. McCoy and Benjamin Thomas, 75–76
    as performance, 79–80
    See also Community Soil Collection Project

making (physical), and sense-making, *101*, 103–5, 108
Malatino, Hil, 100
"many-worlds" theory, 160
markets and rationality, 42–43, 55–59
Mauna Kea, Hawai'i, 158–60
McCoy, Joseph H., 76–77, 80, 83–88
McGreavy, Bridie, 148
McHendry, George F., 148
McLuhan, Marshall, 10–11, 22n4
McNely, Brian, 15–16

meaninglessness
  autokinesis as possibility, 123–26
  normative constructions of sense and, 117–20
  public disorientation and, 120–23
  rethinking, 112–14
  rhetorical theory and, 114–17
media studies, sensation in, 10–11
memory
  music, coloniality and, 135
  race, the senses and, 78–80
  sensation, knowledge-production and, 82–83
  sensory public memory, 77–78
  soil collection ceremony, 75–76, 83–89, 87, 88
Merleau-Ponty, Maurice, 165
Meskwaki grammar, 148–49
Metastasio, Pietro, 133
microstock companies, 54
Mifsud, Mari, 114, 125
Mignolo, Walter, 131, 141, 149
Mill, John Stuart, 42–43
Miller, Abbott, 53
Mitchell, W.J.T., 54
morality
  in conservative invocations of disgust, 31–34
  moral pollution, 28–31
Mormons. *See* Church of Jesus Christ of Latter-day Saint (LDS)
Mormon Tabernacle Choir, 135, 136
Mosby, Ian, 13
Mowitt, John, 164
Moynihan, Conor, 103
Muckelbauer, John, 147, 149
multiplicity, "sensorium" and, 15
multisensory experiences
  multisensory digital marketing, 43, 49–52
  rhetoric and, 3
  soil, public memory and, 77–78
Muñoz, José Esteban, 105
music, use by church-settlers, 129, 133–38
Musk, Elon, 125

needlepoint, *97, 101,* 102–5, *107, 108*
neo-Sophism, 8–9
Nietzsche, Friedrich, 146
Nixon, Rob, 64
normativity
  autokinetic illusion and, 117–20
  public fixation on, as fear response, 120–23
  rhetorical theory and neurodivergence, 113, 115–17, 125–26

sense modals and sense processes, 132
  socialization, coloniality and, 128–31
  See also colonized sensory archives; *inform*ing rhetoric
not-knowing
  feeling through numbness, 95–99, *97*
  potential in, 105–8, *107*
  sense-making through, 92–95, 109n7
  as space of creative wonder, 99–105, *101*

Obama, Barack, 33–34
olfactory rhetoric
  intersectional ecofeminism, 62–63
  as persuasive device, 64–66
  process for evaluation and action, 66–71
  sensory hierarchies, 61–62
  transdisciplinary aims and, 71–72
Olson, Christa, 15, 116, 117
Ong, Walter J., 10–11, 22n5
On Rhetoric (Kennedy), 153
ontology
  relationality in Western science, 158–60
  revising ontological paradigms, 146–50
  sound as settler-colonial tool, 133–35
  toward pluriversality, 12, 150–52
  See also colonized sensory archives; *inform*ing rhetoric
open and closed systems, 155–57
organs, biological and musical uses, 135–38
Ott, Brian L., 51, 58

parosmia (smell and taste disorder), 1, 2
Parrish, Alex, 61, 63
parsimoniously polysemic imagery, 54
pathos, 7
patriarchy, environmentalism and, 62
Peplinski, Brian, 30
Perelman, Alison, 30
performance
  as antiracist activism, 75–76, 83–89, *87, 88*
  lynching as, 79–80
  See also Community Soil Collection Project
persecution, evoked in hymnody, 135, 136–37
Pezzulo, Phaedra, 122
Pflugfelder, Ehren, 148, 150, 151
phantasia, 8
Pine, Joseph II, 50
Pink, Sarah, 3, 13, 81–82
place, as archive, 128
plant-based meats, 26–27, 29–31
pluriversality, 12, 149, 150–52, 158, 160–61
  *See also inform*ing rhetoric
pollution
  environmental, 65, 67–70
  moral, 28–31

polysemy, as agent of acceleration, 52–55
Poulakos, John, 8
Preciado, Paul, 96
Pred, Alan, 128
presence, in simulated environments, 52
Presence of the Word, The (Ong), 10
Price, Margaret, 150, 161
proliferation, logics of, 48–49, 54, 55
public feeling, sensation as, 15
public memory. *See* memory
publics, as spaces of feeling, 15

Qin Pen, 52
quantum mechanics, 160
Quarterly Journal of Speech (Hawhee), 152–53
queer knowing, 93–95, 105, 108
    See also not-knowing
Quintilian, 8, 10

race
    intersectional oppression and, 62–63, 67, 70
    memory, the senses and, 78–80
    racialized touch, 83
    See also antiracist activism
Rai, Candice, 4, 12–13
Rainforest Cafe, 50
Rancière, Jacques, 114
Ratcliffe, Krista, 137
rationality
    markets and, 42–43, 55–59
    sensation and, 5, 15
    See also digital sense-making
Reeve, Paul, 135
relationality
    open and closed systems, 155–57
    removal of, 158–60
    rhetorical energies in, 152–55
religious persecution, 135, 136–37
    See also Church of Jesus Christ of Latter-day Saint (LDS)
Rendel-Short, Francesca, 96
representation, algorithmic logics and, 56–58
Rereading the Sophists (Jarratt), 9
resensing, 4, 5, 9, 58–59
rhetoric
    fieldwork and, 80–81
    meaning and sensation in, 114–17
    olfactory persuasion, 64–66
    rethinking neurotypical theories of, 112–14
    rhetorical acceleration, 45–46
    the senses and, 3–4, 6–14, 130, 166–67
    textualism and, 164–65
    See also antiracist activism; autokinesis; colonized sensory archives; digital sense-making; disgust in political rhetoric; in*form*ing rhetoric; not-knowing
rhetorical listening, 137
Rhetoric in Tooth and Claw (Hawhee), 5, 66
"Rhetoric of Women's Liberation, The" (Campbell), 9
Rhodes, Jackie, 93–94
Rickert, Thomas, 8
Ridolfo, Jim, 45
Robinson, Dylan, 137
Rodden, D. E., 152
Rosner, Helen, 36
Rozin, Paul, 34

Said, Edward, 128
Samuels, Ellen, 115–16
Sattler, Philipp, 77
scent events, 63
Scheiner, Daniel, 146
Schelly, Chelsey, 151
Scott, Charles, 116
Sekimoto, Sachi, 79, 83
Sekulić, Dubravka, 77
Senda-Cook, Samantha, 148
sense models, 132
Sense of Urgency, A (Hawhee), 14
sense processes, 132
senses
    aisthēsis (sense experience), 129–31, 134, 142
    COVID-19 and, 1–2
    delinking of, 131–33
    hierarchy of, 2, 17, 61–62, 63
    interconnectivity of, 17, 119
    race, memory and, 78–80
    resensing, 4, 5, 9, 58–59
    rewriting of, 142
    rhetoric and, 6–14
    sensory multiplicity, 3, 15, 43, 49–52, 167
    See also specific senses
"Sensing School Shootings" (Eckstein), 4
sensorium, 15
sensory ethnography, 13
sensory rhetorics
    antiracist activism and, 78, 89–90
    characterized, 3, 21n1
    COVID-19 and sensory experience, 1–2
    creative-critical scholarship and, 99–100
    cultural-material intersectionality and, 165–68
    making sense together with, 14–16
    moving forward, 168–69
    rhetoric and the senses, 6–14
    sense-making through not-knowing, 93–95

significance of, 3–6
text outline, 16–21
textualism and, 164–65
See also antiracist activism; autokinesis; colonized sensory archives; digital sense-making; disgust in political rhetoric; *informing* rhetoric; not-knowing
Sensory Studies Manifesto, The (Howes), 3
Sharpe, Christina, 122
Shen Bingqing, 52
sight
  privileging of, 2, 17, 62, 63
  retinal fixation and autokinesis, 117–20
  seeing as embodied experience, 15–16
  sense images in digital marketplaces, 50–51
  trypophobia (aversion to repetitive patterns), 28
  visual rhetoric in research, 11
  See also autokinesis; digital sense-making
Singer, N. Ross, 62–63
skin, as metaphor, 135
slow violence, 64–65
smell
  parosmia (smell and taste disorder), 1, 2
  scent events, 63
  sulfur, association with evil, 31–34, 39n2
  See also disgust in political rhetoric; olfactory rhetoric
social norms. See normativity
Sophism, 8–9
Soto Vega, Karrieann, 56
sound
  church-settler hymnody, 135–38
  decoloniality and, 133–35
  privileging of, 62, 63
  sonic rhetoric in research, 11
  See also colonized sensory archives
spectacle lynching, 79–80
speed, digital marketplaces and, 43, 44–49, 52–55
Stevenson, Bryan, 75, 76
Stewart, Jude, 65
Stock, Robert, 119–20
stock imagery
  algorithmic logics and bias, 55–58
  digital platforms and consumers, 42–44
  polysemy as agent of acceleration, 52–55
Stoller, Paul, 96
Stormer, Nathan, viii
structures of feeling, 142
Suisman, David, 49
Sutton, Jane, 114, 125

Tan Weiming, 52
taste
  as identity marker, 30–31
  liberal taste judgements, 35–37
  parosmia (smell and taste disorder), 1, 2
  rhetorical, 130–31, 138
Tell, Dave, 89–90
Tel Quel group, 164
terra nullius, 136, 138–39
thick description, 96, 164
Thirty-Meter Telescope (TMT), 158–59
Thomas, Benjamin, 76–77, 80, 83–88
Thomson, Julia, 36
Three Steps on the Ladder of Writing (Cixous), 96
Through Everyday Things (Muckelbauer), 147
Tlostanova, Madina, 129
Tomić, Milica, 77
touch
  in antiracism ceremony, 85–88, 89
  peripheral neuropathy, 48
  racialized touch, 83
Toulmin, Stephen, 135
Trans Care (Malatino), 100
trans poetics, 96
trauma, 100–101, 107–8
Trump, Donald, 35–37
trypophobia (aversion to repetitive patterns), 28
Tuck, Eve, 134

Ugly Delicious (television program), 13
uncertainty
  autokinesis and, 113
  public responses to instability, 120–23
  See also meaninglessness; not-knowing
University of Hawai'i at Manoa, 159
Utah, idea of, 141
  See also Church of Jesus Christ of Latter-day Saint (LDS)

Van der Vort, Eric, 31
Van Loon, Juliette, 103
violence
  racial violence and sensation, 79–80
  slow violence, 64–65
virality vs. accumulation, 46
virtual reality, 52
visceral publics, 63, 66, 69–70
vision. See sight
Vitale, Francesco, 156

Wark, McKenzie, 96
Watts, Eric King, 115
Webster, Steven, 38

Wells, Justine B., 21n1, 148
West, Isaac, 123
Western ontologies. *See under* ontology
whiteness
    illusory stability of, 122
    in LDS identity, 135
    in LDS scripture, 131, 143n1
white supremacy
    environmental entanglements, 89–90
    lynching, as performance, 79–80
Whittaker, David J., 135
Why Hell Stinks of Sulfur (Kroonenberg), 32
Wilson, Justin, 76, 84
Wilson, Shawn, 154

Wingard, Jennifer, 141
Witt, Catherine Blanke, 27
wokeness, 26–27, 29–30
wordling, public sensation as, 15
Wretched of the Earth, The (Fanon), 151–52
Wright, Beverly, 70

Yang, K. Wayne, 134, 141
Yergeau, M. Remi, 113, 121, 123
Young, Brigham, 136

Zhao Linshuang, 52
Zion, 136, 141

www.ingramcontent.com/pod-product-compliance
Lightning Source LLC
Chambersburg PA
CBHW072003290426
44109CB00018B/2118